CHALLENGE TO AMERICAN SCHOOLS

The Case for Standards and Values

Edited by
JOHN H. BUNZEL

New York   Oxford
OXFORD UNIVERSITY PRESS
1985

Oxford University Press

Oxford   London   New York   Toronto
Delhi   Bombay   Calcutta   Madras   Karachi
Kuala Lumpur   Singapore   Hong Kong   Tokyo
Nairobi   Dar es Salaam   Cape Town
Melbourne   Auckland

and associated companies in
Beirut   Berlin   Ibadan   Mexico City   Nicosia

Published by Oxford University Press, Inc.
200 Madison Avenue,
New York, New York 10016

Library of Congress Cataloging in Publication Data
Main entry under title:
Challenge to American schools.
1. Public schools—United States—Addresses, essays, lectures.
2. High schools—United States—Addresses, essays, lectures.
3. Curriculum change—United States—Addresses, essays, lectures.
4. Home and school—United States—Addresses, essays, lectures.
5. Teachers' unions—United States—Addresses, essays, lectures.
6. Minorities—Education—Government policy—United States—Addresses,
essays, lectures. I. Bunzel, John H., 1924-
LA217.C44   1985   371'.01'0973   84-20737
ISBN 0-0-19-503556-9

Printing (last digit): 9 8 7 6 5 4 3 2 1
Printed in the United States of America

Preface

When I first approached the authors in the summer of 1983 about their interest in contributing an original essay to this volume, I asked essentially one question: "Is there a particular issue (or set of issues) touching on the problems facing our schools today that you are presently pursuing in your research that you would like to write about in the company of ten or so other colleagues?" They are all widely respected specialists who have very busy schedules, which is why I was particularly pleased when each of them said yes. I knew, however, that that would be only half the battle. My toughest task would be to get each of their essays in my hands by the agreed-upon date. Most of the contributors were academics, who are notorious for not making deadlines.

I adopted a simple strategy. For six months I wrote a letter every three or four weeks reminding each of them of the "due date" that had to be met. "A commitment is a commitment," I said. "The publisher has a tight schedule." "Late papers will jeopardize the whole book." "The date cannot be changed." I became a real pest. One contributor was so intimidated, he told me, that he finished his paper two weeks ahead of time. One day I received a letter from the seven-year-old son of one of the authors: "Every time my daddy gets a letter from you he cries. Then he hits us kids. Please do not send him any more letters."

But the strategy worked. The book went to the publisher on time. And so my biggest debt of thanks is to each of my colleagues.

Special appreciation is extended to Thomas H. Henriksen, an associate director of Stanford University's Hoover Institution, who first talked to me about editing a book on education; John Moore, Hoover's acting deputy director, who provided additional encouragement; and to Dr. Richard Call, president of The Seaver Institute, who from the very beginning took a strong interest in the project. Their support, however, does not necessarily mean they endorse all of the views presented in the individual essays, especially since they were not involved in selecting the authors.

Finally, I am most grateful to Sheldon Meyer, senior editorial vice president of Oxford University Press, for his early enthusiasm about the book and for everything he did to help make it happen.

Stanford
October 1984   J. H. B.

Contributors

Joseph Adelson, Professor of Psychology at the University of Michigan

J. Myron Atkin, Dean of the School of Education at Stanford University

Brigitte Berger, Professor of Sociology at Wellesley College

Denis P. Doyle, Director, Education Policy Studies, at The American Enterprise Institute in Washington, D.C.

Chester E. Finn, Jr., Professor of Education and Public Policy at Vanderbilt University

Nathan Glazer, Professor of Education and Sociology at Harvard University

Gerald Grant, Professor of Sociology and Education at Syracuse University

Robert B. Hawkins, Jr., President of The Sequoia Institute in Sacramento, California

Barbara Lerner, a Psychologist and Attorney in private practice as a Policy Consultant in Princeton, New Jersey

Diane Ravitch, Adjunct Professor of History and Education at Teachers College, Columbia University

Martin Trow, Director, Center for Studies in Higher Education, at the University of California, Berkeley

Contents

PART FIVE: SCHOOLS CLIMATES

PART SIX: PRIVATE EDUCATION

PART SEVEN: THE COURTS

PART EIGHT: ACCESS AND ACADEMIC STANDARDS

Challenge to American Schools

Introduction

JOHN H. BUNZEL

In the last several years there has been a waterfall of words in the form of studies and commission reports on the current state of American education, in particular the nation's high schools. Those which have commanded the most attention include the following: *A Nation at Risk: The Imperative for Educational Reform*, by the National Commission on Excellence in Education (1983); *Report of the Twentieth Century Fund Task Force on Federal Elementary and Secondary Education Policy* (1983); *Action for Excellence*, by the Education Commission of the States' Task Force on Education for Economic Growth (1983); *Academic Preparation for College*, by the College Board (1983); *The Paideia Proposal*, by Mortimer Adler (1982); *America's Competitive Challenge*, by the Business–Higher Education Forum (1983); *Horace's Compromise: The Dilemma of the American High School*, by Theodore Sizer (1984); *Schools and Colleges: Partnerships in Education*, by Gene Maeroff and sponsored by the Carnegie Foundation for the Advancement of Teaching (1983); and *National Conference on Studies of the American High School* (1982).

Although these studies differ in their individual focus, they have a common and unifying theme: the public secondary school system is in trouble. The sharpest and most widely quoted alarm was sounded in *A Nation at Risk*, which warned that "the educational foundations of our society are presently being eroded by a rising tide of mediocrity that threatens our very future as a nation and a people." The increasing concern about the quality of public education is reflected in many of the general recommendations and reforms, most of which are variations on the theme of urgency found in all of the studies:

3

- Our schools are confused about their educational mission and have no shared sense of what their major goals should be or how they can achieve them.

- The weakening of the high school curriculum (sometimes called the "permissive" or "soft" curriculum) has contributed to the decline in academic performance. Students should be required to take more courses that are part of the traditional "core" curriculum—reading, writing, mathematics, science—as well as to get increased instruction in key subject areas like history, foreign languages, and the social sciences. There should be considerably more homework, a longer school day, and an extended school year.

- Teaching-training standards should be improved to reaffirm the nation's commitment to quality education. The recommendations include requiring teachers to demonstrate competence in the subject-matter area they will teach, improving the ways of recruiting and paying them, and reconsidering merit pay and master teacher proposals.

- High school principals should be trained and chosen to provide educational vision and leadership rather than to administer and preside over the school bureaucracy.

- The federal government's minimal obligation to "identify the national interest in education" must not be reduced, but the primary responsibility for our elementary and secondary schools remains with the state and local authorities.

- Closer and more effective partnerships between individual schools and the larger community should be strengthened, particularly partnerships between businesses and our colleges and universities.

- America's role as a world leader and its ability to maintain its international competitiveness can be assured only if more and higher-quality education is available to all students. Equality and quality are not in conflict with each other. They are mutually reinforcing goals in the quest for better schools and educational excellence for all of our young people.

- In the words of one observer, "there is a spirit pervading the nation that, somehow, a promise has been broken, an ideal betrayed."

This is not the place to discuss the different criticisms and reforms of American education that are elaborated upon in all of the reports, except to point out that many of the concerns expressed in the current studies were voiced thirty years ago, when the public schools were under attack by opponents of progressive education. What distinguishes the 1980s from the mid-1950s is that in the last several years the problems of the schools have become a matter of wide public interest. Corporate leaders, legislators, union officials, governors, and presidential candidates, as well as parents, teachers, students, and educators—all have joined the debate about what should be done to set the proper goals and standards for our schools. If this is not the first generation that will have a poorer education than its parents—the former Columbia Teachers College president Lawrence A. Cremin has noted that the National Commission on Excellence in Education was wrong in making such an assertion—it is nonetheless a generation that has been the cause of much anxiety and the object of national attention.

Even a cursory examination of American history will reveal that almost from our earliest days as a nation the public has regarded education as a fundamental value. In more recent times the polling data show conclusively that education has often ranked among the top two or three most important issues on the domestic agenda, to the point that the major concern twenty or thirty years ago was the need to give more of our citizens much greater access to our schools and colleges. During the years of the Vietnam War and Watergate, when such issues as foreign policy, civil rights, and the environment dominated our political life, the subject of education was put on the back burner. But not for long. As people began to worry about the alarming use of drugs and the accelerating crime rate in society (among other issues), they were also troubled by what they perceived to be the deteriorating state of the public schools. There was increasing talk in the country of returning to traditional values, and it was inseparable from a growing concern about the quality of public education. And that, today, is the key term—*quality*.[1]

---

1. It should be stressed that the national concern over the quality of education does not mean that the public holds the schools and the teachers solely responsible for everything that's wrong. Since the 1960s there has been a decline of confidence across a range of social, political, and economic institutions, including the church, the Congress, the Supreme Court, organized labor, big business, the press, and the public school system. "The causes of the problem," writes William Schneider, a resident fellow at the American Enterprise Institute for Public Policy Research, "lie in the area of social change, more specifically, in the breakdown of public and private authority." Schneider's point is not that teachers and the schools are "off the hook" but that people tend to see the crisis in education "as a broad national problem, not a specific consumer complaint." Furthermore, he points out that people are significantly more critical of the national public schools than of the schools in their own community, a pattern that "is repeated in polls dealing with other institutions. . . . They like their Congressman but hate Congress. They dislike the press but like their local newspaper, and so forth. What these results suggest is that people are not generalizing from their own experiences. Their negative attitudes toward institutions—including the nation's public schools—

Of the principal conclusions reached by all of the studies, none has been more vigorously endorsed by the American people than the call to prevent the further deterioration of the nation's public schools. One clear message Americans have given to all of the pollsters is that they believe the schools are today in worse shape than they were five years ago and that the quality of education their children are receiving is poorer than that which they received. Gallup has for ten consecutive years asked the following question: "What grade would you give the schools here—A, B, C, D, or Fail?" As Stanley M. Elam, the director of the Gallup–Phi Delta Kappa education poll, reported in 1983, each year between 1974 and 1980, fewer respondents gave their schools a rating of A or B. The downward drift was "slow but inexorable." Whereas 18 percent gave A ratings in 1974, only 8 percent did so in 1979. Four years later an all-time low was registered. In 1983, 31 percent gave their schools an A or a B, whereas in 1974, 48 percent did so. The percentage giving D's and F's has grown from 11 percent in 1974 to an average of over 20 percent the past three years.[2]

Discipline continues to be the chief problem in the mind of the public, followed by the use of drugs, poor curriculum/poor standards, and the lack of proper financial support. When asked to give reasons to explain why there is a discipline problem, the respondents lay the primary blame on the parents and the home environment; they rank second a disrespect for law and order throughout the society. But close behind is the belief that some teachers are not properly trained to handle discipline problems; that the courts have made school administrators so cautious that they do not deal severely with student misbehavior; that students spend too much time watching television programs that emphasize crime and violence; that punishment is too lenient; that teachers themselves do not command respect; and that teachers have failed to make classroom work more interesting. One-parent families are also mentioned as a reason for the lack of discipline in the schools.

There are, of course, many other frequently cited problems that the public feels the schools must deal with, ranging from the difficulty in hiring good teachers, the lack of interest on the part of teachers and parents, and the issue of integration/busing to the declining moral stan-

---

are drawn from the strongly negative impressions they get about how things are going in the larger society, beyond their personal experience. And they do not seem to be going well." William Schneider, "The Public Schools: A Consumer Report," *American Educator* (The Professional Journal of the American Federation of Teachers), 8 no. 1 (Spring 1984), 13–14.

2. These findings are from George H. Gallup, "The 15th Annual Gallup Poll of the Public's Attitudes toward Public Schools," *Phi Delta Kappan*, 8 (Sept. 1983), 33–47.

dards, drinking/alcoholism, and teachers' strikes. But whatever problems are specified, they are all connected in one way or another to the
public's increasing demand for more accountability and competency in
our educational system. Although there is no solid agreement as to
whether more money should be spent on education, most of the polls
show that the American people are willing to pay higher taxes if they
believe they will get better-quality education in return. When people are
asked why they do not support public education, the reason they most
often give is that they are not getting enough value for the money they
are now spending. The days of simply more and more funding for education are over. As the pollster Peter Hart has observed, in this "era of
educational accountability" there are really four components that are
going to get strong public support: more funding for better quality,
higher standards in both teacher and student competency, back to basics
in terms of the educational agenda, and stricter discipline. "In the old
era," says Hart, "a politician could get by simply by promising a little
more funding or simply by promising a little more strict discipline. In
the new era the politician who is going to be successful in the eighties is
the person who's going to be able to best blend all four of these things
that the public cares about."[3]

In 1983 the Gallup–Phi Delta Kappa education poll sought public reaction to a number of specific school programs and policies, some of which
it had not investigated in several years. It discovered, for example, that
the idea of a voucher system—a plan whereby the federal government
allots a certain amount of money for the education of each child, regardless of whether the child attends a public, parochial, or independent school—is favored today by a majority, 51 percent to 38 percent.
(Only 43 percent favored it in 1981.) It also found, significantly, that
public school parents favor the voucher system by a margin of 48 percent to 41 percent. Promotion from grade to grade based on examinations rather than "social" promotion is endorsed by a substantial
majority (75 percent), the same percentage of the survey respondents
who also want to see students in the local schools given national tests so
that their educational achievement can be compared with students in
other communities. Two-thirds of the parents of children (and those
without children) in the public schools agree that the workload given to
students in both elementary and high schools is too light. Gallup further
reports that although more individuals oppose than approve increasing
the length of the school year in their communities by one month (49

3. Peter Hart's comments were made at the Annual Meeting of the Education Commission
   of the States, in Denver, on July 21, 1983. See p. 9 of the edited transcript.

percent to 40 percent) or lengthening the school day by one hour (48 percent to 41 percent), more respondents favor a ten-month school year and a longer school day in the 1983 survey than in the preceding year's. The public votes nearly two to one in favor of merit pay for teachers (61 percent), only a slight increase since 1970, when the same idea was backed by 58 percent. And in the last five years the public has changed markedly in its view about the importance of a college education. The percentage of those who believe that it is "very important" increased from 36 percent in 1978 to 58 percent in 1983.[4]

The eleven essays of this volume examine some of the problems facing American education today that the recent studies and reports have raised and that have also played a significant part in bringing about a marked decline in public esteem for the schools. Although common threads link all of the papers, the authors often differ in their emphases and accents on critical questions of public policy and how they should be addressed. However, implicit in the analysis and discussion of each of the contributors is the clear recognition that the problems causing the present reappraisal of the nation's school system are deeply layered and cannot be remedied by either quick fixes or good will alone.

Joseph Adelson knew the work of the National Commission on Excellence in Education firsthand. He not only wrote a position paper but also met formally and informally with its members and watched "them take testimony, hear reports, and question witnesses and each other." He says there was little reason to expect the commission to produce the strong report it did. His own, pessimistic paper would be followed by an exceedingly optimistic one—in his words, "it seemed likely that the struggle to strengthen the schools would not gain much from the commission." The first surprise, then, was that the "commission somehow managed to transcend those inclinations toward caution." A further surprise was the degree of acclaim it evoked. Yet Adelson believes that the widespread enthusiasm for reform of the schools may not bear fruit. The bureaucracy and ideological interests that led to the debacle of American education remain in place, determined and increasingly vigorous. School reform will not come easily, if at all.

Robert B. Hawkins, Jr., laments that in public education, the elements of diversity, competition, and parental choice have been nearly eliminated. The consequences, he says, are now obvious to everyone: a crisis in legitimacy and competence, extraordinary public expenditures, and a parental search for costly alternatives to public schooling. Hawkins maintains that the crisis has in large part been caused by the success of

4. Gallup, "15th Annual Gallup Poll," 4–13.

the classic American reform theory of education, which imitated the theories of organization emerging from nineteenth-century industrialization: large size, centralization, hierarchical administration, and standardization. Over the last fifty years, this theory has been implemented beyond the early reformers' wildest dreams. But public education has deteriorated. Evidence now at hand from different scholarly traditions and political spectrums indicates that a different kind of organization of our educational institution is required. What is needed, argues Hawkins, is not more money, bigger schools, and more centrally designed and administered programs but rather opportunities for local communities and parents to reconstitute the political institutions we call schools. We now require a variety of educational institutions that can respond to diverse communities of interests and needs. Such opportunities, Hawkins affirms, are integral to the American tradition of self-governance and well within the competence of local communities.

These days strategies for educational change are often developed in legislatures, but, as J. Myron Atkin observes in his essay, laws are blunt instruments for modifying the provision of a personal service like teaching. Side effects (and sometimes the main effects) of major governmental initiatives produce results that frequently are exactly opposite to those intended. In the process, they weaken rather than strengthen the system.

Dean Atkin views the behavior of teachers and school administrators as usually a more-or-less reasonable response to prevailing pressures and constraints. Those who staff the schools try to be responsive to public need. To do so, they must have a certain amount of autonomy to develop appropriate initiatives. The balance between the politician and the teacher, Atkin says, has been altered significantly in the last twenty years, with the politicians becoming increasingly assertive.

When the public becomes concerned about what it sees as an educational problem, such as the low reading scores of children in primary grades or the inadequate provision of education for youngsters with handicapping conditions, the impulse is to write a law and prescribe a desired level of practice. There is a tendency to identify apparent weakness in the system and standardize procedures in an attempt to eliminate it. In the process there usually is some leveling up, but there also is a leveling down.

Atkin believes it is time to stregthen and build on effective practices instead of solely trying to redress weakness. He also recognizes that effective change in social systems is continuous rather than episodic.

The revelation by the College Board in 1975 that test scores of college applicants had fallen steadily and dramatically since the mid-1960s led to

growing concern about the quality of education and declining enrollments in academic subjects. Continuing criticism of curricular practices
within American schools culminated in the report of the National Commission on Excellence in Education, which launched the nationwide discussion of school improvement in which all of us are currently involved.
At the heart of the debate, as Diane Ravitch underscores, was the question of what constitutes an appropriate curriculum for American students. Professor Ravitch explores the historical roots of this issue,
tracing the origins of the disagreement between those who argue that all
students should be educated in a single track of academic studies and
those who argue in behalf of multitrack, occupationally differentiated
curricula.

Sociology professor Brigitte Berger, who has written extensively on
the role and responsibility of the family, believes that our political and
economic culture has largely been the creation of the middle-class family. She further believes that education for a pluralistic, democratic, industrialized society depends upon the sentiments, values, and behavior
that typically arise within the cultural milieu of this type of family. The
massive attacks of the past decades on the family's educational functions, she contends, have inadvertently robbed education of its main
basis. Unlike many American intellectual leaders, she affirms that the
great majority of Americans continue to have faith in the sound judgment of the middle-class family and its ethos. Arguing that educational
reform cannot succeed without the help of the family, Professor Berger
points to the accumulating evidence that, wherever parents are guided
by the middle-class ethos and take their socializing and educational
functions seriously, our schools are the great beneficiaries.

Acknowledging that "teacher unions are here to stay," Chester E.
Finn, Jr., sets forth a series of conditions that make it more possible
today than in the past for the unions to be constructive partners in the
nation's quest for educational excellence. These conditions include intense public pressure to make significant reforms in school policy, the
entry of influential new participants into the policy process, the dissatisfaction that many leaders themselves feel, the demonstrated importance
of a "team" approach to the enhancement of school effectiveness, major
innovations in organizational theory, and the maturing of the labor-
management relationship in a number of school systems. Professor Finn
also examines the sources of teacher unionism, the genres of union activity in education, the large doctrinal differences between the National
Education Association and the American Federation of Teachers, and
the responses of the two unions to the "excellence movement" that has
been sweeping through American education, particularly at the state

level. Finn concludes that teacher unionism can be compatible with high-quality public education but warns that "whether this will in fact turn out to be the case in most American schools depends on both the perspicacity of the union members (and leaders) and the wisdom of those with whom they must contend—and neither of these attributes can be taken for granted."

Gerald Grant focuses attention on schools with a strong positive ethos, by which he means schools led by those who clearly enunciate a character ideal. Intellectual and moral virtue are there seen as inseparable. While intellect is important, the maximization of test scores is not the highest aim. One also wants, says Grant, harmonious development of character. The ethos is evident in the high expectations teachers have for students and is reflected as much by what people do as by what they say. It is also expressed in the kinds of judgments or evaluations teachers make—that is, they take account of both intellectual and moral virtue. In these schools, catalog rhetoric about mind and character comes to life in the discussions teachers have about students. Furthermore, these judgments are applied to both the individual and the community: the student is expected to meet the standards of the community, but the community is also responsible for meeting the needs of the student. As Professor Grant emphasizes, the critical responsibility of leadership is to ground daily decisions in an interpretation of the shared ethos, to choose the best means to the agreed-upon ends. The leaders of such schools are chosen because they exemplify those values; they are the "best of us," persons capable of symbolizing the ethos and drawing others into it.

It is easier to create such a context in private schools where parents voluntarily join together in mutual orientation toward valued intellectual and moral virtues, be they Quaker or Hebrew or Catholic or "Andoverish." The question Grant raises is thus the following: Is it possible to create schools with such an ethos where less agreement about ends exists, where a substantial proportion of the students and even many teachers did not choose that school, and where some may be attending against their will? In such instances, must we settle for weakly normed schools tied together by a system of rules and procedures that can at best only ensure that one of the disparate elements within the school gains an edge or preference on the other? Or, asks Grant, is it possible to create public schools with a strong ethos in both intellectual and moral terms?

Denis P. Doyle turns his attention to the future of private schooling in America. Not only are private schools growing, but among the middle and working classes they are experiencing a growth rate of more than 8 percent a year. Furthermore, the quality of private schools is frequently higher than that of comparable public schools. As Doyle points out, poor and minority youngsters do better in private schools than in public schools. He goes on to say that when the myth about the sanctity of the public school is finally revealed, there will be a successful clamor for public aid to families who enroll their children in private schools. The middle class generally gets what it wants, he argues, and the most likely form of public aid will be tax credits. But that idea does not help the poor, which is why we are left, in Doyle's terms, with a public policy anomaly: the people the public schools were created to serve—the poor and dispossessed—are most badly served by the public schools and are least able to attend the schools that can meet their needs. The solution, he contends, is a low-income, means-tested voucher system designed to extend the benefits of choice to the poor. Inasmuch as equality has not served the interests of the poor, liberty for the poor and the disadvantaged is now called for—and, as Doyle emphasizes, that means the opportunity and obligation to choose.

Barbara Lerner's essay takes us inside the courtroom to show how federal judges end up making educational policy for the nation. Describing her recent experiences as an expert witness for the defense in federal court cases dealing with education, she explains why they caused her to revise her earlier assumption that federal judges were imposing their own, personal policy preferences on American schools. She paints a vivid portrait of the dilemma federal judges face as they struggle to implement two conflicting interpretations of the Fourteenth Amendment while relying on evidence presented to them in the trial courts by educational experts. In most cases, these are the same experts who presided over the tragic declines in achievement and discipline in American schools in the last two decades. What emerges is a clear analysis of a fundamental ambiguity that has resulted, in modern times, in the incorporation of empirically discredited educational theories into the very fabric of constitutional law.

The decline in the quality of American secondary education since World War II has given new urgency to the old problems of underprepared students who enter American colleges and universities. Among the sources of the problem, as Martin Trow points out in his essay, are the recruitment of academically less able people to teaching, the weakness of their education and professional training, the organization and content of secondary education itself, and broader changes in American society outside the schools. Professor Trow believes that colleges and universities can respond to these problems in a variety of ways: for example, by clarifying what they expect college-bound stu-

dents to learn in high school, by providing remedial courses for students
after they enter college, by raising their standards for entry, by providing special help to groups of high school teachers and students, by initiating new channels of entry to high school teaching, and by
establishing a variety of supporting links with nearby schools.

The problem addressed by Nathan Glazer—which he claims is a "peculiarly difficult, indeed intractable," one—is that all efforts to raise
standards in education run up against the certainty that, whatever standard one sets, some people cannot meet it. This is true of teachers (to
improve the quality of teachers), standards for graduating high school
students (to ensure basic competences assumed to come with high
school education), and standards for college entry (regardless of the college). If one assumes some standard distribution of talents, there will
always be people who fall below some level. In most countries, the problem this creates is that of a class factor in achieving the standard set: the
lower the class, the lower the number of those who reach the standard.
This creates a problem for people who wish to democratize higher education by increasing the proportion of students of working-class origin.

But, as Professor Glazer points out, in the United States the problem is
exacerbated by ethnic-racial factors. Simply put, more blacks and Hispanic-Americans fail (though the latter less proportionately than the former). The raising of standards comes into direct conflict with the effort
to achieve proportions of blacks and Hispanic-Americans at each level of
the educational system that match the proportions in the population at
large. Believing this to be the biggest issue in the raising of educational
standards, Glazer discusses various strategies to deal with the problem—placing less emphasis on tests, lowering the standard set (everyone passes the competence test), special tutoring for those that fall
below, and so on—and analyzes their implications.

PART ONE

Change and Choices

1

Four Surprises, or Why the Schools May Not Improve Much

JOSEPH ADELSON

The report of the National Commission on Excellence in Education, *A Nation at Risk*,[1] has become so familiar that it is hard to remember how surprised we were when it appeared. Most of us interested in education were entirely unprepared for its tone and emphasis. It had been assumed we would get a characteristic product of the committee process— a report temperate and evenhanded, which might well mean, in practice, an exercise in the vacuous, the sententious, and the banal.

From what one could learn of the commission at work, there was little reason to hope otherwise. As it happens, I had been asked to write a position paper for the commission; hence I was able to meet with them formally and informally and to watch them take testimony, hear reports, and question witnesses and each other. During a long afternoon, one could see few signs of fire in anyone's belly. To the contrary, the commission membership appeared so diverse in background and disparate in views that an essentially political document, marked by restraint and compromise, seemed to be required if a report was to be issued at all. The commission's able staff had been assiduous in providing the widest possible variety of data and opinion: work showing that American youngsters were doing very poorly in international comparisons was balanced by arguments that those findings were weak, misleading, and not to be taken too seriously. A pessimistic paper on American education, such as my own, would be offset by an exceedingly optimistic one. All in all, it seemed likely that the struggle to strengthen the schools would not gain much from the commission, that its report would, at best, provoke the usual one-day Washington flurry, then be forgotten.

* * *

The first surprise, then, was that the commission somehow managed to transcend those inclinations toward caution, to write a report that was straightforward, outspoken, at moments nearly fierce. The second surprise was the acclaim it received, and the—continuing—attention it gained for the problems of American education. Why a chronic crisis is suddenly perceived to be acute, why one event strikes a nerve while another, similar event does not, why we unexpectedly develop the collective conviction that *something must be done*—those are the mysteries of the zeitgeist, penetrable only by hindsight, if then.

It is important to bear in mind that the report made no new discoveries. The sorry state of the American schools had been evident for many years. If there was a true mystery, it was not that the report said what it did, or attracted attention, but why it had taken so long, why enlightened opinion had not previously been fully engaged. One could hear a good deal about the problems privately—parents retelling some of the hair-raising stories brought home by their children, or college teachers reporting the most recent solecisms encountered in student compositions. There is a local teacher who compiles a catalog of the worst howlers he has come across in papers graded during the past year; he distributes it to colleagues, to their vast amusement; and one senses they laugh to keep from crying, there being nothing quite so frustrating as the semiliteracy they confront almost daily.

Nor was the plight of the schools known only privately. A number of journalists—notably Gilbert Sewall of *Newsweek* and Gene Maeroff of the New York *Times*—had been writing trenchant stories (later books) on the problems of education and what might be done about them. One annual ritual was a story reporting the latest decline in SAT scores. Another annual event was the Gallup poll of public opinion about the schools—sometimes slightly up, sometimes down, but on the whole bleak. In a number of state legislatures, plans for the competence testing of high school seniors were being debated, at times carried out. Looking back, we can now see that by the late 1970s a critical mass of writers, intellectuals, and academics—few of them deeply in the education establishment—were beginning to be heard on the failures of the schools: Diane Ravitch, Chester Finn, Dennis Doyle, Tommy Tomlinson. At the very end of that decade, one was aware that a number of large studies of high schools were under way—by James Coleman, Gerald Grant, John Goodlad, Ernest Boyer, Theodore Sizer—all initiated by a mounting uneasiness about the condition of secondary education.

So there were many straws in the wind; but then there always are. At the time, it took great optimism to believe that we would soon see fundamental changes in thinking about the schools, let alone changes in practice. There were bureaucracies to be found at all levels of the education system, from the local to the national, and they tended to be sluggish, defensive, unwilling to undertake change, unable to grasp the nature of the complaints being made, or too preoccupied with finances and housekeeping to give more than cursory attention to issues of pedagogy.

If the bureaucrats of education were generally inert, the soi-disant intellectuals—scholars and theorists—were likely to be testy and aggressive. The disinterested observer could sense in them an emotional raggedness, a quick-on-the-trigger sensitivity to criticism. They often saw themselves as samurai who had been given the task of defending the system that had emerged during the 1960s. That system, one would be told, might have its faults, but nevertheless represented a triumph of humane values and democratic ideals. Threats to the system were seen to be political in inspiration. In private conversation, one would sometimes hear amazing things: that there was an orgy of bookburning in the schools, set in motion by the Moral Majority, or that the high schools had no function except to keep youngsters out of the labor market, so as to maximize corporate profits. Public discourse was generally more guarded, but even there it was not difficult to perceive an embittered ideological animus, two noteworthy examples being the efforts to discredit Marva Collins's work in her Chicago school and the innuendo and obloquy that greeted the important Coleman, Hoffer, and Kilgore research on high school achievement.[2] By hindsight, once again, it might appear that so much touchiness bespoke a dwindling sense of inner confidence; but the more common reaction was to despair for the immediate future of education, dominated as it appeared to be by a curious mixture of mediocrity (in personnel, techniques, and ideas) and ideology (egalitarian, individualistic, utopian).

Another reason for pessimism was that many defenders of education would hint that the critics were actuated not by politics alone but by a covert racism as well. To worry openly about the collapse of cognitive skills was taken to be a surreptitious way of questioning the competence of blacks. To be sure, there were enough instances of poor black performance to warrant alarm about their schooling; but the general level of intellectual quality was at least equally worrisome. A university professor might, for example, read a term paper containing serious grammatical errors in almost every sentence, then learn that the writer was a college senior with a high grade point average, preparing to attend graduate school, the child of a successful professional, and a graduate of a fast-track suburban high school. Or be asked to sign a permission slip drafted by another college senior (white, middle-class) containing three spelling mistakes in two sentences ("herby," "permision," "signiture"). In fact, the problem of black achievement is less troubling, because it is less puzzling. But how is one to understand a youngster who has had the best of everything, yet after sixteen years of schooling is unable to write a comprehensible sentence? And how is one to understand an educational system that passes that youngster through a competitive high school, a selective university, and into a good graduate program? Race was only one of the many questions troubling the critics, yet the conversation on educational quality was conducted so allusively and so euphemistically that it often proved difficult to make that plain.

A final reason for pessimism: the critics of the schools were not them-selves powerfully situated and, looking about them, did not see the prospect of strong institutional support. Above all, they found them-selves thwarted and puzzled by the indifference of the universities. After all, it was higher education that felt the failings of the schools most directly; yet, those failings did not become a matter of institutional con-cern. It was not hard to see why: the universities felt that the schools and, even more, their ecology, the schools of education, and the teacher-training apparatuses, and the accreditation procedures, were a brier patch of ineptitude, stubbornness, and entrenched interests—un-reformable, hopeless, best left alone. So there would be little help from higher education.

Then *A Nation at Risk* took the country by storm. Against all expecta-tions, the nerve had been struck. A public long unhappy about the schools, but held at bay by bureaucratic inertia, intimidated by expert opinion, kept in check by a solipsistic legal system, had at long last found its own interests voiced, and by the most unlikely agent of re-demption, the federal government. Other reports were to appear in the following months—Goodlad, Boyer, Sizer—but the commission, in pre-ceding them, also adumbrated them, or seemed to, so that these later works were accommodated into the "paradigm" already established. A bandwagon was soon rolling: the pundits and politicians who had shown no previous interest in education, let alone in its quality, quickly added their voices. So did, *mirabile dictu,* the National Education Asso-ciation, until that moment noted only for a fastidious distaste for the idea of excellence, thought to be elitist, perhaps illiberal. Yet these ele-ments, the opportunistic and the merely fashionable, were only the smallest part of the reaction. What seemed far more important were the actions taken locally or at the state level to revamp curricula and to in-crease requirements for graduation. Even these actions, important as they were, were understood to be surrogates for those changes of the spirit felt to be really needed. They were to serve to signal parents and teachers and the young themselves of the communal wish to be—once again—serious about schooling. More time was to be devoted to academic subjects, and more homework was to be given, and done. When feasible economically, the school year and school day were to be lengthened. There were to be orderly classrooms and more systematic, focused, attentive instruction.

The tide had turned. Perhaps there would be further struggles, even some minor setbacks; but now it seemed clear to all that corrupt progressivism, the dominating mode in American education, had had its moment, had failed wretchedly, had been seen to fail, and had recognized its failure. What many parents suspected, and what many teachers knew in their bones, was confirmed each time new findings appeared. For example:

The number of American youngsters scoring over 650 on the verbal portion of the SAT declined 45 percent in the ten-year period 1972–82.

In the most meticulous cross-national research yet carried out, comparing American, Japanese, and Taiwanese children, Stevenson found that in mathematics "only one American child appeared among the top one hundred fifth graders" and that "among the twenty American fifth-grade classrooms, in not one classrom was the average score on the mathematics test equivalent to that of the children in the worst-performing Japanese classroom."[3]

Stevenson's prose is unemotional, yet he nonetheless terms these (and similar) findings "devastating," as indeed they are, made all the more so by the fact that the American children were more advantaged than their Asian counterparts, coming from well-educated families and attending much smaller classes. Still, one felt that the pain occasioned by these findings could be borne, given the belief that reform was at hand.

The third surprise—a most unpleasant one—was the slowly dawning recognition that the tide may not have turned after all, that despite the reports and the resolve, the movement for reform might well be blunted, that the disarray of its opponents, though real enough, had been only momentary, that the forces against reform were unpersuaded and unchastened. It is that supposition, that sad possibility, that this paper will examine.

As soon as the reform of education became a public issue, one began to notice efforts, witting or not, to change the subject, to divert the discussion to other questions. The most obvious form this took was political: each presidential candidate, declared and undeclared, rushed into speech. Planks were drafted, platforms rewritten. The true course of education had been subverted/had been enhanced/would be moved forward by the new/old administration. New programs were needed. New programs were not needed. More money was needed. More money was not needed. In other instances the discussion was moved to issues closer to education, yet secondary in importance. Merit pay for teachers: it may or may not be a good idea, but its importance is questionable. It is hard to see how, even over time, it would produce a significant improvement in teaching and learning. Yet, the issue of merit pay, pro and con, absorbed a considerable amount of discussion and debate. Another example was the controversy about the competence testing of current teachers. It is unclear what effect it would have beyond harassing an already beleaguered group.

Another diversion was that many of those strongly in favor of academic reform also favored, quite as strongly, some other purpose for the schools, usually moralistic: instituting prayer; monitoring the school libraries; scrutinizing the curriculum in sex education, or getting rid of it altogether; eliminating the relativistic approach to moral education; teaching values through literature or philosophy; and so on. Most of us will find some of these proposals lamentable, and others laudable; the problem was that their being linked to academic reform tended to confound separate domains and much of the time to alienate one or another type of parent—for example, those who might favor intellectual achievement, yet were modernist (or traditionalist) in moral outlook.

These diversions and confoundings were more annoying than disturbing, were disturbing only insofar as they suggested an increasing diffusion of purpose. What was troubling, and unexpected, was the appearance of rhetorical strategies that seemed to aim at denying the very existence of problems in education. In various ways, these problems were said to have never existed, to have been trumped up, to have been trivial, to have been distorted, to have been misunderstood, to be only a small part of the total picture, to be a thing of the past, and so on. To a clinician these devices seemed eerily familiar: denial, negation, splitting, externalization, displacement. For the last few months, I have been noting examples of these defensive tactics as they appear in the press. Here are the major themes:

"Things really aren't so bad." Stories reporting that though there may be minor problems in the schools, these have "been blown out of proportion."

"Some things may not be good, but other things are first-rate." Upbeat accounts of successful ventures, aiming to provide "a balanced picture."

"Those who criticize the schools do so out of base motives." These stories personalize, drawing attention away from the problem itself and toward the personality of the critic. A choice example is this statement from a press release: "A large part of the public's confusion [i.e., why they mistakenly believe there are problems in the schools] comes from university scholars trying to attract attention to themselves."[4] The speaker is President Derek Bok of Harvard, the celebrated shrinking violet.

"Perhaps things were bad at one time, but that was long ago." Stories that historicize the schools' problems, suggesting they are safely in the past, and long since resolved. This motif usually accompanies enthusiastic accounts of new approaches to familiar difficulties. A recent example can be found in *Time*'s account of the Reagan administration's calling attention to discipline problems in American schools. The story stresses the "dismay" of educators at the President's initiative, argues that the administration's data are dated, and offers in rebuttal several heartwarming anecdotes about chaotic schools now become pacific. In fact, the data are not all that dated and are the most recent findings available; the story offers no newer evidence, aside from those anecdotes and some indignant opinions. The thrust of the story is to suggest, quite incorrectly, that discipline is no longer a problem in the schools.[5]

Finally, and above all: "Those who criticize the schools have a political end in mind. They are trying to turn back the clock."

This last theme, openly ideological, deserves our close attention. Some of the motifs mentioned earlier seem to have little behind them; they are efforts at amnesia, or simple outbursts of Pollyannaism. But the ideological strategy is another matter entirely. It is principled; it is determined; it is intelligent; it is adversary. It takes the view that reform is reaction, that the pursuit of excellence will endanger worthier ideals, that the movement for reform is a stalking horse for the recrudescence of dangerous values. The reform proposals are seen not merely as misguided but as illegitimate, as a subversion of the proper ideals of American education. The position taken is *revanchiste:* the new era must be resisted, then overturned.

In the softer, attenuated version, the *revanchiste* idea is not taken to its limits: changes must be made, yet without our giving up the accomplishments of the past. We see its quintessential expression in the press release mentioned earlier, chronicling the outcome of a summit meeting of thirty-nine university presidents who, prompted by the public con-

cern about education, convened and considered and conceived ten recommendations for the universities, each and every one vapid, self-
important, and condescending: "Providing opportunities for the continued professional development of superintendents, principals, and
other school leaders"; "Strengthening existing affiliations with elementary and secondary schools or initiating new ones"; "Serving, where
needed, as sources of advice in the shaping of public policies affecting
education"; and so on.

One would not expect much bite or penetration from a summit-level
communiqué, and certainly not from one issued by university presidents. Still, one had hoped for a bit more than these fatuities. No institution is more grievously harmed by the erosion of talent this nation is
witnessing than the university is, and one might presume that the universities would see it as their duty to preserve and support that talent.
We find, though, that the presidents give almost no attention to what
caused the fuss in the first place. The concern rather is to allay anxiety,
since "too uniformly gloomy" a picture has been painted for the public.
We are reminded that the "significant achievements" of the recent past
must not be forgotten; these consist of improving achievement in younger children (in fact, an arguable conclusion) and of "improving access"
to the schools.

Anyone steeped in current commentary in education is soon aware of
the word *access*—generally preceded by *providing* or *improving*—part
buzz word, part code word, and a delicate way of adverting to universal
secondary education and, more particularly, to the presence of blacks
and other minorities in the senior grades of high school and the colleges.
It is the succinct expression of a somewhat more complicated idea: that
there is an implacable trade-off between excellence and equality (now
more commonly called "equity") so that encouraging a democratic
school system produces a decline in achievement. Equality means leveling, which in turn means intellectual mediocrity (of course, it is not put
so crudely); mediocrity is the price we pay for universal education. That
is by no means a new idea; to the contrary, it is a very old, conservative
idea, albeit with a somewhat different moral emphasis. It has now become the conventional establishment-liberal idea. One can understand
its appeal. It is centrist, moderate, enlightened, above all symmetrical:
excellence and equity in balance, on a seesaw, so that a rise in one virtue
induces a fall in the other.

It is also a comforting idea, permitting one to take long views and to
look well past today's troubles. Unfortunately, it is more appealing than
useful as an explanation of intellectual decline. Even if we limit ourselves to the two findings mentioned above, it is plain enough that

widened access has little to do with it. The American portion of the cross-national study was conducted in Minneapolis, which has few minority families. The sharp decline in top SAT scores cannot have been much affected by universal secondary schooling. For some years now, poor American performance in international comparisons has been explained by the high retention rates in our secondary schools; but other countries—Japan notably—now show similar rates, while maintaining much higher standards of achievement.

Nevertheless, the fear of excellence is real enough, when the case can be made that the disadvantaged are at risk. Here, for example, is the story of a contretemps now taking place in my own community, as reported by one of the local newspapers:[6] it tells us a great deal about what can intervene between intention and outcome when higher standards are sought. The school administration had proposed some modest increases in high school graduation requirements, essentially along the lines suggested by the various commission reports. No matter that they were modest; there was an immediate uproar. The plan agitated "angry teachers" who were said to consider it "simplistic." It was also deemed reactionary: a high school principal is reported as saying that it reminds him of the curriculum twenty years ago. The new plan would require three years of math and science, so that "even marginal students would have to pass basic chemistry, physics, algebra, geometry, and logic to gain their diplomas." That might well raise the dropout rate, now very low. Mandating courses may mean eliminating electives, which students are said to like. "Electives have pizzazz," a teacher is said to have said. Besides, college-bound students already take many courses in science and math, so why have requirements? Besides, the teachers are angry because they were not adequately consulted. Besides, the community is angry because it was not adequately consulted. Besides, the administration's proposal evades the real issue, which is the presence among students of "passivity, apathy, linear thinking, and dependence on authority." A local professor of education is quoted to this effect, along with the observation that what is really needed, before we rush into things, is more research, to tell us how to "involve students more deeply in learning." The story concludes with an attack upon *A Nation at Risk*, depicted as *fons et origo* of the nation's descent into pedagogical darkness.

One finds it hard to imagine that such arguments could delay change. Given the national climate of opinion, who would not support so slight an elevation in requirements? Yet, the school administration surrendered immediately, putting up no resistance. It appointed a forty-person committee, representing teachers, students, and "the community," deputed to draft a new curriculum. That committee would in turn break up into smaller groups to hold public meetings, hear witnesses, draft reports, and so on, until ultimately changes would—or perhaps would not—emerge.

One also finds it hard to imagine that this farrago of shopworn and discredited ideas retains the power to compel belief. Yet the ideology persists, undaunted. In one of its major variations—liberationalist—it holds that traditional schooling enslaves the spirit. Though we may achieve a rapid acquisition of skills, we do so at a terrible cost in creativity, independence of mind, joy in learning. The criticisms commonly directed against liberationist practice, that it encourages ignorance and intellectual incapacity, are treated disdainfully, since it is held that objective methods of assessment are both invalid and morally meretricious. Traditional schooling is seen to reflect an unwholesome devotion to such values as "cognitivism" and Social Darwinism. The critic, in short, is seen to be a fusion of Gradgrind and Snopes.

In the left variations, class or ethnicity outweighs all else. Here is a capsule summary of the position: "The schools are one way the privileged have chosen to intimidate, humiliate, emasculate the poor and the blacks. Tests, grades, and the like are of no moment, since they do not relate to the actual conditions these youngsters will confront—unemployment or a continuing economic degradation. Tests are little more than a means of oppressing the victims, then blaming them. All the talk about discipline is a smoke screen. It is based on straight racial bias and is a subterfuge for getting rid of the blacks. If there are real problems, which is doubtful, they developed because the true needs of disadvantaged youngsters are not being met."

The two variations are united in a disdain for the idea of merit. In the liberationist view, the striving for merit is seen to diminish any love for the activity itself. In the left view, that striving produces differences in rank, distasteful and unjustly achieved, as those beginning behind are destined to remain behind. The use of *merit* as a *Schimpfwort* now extends to the term *excellence* itself, to judge by the scorn conveyed by Irving Howe and others at a recent conference of intellectuals; and it should be no surprise to us that at least one speaker at that meeting singled out the commission's report as an example of a deplorable drift in American life.[7]

"Given the willpower, we have the knowledge to increase school learning, and raise our national achievement standards."[8]

Reading that sentence prompted a moment of surprise. It is from congressional testimony given by H. J. Walberg, a leading researcher on classroom learning. What surprised me is not the statement itself, which is unquestionably correct, as Walberg's excellent review of the literature has shown;[9] it was the word *willpower*, a term so old-fashioned, so nearly anachronistic that one rarely sees it used, not by an academic. Yet, when that brief instant of surprise had passed, it struck me that *willpower* or some equivalent—effort, drive, energy, commitment, some word connoting intention and purpose—would indeed be needed in discussing both the immediate past and the probable future of American education.

We are, of course, more comfortable in discussing these matters by reference to tangibles: the economy, the labor market, demographics, and so on. What will the supply of teachers look like in the next decade, and what incentives will be available to increase it? Are there changes in prospect for school financing? What would be the impact of tuition tax credits in states willing to adopt them? These "realities" are or will be of vital importance in understanding the present and future of American schooling. Who can doubt that the outflow of talented women to other professions has had, and will continue to have, a profound effect on teaching quality? Who can deny that many of the problems of the schools have been due to the population anomalies of the last generation: larger families and crowded age cohorts, which contribute in the first case to lowered intellectual capacity and in the second to a staggering increase in such pathologies as drug use, criminal violence, and illegitimate births, all of these having the deepest impact on the climate of schooling? It is perhaps worth mentioning here that the lowering of family size and birthrate, though little noted by writers on education up until now, will quite likely be the single most important benign influence on American schooling in the next decade.

Nevertheless, there seems to be no calculus of tangibles that allows us to comprehend fully the debacle of American schooling in the recent past. It is the underlying argument of this paper that it is far more important to understand those ideas, true ones or false ones, that allow us either to overcome or to succumb to the hard facts of life—above all the ideologies and illusions, the illusions fed by ideologies, and the ideologies fed by illusions.

At almost every moment during the last two decades, the schools and the young have been held hostage to our fantasies. Why in the world did so many university professors allow themselves to believe that the college students of the 1970s were so remarkably gifted? They were not, yet that illusion contributed to grade inflation at the universities, which led in turn to the despoliation of the high school curriculum. Why did so many social scientists, many of them familiar with the psychometric literature, allow themselves to believe that minority students functioning two standard deviations below the mean in aptitude and achievement would nevertheless do successful work in the most competitive graduate and professional programs? Why did we believe that schools incapable of teaching correct spelling would nevertheless be able to convey the highest degree of moral, psychological, and social insight? Why were we unable to perceive and reflect upon the uncertain relation between schooling and later achievement—why it is that a James Joyce could be delivered out of the most rigid Jesuitical circumstances, whereas a hundred Summerhills have yet to deliver a James Joyce? Why did it require an accumulation of empirical work to confirm the obvious, that learning is best achieved given enough time, and enough effort, in an orderly milieu; and why has that simple finding met such outrage and condemnation?

Two final questions: Why did some of us develop the illusion that these and like illusions would be easy to overcome? Why did we assume that the exposure of false doctrine to experience, or to careful empirical test, would be sufficient to change belief? I would guess we assumed so out of innocence and wishful thinking, almost as a counterpart to the innocence and wishful thinking in the utopian ideas we ourselves sought to correct and overcome. We were also too drawn to the metaphor of the pendulum, the view that cultural and intellectual life moves regularly from one pole to another. Although that view is by no means entirely false, our error was in failing to grasp the many ways in which ideologies are embodied in human lives. They provide a career, or a personal identity, or a badge of status, or a measure of religious faith. We did not anticipate how much would be at stake and hence how bitter the struggle would be.

2

A Strategy for Revitalizing Public Education

ROBERT B. HAWKINS, JR.

We are bombarded with messages from political and educational leaders that we have reached a point of crisis in education. Yet a closer look at recent history shows that our education system has been in crisis since 1957. In that year a little, Russian-made, beeping object in outer space was used to mobilize public support for federal and state reforms of primary and secondary education. Today it takes a mere national commission to focus public attention on the risks associated with a failing public enterprise. The crisis is more intense.

How can this have happened? Our schools have not been ignored for the last twenty-five years. On the contrary, the implementation of the progressive liberal agenda for school reform has continued unabated: public education has been extended to nearly all Americans, school consolidation has continued, federal compensatory programs have been created on demand, school expenditures have kept pace with or exceeded inflation, many states have taken steps to equalize expenditures, and schools have been professionalized.

Given this devotion to the cause, one must wonder, Why is there now a crisis in public education? Why have test scores declined for students from all socioeconomic levels, when school expenditures have outpaced inflation? Why do our schools seem to lack purpose and direction? Why are parents from all socioeconomic groups increasingly willing to suffer economic hardship to send their children to private schools? Why do they perceive public education, which was once deemed a public good, as turning into a public bad? These questions are especially relevant when we have carried out most of the policy recommendations that were supposed to make our schools models of efficiency and effectiveness.

Given the widening chasm between reform theory and educational reality, one should cast a skeptical eye at recommendations that seek only more of the same. If traditional "reforms"—more money, larger schools, increased professionalization, and more centralization—have in fact been positively associated with the decline of our public schools, then we should look at other ways of reviving public education.

The basic problem facing our public school system is the complete failure of its political organization. This is the crisis that has been gaining momentum over the last forty years, as our schools have become centralized. It is not a crisis caused by the provision of more education to more students. Rather, it is a crisis of divided fundamental interests, a situation in which parents, students, teachers, and school boards are members of opposing teams. We have created organizations called schools that disjoin parent, student, community, and education.

The solution is not more programs that intrude into the classroom or impose intolerable administrative burdens on school officials. A necessary condition for any meaningful educational reform is significant change in the political and structural setting of public education.

Education policy and administration have been guided by a set of assumptions, which we will call the Reform Theory of Education, that has probably gained more success in terms of being put into practice than any other set of ideas in America in the nineteenth and twentieth centuries.

The notion of the common school has been the critical organizing concept for public education over the last 125 years. Public schools were to be "common" in the sense that they would be open to all and would make up a single, comprehensive, public school system. Horace Mann, the first secretary of education in Massachusets, expressed the basic premise. To him, education, "beyond all other devices of human origin, is the great equalizer of the conditions of man—the balance-wheel of social machinery . . . it gives each man the independence and the means by which he can resist the selfishness of other men."[1]

Mann began the movement for a public school system based on that philosophy. (Mann would have accepted the economists' notion of a public good, since Mann's public schools were to be the balance wheel of the social machinery.) Mann blamed the decentralized nature of education for most of the defects of the schools of his time, such as incompetent teachers and inadequate fiscal support.

While Mann was not as successful as he would have desired, he was responsible, along with other state superintendents, for articulating a

public school philosophy based on local centralization and an authoritative role for the states. Since many public school advocates perceived local communities as being parochial, which in this context meant
anti–public schools, they concentrated on establishing the state as the
authoritative instrument of policy.

Although the basic unit of production of education was the common
school, the state-directed instruments of control were to be professionalization, specialization, and standardization. In using these tools,
school reformers were imitating the popular theories of organization
emerging from industrialization. Ironically, it was Woodrow Wilson
who put forward, in *Congressional Government*, a strong attack on America's decenttralized political institutions. He argued for a political and
administrative organization based on the following presumptions:

· There will always be a single, dominant center of power; with the frag-
mentation of power comes its irresponsible exercise.

· The field of politics sets the tasks for administration, but the field of
administration lies outside the proper sphere of politics.

· Perfection in the hierarchical ordering of professional administration is
a necessary condition for good administration.

· Perfection in hierarchical organization will maximize efficiency as measured by the least expenditure of money and effort.

· The perfection of good administration is a necessary condition for
modernity in human civilization and for the advancement of human
welfare.[2]

The words of school administrators and others illustrate how these
abstract assertions began to determine the shape of public education.
David Tyack notes that many rural education leaders wished, with certain modifications dictated by rural conditions, to create in the coun-
tryside the "one best system" that had been slowly developing in the
cities.[3] Educators in Arkansas were critical of their schools because they
failed to utilize the "great economic principle of division of labor, which
has multiplied a hundred fold the production capacity of manufacturing
industries."[4] In Vermont the superintendent of schools held that the
maintenance of small schools is not in accordance with business principles, that the returns are meager in comparison with the time and
money invested.[5] Finally, the same superintendent argued for the inev-
itability of consolidation when he stated, "The intelligence of the times

advocates it and rural conditions demand it. . . . Consolidation is a natural sequence to the evolution of the modern industrial system."[6]

Education reformers saw in consolidation not only a way to bring about the professionalization of education but also the creation of large school systems that would produce effective education services through a marshaling of scarce resources. It was predicted, too, that large systems would be more efficient through the realization of economies of scale and would be more responsive because of their visibility.

Although this body of theory was developed around the turn of the century, its power as policy and myth has remained intact up to the present day. Soon after Sputnik, James Bryant Conant's study of American education claimed that a high school with fewer than 100 graduating seniors was incapable of mobilizing the needed educational resources for an adequate education.[7] In 1959 three noted theorists of education could say with a straight face that "at least 85 per cent of the school districts . . . are too small to provide an effective program of education at any reasonable cost."[8]

These were (and are) the tenets of professional reform:

· Elected boards of school districts should be concerned only with the broad outlines of policy.

· The administration of education should be left to professional administrators, teachers and counselors, and experts in the science of education.

· Education systems should be large enough to allow the realization of economies of scale and to marshal adequate educational resources to provide students with the broadest possible set of educational opportunities.

· Schools should be large enough to provide a large fiscal base, in order to internalize issues of equity. Schools, according to the general consensus, should be composed of at least 5,000 students.[9]

The best means of realizing sound administrative policy was thought to be centralization: consolidation of small schools into large ones, more state financing, and comprehensive state regulation of existing schools. The success of these efforts is indicated by the following table:[10]

Year	School Number	Percentage Distribution of Funds		
		Federal	State	Local
1930	128,000	.4	16.9	82.7
1940	117,000	1.8	30.3	68
1950	83,718	3.9	38.6	57.8
1960	35,676	4.3	38.7	56.9
1970	19,169	8.0	39.9	52.1
1980	15,900	9.8	45.7	44.5

These figures suggest that our public schools have changed dramatically over the last fifty years. We find a steady movement from a highly decentralized system of local schools, controlled in large part by local school boards with broad discretionary powers, toward the organizational goals of school reformers. By 1980, public schools were in the main large organizations, with 63 percent of all students attending schools with over 5,000 students.[11] And though consolidations decreased after 1970, in large part because of declining opportunities, other forms of consolidation or centralization accelerated. Beginning in 1950, state and federal funding began to rise as a percentage of total revenues. With the advent of the Great Society programs, state efforts to equalize expenditures, and court-mandated programs, the authority of local school systems was again reduced.

What effects have larger educational organizations had on the performance and legitimacy of public schools? Reformers predicted that, organizationally, larger school systems would accomplish at least the following:

· Realize greater efficiency, that is, decrease costs for each unit of educational output.
· Make more effective use of educational resources, thus increasing the abilities of schools to educate students.
· Be more responsive to parents and citizens.

But have consolidations and large size produced the much-sought-after economies of scale? A number of studies find few economies of scale and many diseconomies of scale associated with larger school systems. A study by Werner Hirsch was unable to "find significant economies of scale and suggests that consolidation is unlikely to solve the fiscal problems of schools in urban America."[12] A study conducted in California indicated that systematic diseconomies of scale are associated with school systems with more than 2,000 students.[13] And, as Ostrom and others have pointed out, small school systems in rural as well as urban areas can realize economies through contracting for services in both the public and private sectors.[14]

Has quality improved? A growing number of studies suggest that student performance and the best use of educational resources diminish beyond a certain size. Max Kiesling's landmark study found size to have a negative relation to achievement: "many of the gross relationships, especially in grade 12, seem to attain a maximum at some size level in the neighborhood of 1200 to 1600 pupils in ADA and then to decline, while after the three control variables are introduced, the entire relationship becomes negative and linear."[15] Niskanen, in a 1973 study, made similar findings for California's schools. There is an important relation between school size and student self-confidence and life performance: the latter have been found to decline as school size increases.[16]

Finally, how have schools fared in terms of their responsiveness to citizens and parents? A number of different measures give us some idea of what citizens think and feel about their schools and what they would like to see in the place of the existing system. According to many of these indicators, citizen support and approval for our public schools has been decreasing. Over the last twenty years there has been a 30 percent decrease in the number of bond issues passed through local elections to support public schools.[17] The number of citizens choosing to abandon the public schools in favor of private schools has increased not only overall but also among most socioeconomic classes.[18] Many polls have found that favorable ratings on performance have been dropping for ten years.

What is more disturbing is the divergence between the professional educators' views on how educational problems can be solved and those of the public. The public's commitment to the notion of public education has remained firm. Over the last five years, a high level of public consensus has formed on what is really wanted from the schools: a return to basic education and to the teaching of basic American civil values through local systems that are responsive to local values and preference.[19] The policies recommended by professional reformers have not brought about the desired and predicted results.

As one looks at today's schools, one does not see systems rationally run and directed by boards of directors and professional administrators. One would be hard-pressed to state that the present system was the product of reflection and choice. Rather, one sees local school districts buffeted by lawyers and the courts, regulated by state and federal agencies, subjected to unionization, and attacked by critics.

This situation should not surprise anyone. As local choice and oportunity have been closed off to citizens through consolidation and bureaucratization, frustrated communities have sought redress of other levels of government as well as through the courts. Most reformers have been either against local control or apolitical. Most have believed that once local political influences were reduced, the rational application of modern administrative and educational theory would create an education system capable of solving most of society's problems. We now see that the system they sought to create had very real limitations. It is indeed ironic that reformers, who prided themselves on having organizational genius, may well have created organizations incapable of meeting the demands of a complex, modern society.

In most of the political and administrative literature about education and its reform, the organizational unit—the common school—is the unit of analysis. Our basic unit of concern is the citizen.

Robert Nozick, in *Anarchy, State and Utopia*, founds his philosophy on the assertion that the rights of individuals are "so strong and far-reaching that they raise the question of what, if anything, the state and its officials may do."[20] If we begin our efforts to cast a democratic theory of education reform from this vantage point, we must ask what role the state should play in the provision of education services.

We can draw guidance from the *Federalist Papers:* America's experiment in self-governance was based on an assertion of the fundamental rights and obligations of individuals as citizens, both as constitution makers and as persons of authority in the conduct of daily public affairs. Alexander Hamilton, in the *Federalist* no. 1, set forth the moral and political issue that political organizations would have to face if the new constitution were adopted:

> It has frequently been remarked that it seems to have been reserved to the people of this country, by their conduct and example, to decide the important question, whether societies of men are really capable or not of establishing good government from reflection and choice or whether they are forever destined to depend for their political constitutions on accident and force.[21]

A number of important prescriptions for a democratic theory of education are implied in this statement. The first concerns the critical role that individuals, as citizens, must play in forming their political communities, through the process of constitutional design and ratification. In our federal system, citizen choice operates at the federal and the state levels; in addition, where states have conveyed local ruling powers, citizen choice must determine the terms and conditions under which local

governments and schools operate. The governments or public organizations created through these processes are strictly derived from citizen
authority, or at least should be. Their responsibilities are fulfilled by the
choice-making process that extends from the formation of governmental
entities to their maintenance and modification.

The Founding Fathers also held that if America's experiment in self-
government was to succeed it must be based on reflection. By this they
meant that if choices are to be the results of anything more than mere
chance they must rest on rational grounds. If citizens are to determine
the terms and conditions under which public enterprises operate, they
must have the opportunity to consider the merits of different ways of
doing things and the opportunity to experiment—to accept, reject, and
change their institutions after new evidence is collected and reflected
upon.

By eliminating the opportunities to choose and the very bases of reflection—local experiments and the local settings in which education
policy can be publicly debated—the present organization of education
has violated the basic moral and practical premises of American government.

The ability and need to choose and reflect can be embodied in a set of
guiding principles for the organizing of education such as the following:

· In the context of the American experiment in self-governance, choice is
  a fundamental political right and moral imperative. Thus, as a principle of design we must require political organizations to maximize citizen choice and control over their political organizations.

· Issues of politics and organization are clearly inseparable. Citizens as
  constitution makers and as political decision makers should determine
  the terms and conditions under which public enterprises operate, and
  they should oversee day-to-day decisions.

· Public education is public in that it derives its authority from various
  publics and thus should be accountable to those publics.

· There is no necessary connection between a particular activity and a
  public bureaucracy. There is plenty of room within our political culture
  for diverse ways of realizing public goals. Education should be public
  in its finance and opportunity, not in the organizational means by
  which it is accomplished.

· Diverse communities of interest have different preferences for educational goods and services, thus creating needs for different modes of
  organization.

While education theorists and reformers seem to lack agreement on the goals that primary and secondary schools should pursue, the public does have a good idea of what it wants from its schools and how it wants them organized.

Citizens want students to be educated in a broad and basic set of subjects. There is also a general consensus that our public schools should, to the maximum extent possible, be self-governing institutions whose terms and conditions for operation are determined by locally elected officials. There should be provision for parents to select the public schools of their choice. These preferences suggest an important and new role for the states. Rather than funding specific programs and prescribing administrative detail, they should set standards of performance, reward good performance, and protect the fundamental civil rights of liberty and real choices for all children.

In Hamiltonian terms, we could state that the goals of education should be to provide students with the necessary training to allow them to discharge their obligations as citizens—that is, to be able to reflect and choose, to acquire the necessary skills to be participating members of our commercial republic, and to be conversant with the philosophical and moral underpinnings of America's experiment in self-governance through civil communities.

For policymakers to design a set of state policies that will implement a democratic approach to education reform, they will have to reflect on existing evidence regarding the merits of alternative ways of organizing education: their political, fiscal, economic, and organizational feasibility and their likelihood of accomplishing the state and citizen goals.

The role of the state in bringing about educational reform is critical. Even with increased federal funding and regulation, the states still are the critical legal and political ground on which reform must proceed. Since education has never had any of the home rule protections that many local governments in the United States have enjoyed, local school districts, citizens, and special interests must seek state policy changes and statutory changes if they wish to implement reform. This is true even if what is desired is permissive legislation that allows citizens and local districts to seek reform, for state legislation authorizes such reform transactions by conveying decision-making capabilities to different organizations and individuals. If a group of local citizens were to begin to design new educational institutions, they would first array the evidence regarding the organizational structures most likely to realize their goals, perhaps in the following ways.

They would obviously want a school system that could meet their goals in the most efficient way. This would not mean that educational products would be standardized like items on a Ford assembly line. Rather, it would mean that, given a set of goals, they would be able to design systems to maximize those goals. A reading of most of the studies indicates, however, that our citizens should expect diseconomies of scale from larger school systems. Where one draws purely economic lines is hard to determine. At issue is the quality of the outcomes from schools of different sizes. As Kiesling and Niskanin have found, there appear to be negative learning experiences associated with school systems of more than 1,600 to 2,000 students. (Coleman did find small, yet positive, relations between size and performance, but these were cancelled out by behavior problems in the larger schools.)[22]

Yet even if there could be economies of scale, there is no clear reason why local communities must consolidate their schools into larger systems. There exist a number of options that have not traditionally been considered respectable by school administrators. Where small school systems are incapable of producing the desired product or of doing it efficiently, they may choose to do what many small towns in Vermont do: provide their high school students with vouchers to attend public high schools of their choice. Or a school could contract with adjoining school systems to provide the desired education product or contract with a private provider, college, or university. What is being articulated here is nothing more novel than the contract cities' approach to providing public services, which has worked quite effectively.

The issue of efficient and effective organization goes beyond economies of scale. John Goodlad, after studying numerous schools, concluded, "Indeed, I would not want to face the challenge of justifying a senior, let alone junior, high of more than 500 to 600 students. . . ."[23] He came to this conclusion because, according to their measures of an effective school, "most of the schools clustering in the top group of our sample on major characteristics were small, compared with schools clustering near the bottom. It is not impossible to have a good large school; it simply is more difficult."[24] In sum, smaller schools are able to create effective teamwork between principals and teachers, between teachers and students, and finally between all of them and the larger community. They are able to build and sustain an identity that translates into higher educational outcomes.

Clearly, a necessary condition for the continuance of our experiment in self-governance is the development of students who have high levels of self-discipline and self-confidence. This is one area where small schools play an especially important role. Etzioni argues that external discipline and hierarchical structure tend to create passive and compliant students.[25] The size of the school appears to have an important impact on the development of self-discipline and self-confidence.

Barker's study of schools found that one of the casualties of school consolidation was what can be called the reduction of civic space—that space where students can be actively involved in the activities that build self-confidence and self-discipline. When ten high schools are consolidated into one, there is a 90 percent reduction in opportunities to participate in important growth-inducing activities. Nine of everything have disappeared: from class presidents to lead roles in the student plays. Thus, it is not surprising that Barker found a negative relation between self-confidence and school size. Goodlad found similar student activity patterns, which are in part a mere function of size, since it takes more students in a small school to undertake the same range of activities.

Yet small size is not the be-all and end-all. Colman's study suggests that larger schools can provide a broader range of courses. In an age of increasing specialization, there is a need for specialized high schools like the successful specialized schools of New York City. Most school districts do not have the resources to provide such costly institutions. There is thus a growing need to be able to support specialized high schools by allowing them to recruit freely from large metropolitan and rural areas.

If we also take into account the demands of specialized communities for specialized education, we can see that the demands made on current common schools are clearly beyond their capabilities.

If a new organizational theory is to correct the defects of "common" schools run by professional administrators, it must be one that makes educational organization dependent on the choices of citizens and the demands of the services being performed. In a very real sense the organization of education should be emergent: emerging from the political and educational forces within the community, within the general confines of statewide education goals and requirements.

If citizens in California were to act on their preferences for, say, very small elementary schools, those schools could feed into small common high schools and into larger specialized high schools, with students having a broad range of choices among schools. But if they attempted such a reorganization, they would find numerous obstacles in their way. First, state law is rigged in favor of making school districts bigger: there are only three pages of regulations that control the process of consolidation and forty-five that control deconsolidation. To begin with, citizens would have to draft a plan and to submit it to a county school planning commission, whose members would be composed of the exiting school system and who would have the authority to approve or deny the process. Furthermore, if students wanted to transfer from one public school to the next, they would need the permission of the leaving and receiving superintendent of schools. Students may petition to the county school board to have a denial overturned, but this is seldom done.

In short, state law favors present producers by increasing the transaction costs that citizens must pay in order to change the governance and organizational structure of their schools. This shows how important the role of the state and state policy-making are in setting the ground rules by which education reform can take place.

States play a number of important roles in determining the quality and cost of local education. Through their allocation of more or less authority to school districts, administrators, and parents, they can create powerful incentives for effective or ineffective schools. Through programs that distribute funds and regulate behavior, they create incentives for certain types of behavior. Finally, they have the power to set the goals for their local school districts. In fact, one educator makes this the key goal and responsibility of the state: the articulation of a comprehensive and consistent set of education goals.[26]

How often these allocations of authority, programs, and state goals work productively is a question increasingly asked of state education efforts. The Democratic state senator LeRoy Greene, the longtime chairman of the Assembly Education Committee in California, maintains that there are two basic problems in the approach that the state has used to fund programs: namely, (1) that program funds are awarded to schools on the basis not of performance but of numbers of disadvantaged students and (2) that the state has mandated all procedures for educating students, thus eliminating flexibility and incentives for local leaders to take responsibility for the success of the schools.[27] His solution is to earmark a significant portion of state monies over the long run, to be distributed to schools on the basis of performance. The key role of the state would be to identify what it desires from schools and to reward schools that are successful. If this is to be a viable strategy for states, a corollary is that state law must provide local authorities and local citizens with the organizational flexibility to realize those objectives.

In a recent article on education reform, Diane Ravitch notes that while reformers have scoffed at incremental change, "experience suggests that small changes are likely to be enduring changes." She also suggests that in order for reforms to be effective, they must "appeal to teachers' educational ideals, respect their professionalism and build on their strengths."[28] Goodlad offers what parents would like to see in reformed schools: "most of the parents we surveyed would take power from the more remote, less visible, more impersonal authorities heading the system and place it in the hands of the more visible, more personally known, close-at-hand staff of the school and parent groups close to the school."[29]

In the light of these recommendations and of our general theory of organization, we will outline four models that are relevant and have some chance of being passed by state legislators and implemented by local communities. They are teacher partnerships; performance funding; deconsolidation, including schools without boundaries; and public school vouchers.

Teacher Partnerships. In the last twenty years teacher unions have made tremendous gains in membership and influence in state capitols. Yet there are inherent contradictions between teacher professionalism and membership in strong state and national unions. A further undermining of professional authority and integrity is to be found in the structural relationships between teachers and administrators. If one looks at major professions like law, medicine, and accountancy, one finds that professionals lead the organization and define and produce the product. Those responsible for administering the organization are generally paid less than the professionals and exercise little actual authority. Education is one of the few professions where these relationships are reversed. Administrators are the highest paid, have great influence over factors going into the product, yet do not produce it.[30] One education expert has described the situation:

> Thus, teachers, who directly affect the quality of the students' education, presently exercise the least control. Decisions ranging from time spent on curriculum units to the brand of chalk to be used are made at the district offices, and the consequences of those decisions filtered down through the ranks of the teachers. Many teachers, needless to say, resent this structure, finding it demeaning and unprofessional.[31]

Clearly, there is not much reason to think of oneself as a professional if one has little or no control over implementing one's professional knowledge. And if we are to follow Ravich's recommendation that changes must build on teachers' educational ideals and professionalism, we must seek reform that moves teachers back into the role of professional educator. One possible remedy is the creation of teacher partnerships.

A teacher partnership is a legal entity that would contract with a school district, state, or other public or private institution to provide educational services. Personnel, pay, responsibilities, and assignments would be determined by the partnership and not by the school district.

Natural divisions of labor would emerge from within the partnership, allowing members to choose the assignments that maximize their effectiveness and that enable them to meet the conditions of the contract as set down by the district; these are considerations that have not seemed of great importance in traditional education reform theory but are in fact critical in the teacher-school relationship.

Partnerships and school districts could enter into different types of contracts. Partnerships could be paid on a per-pupil basis for certain courses and a flat fee for other courses, or they could sell curricula for a fixed fee. Schools would not determine teaching approaches or the content of curricula. Rather, districts would articulate their needs, specify outcomes, and the manner in which outcomes would be evaluated.

Partnerships would restore the authority and professional standing of teachers, but such programs would meet resistance. Superintendents and principals would lose much authority to teachers. State law would have to specify the required characteristics of partnerships and the conditions under which partnerships could be formed. Of particular importance would be the conveyance of authority to parents and teachers to petition school boards for the acceptance of partnerships as models of delivery of educational services.

Performance Funding. Merit pay is seen as one of the most significant approaches to performance improvement, but it runs into a number of structural problems, such as the inherent administrator-teacher conflicts in the determination of merit and the selecting of those who should be rewarded. (One of the attractions of the teacher partnership system is that it bypasses this problem.) The solution is an often neglected approach: performance-based funding.

One of the perverse aspects of many compensatory programs is that they are penalized for success. Once a student has achieved a given level, the compensatory monies are withdrawn from the school. Performance-based funding would rectify this state of affairs by giving schools an incentive to compete with their own past scores and with other schools, to improve their performance in attaining goals defined by the state. Performance-based funding is a funder's policy tool. It offers incentives to schools to compete for public monies as a means of stimulating movement toward the realization of goals chosen and defined by the funder.

In California a pilot program is being designed: individual schools will compete with their own past year's record on state-administered tests. Schools that improve their performance will receive a pro rata share of the total incentive appropriation, based on the actual increase in test scores and the number of students taking the test. Rewards for schools will always be based on performance improvement over the preceding year.

There are a number of options in using this tool. If the state desires to foster great authority in local schools, it could choose to pass monies through the school district directly to the school. Or it could use a pass-through formula by which the school gets 70 percent of the monies and the district 30 percent, though to make the incentive effective it must be strong enough to encourage participation. Such programs could be made optional or mandatory; performance measures other than test scores could be used; and large school districts could even solicit monies from foundations and corporations.

Performance-based funding has some very attractive political ramifications. First, it need not cost more money, but can come from a re-allocation of existing monies. But states must face up to some tough questions. How much money should be allocated through performance-based funding? This is a question of determining the critical margin. The answer is that probably less than 5 percent of state education revenues need be utilized to have a positive effect. States must also have the capacity to administer fair and valid tests and to evaluate the effectiveness of the system. Moreover, they must determine how to reward schools that have topped out. Yet these are technical questions, for which technical competence exists. Performance funding holds the promise of creating strong incentives for schools to build education teams to compete for the desired rewards.

Deconsolidation Strategies. Many states, either through statute or through fiscal policy, encourage the creation of larger local school districts. The purpose of deconsolidation strategies is not to mandate the creation of 100,000 small school districts throughout the United States. Rather, it is to make state law neutral with regard to school district organization and to give citizens greater control over their school systems—in terms of authority, to transfer the right to determine school structure from remote administrators and regulators to citizens.

The logic of deconsolidation is quite clear: it is the creation of neutral organizational forms in state law that would permit local communities, teachers, and school administrators the freedom to develop organizations that are best able to maximize the particular education values they prefer (within, of course, state goals). The goal is to encourage the emergence of effective schools.

Deconsolidation is one strategy, but there are alternatives that could have the same effect. There is no reason that parents and teachers within large school systems cannot create school systems within systems. Although this approach is similar to that of school-based management, it differs in that it would create a confederation of schools. Local communities could have the right to petition the school district for an election to determine whether a school subsystem with broad independent authority should be created in a given community. If the petition had enough signatures, the large district would call for an election to decide the issue.

To implement such strategies, reformers must take a long look at state law and regulatory policy. Making state law neutral with regard to organizational structure necessitates a serious study of the requirements for forming new school districts. Key areas of concern would be the petition requirements for citizens wishing to form a new district and the reduction of the authority of state and county regulatory committees that can significantly affect the outcome of deconsolidation efforts. State law would also have to lay down the general procedures for reallocating bonded indebtedness and other assets or liabilities of existing districts.

The creation of schools within schools is a more gradual and incremental step. The critical question to be addressed is how to effectively allocate authority between two different school systems so that each has adequate authority in its own sphere of competence. Fiscal relations between two such systems should be specified in state law so as to prevent the loss of self-direction that always occurs when one unit of government controls the fiscal resources of another. Principals and teachers must have adequate authority if they can be expected to invest their time and professional skills in building an effective school. In short, if real authority is not given to confederate schools, then such schemes will merely lead to more administrative reorganization that ultimately ends up as more centralization.

Public School Vouchers. Public school vouchers would allow families to send their children to *any* public school, to the extent that places are available. The purpose of enrollment alternatives is to give families the right to select the appropriate public school for their children, thereby encouraging public schools to respond to student and family preferences. Public voucher programs would cause public schools to compete with each other by offering different styles of classroom teaching, emphasizing different subjects, and providing specialized high schools. Schools would be dependent on the choices of citizens rather than the other way around.

Two objectives are being sought in public school vouchers: first, to put competitive pressure on individual schools within a system and, second, to put pressure on the system by allowing parents to transfer their children out of the district. A state could consider giving parents the right to send their children to magnet schools outside a given district, or to allow workplace enrollments.

A number of options can be considered. Open enrollment would give families the right to send their child to any public school within an area or within a state; or it could be limited to a single district that could offer a broad range of choices.

Some states, such as Missouri and Michigan, allow interdistrict transfers as a means of voluntary integration. States could also add premiums to increase the incentives for schools to integrate.

A number of important factors must be considered in the implementation of a public voucher scheme. One of the most important is transportation. In large urban areas with good public transportation systems, costs of implementing this program could be relatively low. Yet even small costs could be a barrier to certain families. If a state wanted to encourage open enrollment, it would pay some or all of the student transportation expenses.

In states with fiscal disparities, there will be a cost factor that must be addressed in legislation. Students wishing to transfer from low-cost to high-cost districts would have to pay the differential, or state monies could be used to make up the differences. State legislation would have to resolve whether a student would take with him not only his state contribution but also his local contribution. The strongest incentives for local schools to be responsive would be for students to take all of their monies with them.

Finally, states must determine where the authority resides to initiate the transfer. In California, students wishing to transfer from one district to the next must receive the permission of the leaving and receiving superintendent. Clear authority is allocated in favor of the school and against the student moving. If states wish to encourage movement, then they must reduce the transaction costs by making acceptance by the receiving school the only condition for a student who wants to move.

This one change in law and practice—public school vouchers—would probably do more than anything else to make public schools responsive and efficient organizations. Vouchers would create external incentives for schools to become effective. They would create strong incentives for adopting what Goodlad sees as the guiding principle of effective schools, "that the school must become largely self-directing. The people connected with it must develop a capacity for effecting renewal and establish mechanisms for doing this."[32] Unfortunately, public monopolies seem to have few incentives for self-correcting behavior. Removing their captive student bodies might be a first step toward providing the incentives for self-correction and growth.

Public education is in a moral quandary. One of its missions has always been to educate tomorrow's citizens in the American experiment in self-governance and to be full participants in our commercial republic. Yet it tries to accomplish these purposes through political and administrative organizations that violate most of the principles of democratic government. School systems are at present public monopolies that reduce citizens to clients and district superintendents to agents of the state, that treat teachers as assembly-line workers, and that give parents litttle real authority. It is all of these factors that have caused and will continue to cause a crisis in public education.

It is ironic that the remedies are so simple and direct. There are remedies that can reaffirm the role of public education, return the teachers to their rightful role as professionals, and give Americans a range of real choices about the public education of their children. By squaring the organizational form with the logic of our political institutions, schools could again take root in the fertile soil of self-governance.

The odds of this occurring are at best problematic. It may well be that educational policy and implementation are not responsive to attempts at rational planning. In our time the public interest groups connected with education are so powerful that they can stop real reform. If they do so, then we must rely on rot: our educational system will get so bad that parents will desert the public schools. Let us hope that this will not be so. Let us hope that the fifty state legislatures will take an easier path to reform. Let them ignore grandiose schemes to rebuild our public school system. Ask them for no new programs. Merely urge them to unleash the resources and power of citizens, teachers, and principals, to rebuild a diverse and locally rooted set of public schools Then, and only then, will Americans have educational institutions that can do what must be done: provide quality educations to our children, who will carry on our glorious experiment in self-governance.

3
Changing Our Thinking about Educational Change

J. MYRON ATKIN

The education reform fervor triggered in early 1983 by the report of the National Commission on Excellence in Education, *A Nation at Risk*,[1] was greeted with trepidation by teachers and school administrators. Given its indictment of the quality of public education and its focus on the "rising tide of mediocrity" in the nation's schools, it was not clear whether the report was a prelude to educational improvement or the beginning of a new wave of attacks on schools and teachers. Judging from the polls, the public seemed to be in a mood to take constructive steps to improve the quality of public education, but teachers and school administrators had become gun-shy over a period of three decades as a result of previous reform efforts that assigned blame recklessly, raised expectations unrealistically, and led to legislative and other initiatives that sometimes had effects on teaching exactly the opposite of what had been intended.

As reports continued to be issued on the state of American secondary education in the months following *A Nation at Risk*, it became clear that an extraordinary phenomenon in the history of American education was taking place. Each new statement—Ernest Boyer's,[2] John Goodlad's,[3] Mortimer Adler's,[4] the College Board's,[5] the Twentieth Century Fund's,[6] the National Science Foundation's[7]—captured front-page attention, editorial comment (usually favorable), and even significant time on the television network evening news. Public interest in the quality of education clearly was deep. The mood for change was strong. It even began to appear that legislators were willing to appropriate more money for education if they could be convinced that the additional funds would produce higher quality.

The theme of the reports, taken as a group, was that the school curriculum had become soft, particularly for children with strong academic ability; that standards were poorly defined and low; that the quality of teachers seemed to be declining; that teacher education programs were weak; and that schools were not meeting the needs of business and industry as well as they should. Most of the recommendations for improving schools were couched in general terms, but the reports converged on the remedy that a common curriculum for all children should be reinstated and that clear goals and expectations for pupils in the subjects of English, history, science, and mathematics should be formulated. Teachers at the secondary school level should major in the subjects they were to teach. Some of the reports suggested that schools should be less preoccupied with training youngsters for specific occupations than with making sure they possess basic skills, especially in written communication.

The suggested educational reforms may not have seemed particularly startling, even if the public appetite for them was; but in addition to the extraordinary publicity attendant to release of the reports, the lineup of those who were pressing for change in the educational system was different and noteworthy. In the period immediately after the launching of Sputnik I, in 1957, those who exerted maximum influence on the tone and substance of educational reform were university professors who were experts in the subjects taught in secondary and elementary schools. They provided the driving force and conceptual leadership for new programs in the teaching of biology, physics, mathematics, social science, and language. It was a major feature of the education reform scene ushered in in 1983 that for the first time in recent memory major business leaders were identifying education as a key national problem and priority. Chief executive officers of some of the country's major corporations began to involve themselves in coalitions to improve public education, giving of both their time and their influence. The country's productivity and trade position were seen as threatened, and the cure lay in part, the public was told, in producing a more efficient work force. The California Business Roundtable consisted of several-score corporation presidents (not their public affairs officers), who devoted significant energy and intelligence to learning about the state's educational problems and what might be done about them.

Just as significant, state-level politicians from coast to coast rediscovered the issue of education. Through most of the 1970s, education committees in the state capitols represented virtually the last choice for freshman legislators with verve and ambition. Governors, too, preferred to focus on social welfare programs, prisons, environmental issues, agriculture, and industrial expansion—anything, it seemed, but education. Before 1983, most politicians saw little advantage and considerable risk in emphasizing issues associated with educational improvement. Schools were being closed in every state because of the decline in the numbers of children. Money was tight. People feel passionately about their schools, particularly those who send their children to them, and politicians saw little to be gained by becoming associated with the unpopular decisions necessary to shrink a huge enterprise with a strong emotional foothold in virtually every community, while dealing with a powerful, large, and increasingly assertive union. Suddenly, it seemed in 1983, politicians were featuring education improvement in their major speeches and in their election platforms. Even those with national political aspirations, such as Gov. James Hunt of North Carolina, were asking to be judged on the basis of their records in education.

While the renewed interest in education seemed encouraging to many teachers and school administrators, there was still apprehension and skepticism. Would the nation hear once gain that the problems in the schools are caused by teachers who are too child centered, or insufficiently informed about their subjects, or too preoccupied with raising their own salaries? Would there be a tendency to find scapegoats or to blame the victims? Just as much a cause of concern among informed school people, would there be initiatives by an awakening public that might actually impair the ability of schools to improve educational quality, however well motivated those initiatives might be? If so, it would not be the first time that the best of public intentions became associated with changes in schools that did not have the desired effects, and in fact were counterproductive. Educational change is tricky business. How does one balance the imperative of political will and the advantages of informed professional latitude? Which changes are best planned by state education departments and which by teachers and administrators in local districts? How does one best influence a "system" of about three million teachers who work for 16,000 different employers?

When Americans look for solutions to problems in the field of education, as in most areas of public concern, they usually begin by examining the possibility of writing new laws. School codes—laws and accompanying regulations—now run to tens of thousands of pages in many states. Children do not read well? Pass a law that requires the demonstration of reading ability at a certain level before the child may be moved to the next grade or awarded a high school diploma. Concerned that handicapped children are not receiving instruction geared to their distinctive needs? Pass a law that requires an "individualized education plan" for each child; in addition, require that the plan be negotiated by the teacher with the parents to give those with the most at stake a chance to participate in the process. How better to assure accountability? Legislative responses to serious problems seem deeply satisfying. The laws often have a direct appeal and an apparently compelling logic. They are usually preceded by considerable study and debate. Those responsible for the initiatives work hard for them. The prime movers feel a sense of concrete accomplishment.

Examine the results of each piece of legislation designed to improve educational outcomes, however, and you begin to note results that do not always correspond to the intent to those who wrote the laws. With the passage of "minimum competency" laws, for example, test scores, at least for some children, go down, not up. Pass a law requiring an individualized education plan for each child, and service to handicapped children declines rather than expands. How come?

At one level, new laws are symbolic expressions of shifting public attention and priority. They reflect a new focus of public interest and sometimes crystallize consensus: we had better take the plight of handicapped children and their parents more seriously; our school system is not doing well enough for youngsters who need basic reading skills; non-English-speaking children need special attention. Insofar as such declarations represent a new resolve by the public to attend to a matter whose priority is elevated, little harm is done. Public schools are public institutions. Politics is an expression of the public will. Schools have always been subjected to intense political pressures. To secure the necessary financial support, they must be responsive. However, when legislators move beyond an affirmation of intentions to frame laws governing specific educational practices, to be followed by regulations that prescribe the details of how teachers are to work with children and which tests are to be administered for which purpose, the results become unpredictable and often seemingly perverse. This is the situation in much of the United States today.

For example, with respect to the minimum competency legislation, the intention and the message to teachers and school administrators are clear enough. We have a large population of youngsters in school who are not learning basic skills associated with reading and computation. The situation is undesirable and perhaps intolerable. The law directs renewed attention to the educational needs of this population. Unless the examinations are passed, the child does not advance in the educational system or does not receive a diploma.

As intended, after such laws are introduced, reading scores do go up for youngsters who before the law was enacted did not possess the skills required to pass the examination. Children who did not read and compute are now reading and computing. But success is not that simple (though accomplishment is seldom acknowledged). It is noticed, too, that scores for the most able children begin to decline at the same time. What is happening?

Determining causality is always a difficult issue in understanding social phenomena, but it seems reasonable to conclude that without an increase in resources, which typically is the case when new demands to serve the educational needs of a large population of youngsters are imposed, the other children receive less time from teachers. Here is one way it happens: because of new test requirements, a school superintendent or a principal is expected to raise the skill levels of a significant number of the youngsters in the school quickly, as many as 20 or 30 percent of the children in some instances. The administrator examines the resources available to meet the educational needs of all the youngsters in the school and decides to give priority to those policies that use available resources to serve the most children. The decision is made to close small classes and reassign their teachers. The principle seems reasonable, fair, uniform in application, and easy to explain: concentrate the available teaching force in classes that enroll the largest number of children.

It turns out, however, that the large classes are the introductory courses in a subject or the remedial courses intended to teach the minimally required skills. The small classes are often those in advanced biology, or calculus, or the third year of a foreign language. The minimum competency movement, so reasonable in intent, seems to lower the educational accomplishments of a district's most able students because it deprives them of a chance to do advanced work, an outcome no one intended and few people predicted.

Minimum competency laws are passed at the state level. The Education of All Handicapped Children Act is a federal law. It is unusual for the federal government to become involved in matters of education. The Tenth Amendment to the Constitution reserves to the states those functions not explicitly assigned to the federal government, and education is not mentioned in the Constitution. In areas of clear federal responsibility, such as strengthening the national defense and assuring equal protection for all citizens, the Congress has a role. The Education of All Handicapped Children Act was passed in 1975. It flowed directly from principles that were enunciated in the 1960s and early 1970s as part of the civil rights movement. Handicapped children were seen in the minds of those who lobbied for them and of those in the Congress as a minority group, like blacks or Hispanics. They were entitled to the education received by everyone else. The law called for handicapped children to be put in the "least restrictive environment" in every school. This action led to the "mainstreaming" of handicapped children—that is, to their placement insofar as possible in regular, not special, classes.

In many instances such placements prove effective for the handicapped child, though not always. Many handicapping conditions require almost constant adult supervision. Mainstreaming has sometimes resulted in a reduction of service to the afflicted child. Putting that outcome aside, however, we can say that the placement of handicapped children in regular classrooms almost always requires a level of attention from the teacher that is disproportionate to the attention given other children. The regular teacher is often ill prepared to work with youngsters who are mentally retarded, emotionally disturbed, orthopedically disabled, or visually impaired. The impulse to mainstream is humane. Often, though not always, it is in the best interest of the handicapped child. But there is a trade-off. The disproportionate amount of time that the teacher must work with handicapped youngsters is time taken from the other children.

Advocates of new social policy initiatives attempt to support their policy preferences with research whenever possible. When the new laws affecting the education of handicapped children were passed, there was indeed a considerable amount of education research indicating that the educational achievement of children with handicapping conditions was often improved by their being required to meet the standards held for other children, and in the same settings. However, about 90 percent of the studies that had been done on mainstreaming at that time addressed only the issue of how such a practice affects the children to be mainstreamed. Only a few studies gave any attention to the effect that such a practice has on the teacher or on the other children.[9]

In the same Education of All Handicapped Children Act, and as if to give another example of how laws about the details of teaching practice can be mischievous, the Congress incorporated a requirement that an "individualized education plan" be developed for each child, to be negotiated between teacher and parent. Such a plan was advocated by specialists in the education of handicapped children. Representatives and senators were also impressed by the effectiveness of such a practice in serving the needs of handicapped children in many districts. It seemed to represent sound practice where it was used, and it provided an uncommon degree of accountability. Impressed, the legislators wrote the requirement into law.

Soon afterward, it was noticed that in order to develop the new plans for each child, teachers began to spend an increasing share of their time in conference with parents and in providing the written documentation that the law and subsequent regulation required. The written document—the individualized plan—became the instrument for monitoring compliance with the law. Administrators, parents, and the education auditors took the plans seriously. The result: teachers spent less time with the children. They were busier conferring with parents and keeping the written records that the law demanded. Since new teachers usually were not hired, direct service to handicapped children actually declined. To a degree, the preparation of the written document became a surrogate for personal service to youngsters.

Global definitions of educational problems tend to breed global solutions. Most legislators have a penchant for translating good ideas into legal requirements. It is the only tool at their disposal. They aren't stupid, of course, or mean. But the public expects them to act on problems, not necessarily with much thought about which problems are most amenable to legal redress and which to other methods.

Laws are blunt instruments. There is little understanding or appreciation of the fact that the provision of a personal service, such as teaching a child to understand the binomial theorem, often requires a degree of sensitivity and accommodation at the site where the service is provided that enables the person providing the service to adjust his or her approach depending on circumstances. Out of frustration with what we see as poor service, we attempt to assure at least a minimum level of accomplishment and accountability, but such attempts almost invariably lead to a standardization of practice. There frequently is some elevation in minimum accomplishment as a result, but there is usually a leveling down as well.

This argument is not meant to minimize the importance of accountability on the part of teachers and school administrators. The issue, rather, is one of how to achieve a balance between the initiatives best taken by the public's elected representatives and those attempts at enhancing quality that are best left to the professionals who operate the system. The tension is not new in American education, but the momentum in recent years has been clearly in the direction of greater political assertiveness and reduced professional discretion.

To strike the most effective balance between politicians and teacher, it would be helpful to have a clearer picture of the kind of teacher the country wants. If teaching is something like plumbing, then it is appropriate for the public through various laws and codes to specify in considerable detail the standards to be applied in judging adequacy. Those who practice the craft must understand the requirements, but there is not much latitude associated with how an individual task is to be accomplished. If teaching third-grade arithmetic is like soldering a joint, then some individual discretion is required, as in any craft, but not much. The emphasis is on skill. On the other hand, if teaching mathematics requires that the teacher make adjustments based on the motivational level of different children in the class, on his or her understanding of the intellectual level at which different children are functioning, and on a comprehension of the subject matter sufficient to know which of the children's questions have intellectual mileage and which do not (and which should therefore dominate in classroom discussions), then considerable latitude is necessary at the level of classroom instruction. It makes little sense to try very much presecription of practice from afar.

Moving to a different issue associated with the current legally rooted strategies for educational change, we note that a partial result of the recent pattern of problem identification, legislation, and regulation in education is that the public identifies one troublesome matter at a time, then directs virtually all attention to it. There is concern about gifted children and the space race in the late 1950s, and a massive attempt is made to improve the quality of the curriculum in science and mathematics. It turns out that the schools respond positively. America is first on the moon. High technology thrives. But the country does not seem to notice. In the time it takes to respond discernibly to the identified problem, the public has shifted its attention to a different criticism of the schools, this time the distressing achievement levels of the poor. The nation and the schools redirect energy toward that population, again with success. Within a decade, test scores go up for those who used to do least well. But again the achievement does not seem to register with the public. Instead, there is a new outpouring of publicity about declining test scores for the brightest children and America's diminishing position in world trade. Priorities in education change with unpredictable frequency and intensity. The schools are told to work on one feature of the system with little understanding of what is as a result happening to others. And there is little acknowledgment of the volatile and impermanent nature of the public attention span.

One of the most troublesome aspects of the American inclination to change priorities quickly is that teachers become demoralized. As a group, those who staff the schools want to serve youngsters and please the public. Very few people enter the field because of the financial rewards or, these days, the job security. Teachers and school administrators are no more or no less conscientious than others. When the nation says it wants to train scientists and mathematicians, the schools respond; and they succeed. Similarly, monumental progress is made on teaching basic skills when the public sends the message to schools that this is the outcome it wants. However, when the accomplishments of the schools in response to each new declaration of urgency are ignored, discouragement sets in. It is understandable that priorities shift. They do in almost every enterprise. But, somehow, in the field of education teachers seldom receive a message conveying a sense of appreciation for work that has been done well.

The argument advanced here is not that the country should diminish attempt to improve educational quality for a range of children in the schools through the political process. It should not diminish them. Rather, the intent is to question how such a goal is to be achieved without weakening the capacity of schools to provide education, and in particular without discouraging those who must play a major role in doing what the public wants. A possibly fatal flaw in attempts to improve programs primarily through legislative remedies is that expectations at the level of school and classroom are lowered for developing creative responses to problems. When it is reiterated in the various cycles of educational reform that problems and their resolution are universal and that legislators will develop the "solutions," the local inclination to be responsive is diminished. After a while, the expectation is created that problems will be solved primarily by somebody else.

For example, transcript analyses of California high school students reveal that there is considerable consistency in the courses taken by the top 20 percent of students. Putting aside the issue of what actually happens in Algebra I when the door is shut, the titles of the courses taken by the top-ability group are similar as one moves from one youngster to the next. They are probably guided in their choices by college requirements. Similarly, there is consistency in course titles for youngsters in the poorest-achieving 20 percent. They probably know what courses they must take to prepare for the minimum competency examinations. However, there is little pattern in course taking for the middle 60 percent.

Are there too many electives? Are the youngsters preparing for a large number of different occupations? Is there a broad range of ability in the middle group? Is there considerable pressure from the community to offer a variety of courses? The "solution" to the "problem" of patternlessness depends in significant measure on the diagnosis. If the pattern reflects an outdated or no-longer-supported view about choice or a casual response to apparent interests, then a well-defined core curriculum may be indicated. On the other hand, if the population served is enormously varied and if the school has a community-supported approach to help different children reach clearly defensible goals, then a plan to institute a core program might be misdirected. Legislatures do not make these distinctions.

Another example: a school district is having great difficulty teaching youngsters in the first grade whose first language is not English. This problem indeed exists in thousands of school districts across the country. Assume that those who recognize and must deal with the issue understand the limitations of solely legislative remedies. What strategies for educational change make sense?

One approach is to assemble experts: linguists, authorities on language acquisition, successful teachers, sociologists, psychologists, and others. Ask the group to develop a course of study based on the soundest research and most reasonable theories to teach English to six-year-old youngsters in American schools who speak it poorly and who were raised in a different tongue. Millions of dollars might be invested in course development by a determined nation. The task is then to "disseminate" the program devised by the experts to school districts around the country.

This method of curricular development and educational change was prevalent during the 1960s, when school programs were being modified at the urging of the National Science Foundation to develop a cadre of young people with strong education in science and mathematics. Outstanding scientists were assembled. They worked with teachers, psychologists, and other educational experts to prepare new courses. Although these efforts of the 1960s had many beneficial effects, the courses of study developed during that period were seldom used as designed. More-traditional texts continued to predominate (though they began to include topics suggested by the reformers). Where the new texts were used as written, however, the programs rarely met the expectations of the developers. Physics texts, for example, were prepared to help children understand how scientific lines of argument are developed—that is, how scientists think about the issues they work on. The children were often expected to engage in independent inquiry so that they would begin to have firsthand experience with scientific thinking.

When the curriculum developers observed in classrooms where the new texts had been adopted, however, they were sometimes shocked by what they saw. Children were often taking turns reading from the new books. They would then be asked by the teacher to repeat what they had just read. The method of teaching was directly counter to the spirit intended by the course developers. Although books had been written to stimulate original inquiry, reading and occasional lecture, followed by recitation, were still the primary methods of instruction. Somehow the guiding impetus for the new courses did not seem to be captured by teachers, at least not by large numbers of them.

On the other hand, modern topics in science and mathematics were introduced as a result of the curricular reform movement. Texts became more accurate as well. Furthermore, teachers were motivated at a high level because outstanding scientists and mathematicians, by redirecting their own activities toward issues of precollege education, were underscoring the importance of secondary school teaching to the country. In addition, considerable amounts of money were devoted to new programs of in-service teacher education, often during the summer months, in which teachers were subsidized to learn about the new topics. There were thus many beneficial effects, but large-scale teaching in the spirit of the course developers was not one of them.

The implementation of new educational programs is a difficult and sensitive matter. Teachers vary enormously in their training, their interests, and their tastes. So do children. So do individual communities. Different high schools have different expectations of their children and teachers that are complex and special—and uncomprehended in a policy-making body far from the school. A text-writing team has as much difficulty as a state legislature in designing courses and teaching approaches that they can expect to be instituted with fidelity.

Is there an approach to fostering educational change that holds more promise of success than those typically employed do, or are the current strategies for change in schools the only ones available? The answer is that there are indeed other methods, but they are relatively untried on a systematic basis, and there are weaknesses associated with them, too. To stay with the same example, if one wants to improve the teaching of English to youngsters in the first grade who speak it poorly and for whom it is not the first language, it might at the outset be noted that because the problem is widespread in the United States there already are thousands of classrooms where teachers are wrestling with the issue. While there may not be a single, ideal approach in evidence anywhere, some teachers are clearly more effective than others. Furthermore, most observers would agree about which programs are best. One strategy for educational change that capitalizes upon rather than ignores the natural variation already existing within the system is to identify the teachers who do relatively well. What particular combination of teaching technique, site leadership, student population, community support, and school organization seems to be operating to have established a praiseworthy program? Instead of solely designing a completely new approach to the problem, those who want to improve schools might search as well for factors that seem responsible for existing high-quality programs. By analyzing their characteristics, one begins to understand how programs in other locations that seem similar in essential points like level of teachers' competence, demographics, and financial support might be improved. The main theme of this line of argument, of course, is the age-old admonition "Build on strength." Do not devote all energies to redressing weakness. An inclination to recognize and capitalize on strength is not only an acknowledgment of success that has arisen within the system; it also provides proven direction for educational change.

An approach broadly along the lines outlined here would place a greater premium than commonly exists on understanding the origins of current practice. Teachers and school administrators are no more capricious, stupid, or perverse than legislators, politicians, businessmen, or professors. As in every field, some are well motivated, some are more able, some are more intelligent than others; but, as a profession, teachers and school administrators strive as conscientiously as anyone else to meet the varying demands on their time and skills, probably more so because they are in the eye of the public continually. School boards, more than 16,000 of them across the country, are monitoring, setting policy, and providing direction. So are state departments of education. So are politicians. So are journalists. If a program for teaching reading, science, or mathematics exists in a school district, it has obviously met the usual impediments to innovation successfully. It becomes important, then, to understand how a new practice has taken root, how inertia was overcome, how competing interests have been accommodated, and how the resources were identified to establish the program. Instead of continual remediation, policymakers might begin to look at what's right and try to understand it.

The imagery employed here is that of biological evolution. Natural variation exists in a system as large as American education. Some of the variation is adaptive. The strategic task becomes one of finding out how the particular niche for the program was created and of reproducing or tailoring it to new settings.

Among the advantages of such an approach to educational change is the fact that the new school programs thus identified are credible to teachers and administrators. If practices exist, then those who currently teach have reason to believe people already staffing the schools have the capacity to make improvements. Strategies for educational change that build on strength also have the advantage of raising the self-esteem of teachers, a significant goal in today's climate of criticism and crisis.

Strategies for changing schools are centered almost exclusively on the system of public education. More than independent schools, of course, public schools are regulated by and legally accountable to political bodies. Despite the extraordinary attention to the deficiencies of tax-supported education, there has been very little public interest in or movement toward non-public schools, at least so far. In 1976, 10.5 percent of the children in elementary and secondary schools were in non-public institutions, including parochial schools. That figure climbed to 10.9 percent in 1980. (In 1960, the figure was 13.3 percent.)[10]

It could be otherwise. In the national concern about and impatience with the educational system, one might expect attempts to seek an alternative. Such a possibility is highlighted by periodic attempts to introduce tuition tax credits and school voucher plans. Such initiatives may yet prevail. So far, however, despite the personal support given these two measures by the President of the United States, other politicians, business leaders, and the general public seem to be rejecting the private school option.

While there are many reasons for continued attention to the improvement of public education, and while it would be difficult to predict how long the emphasis will last, one explanatory factor may well be associated with our urgent search for national identity and purpose. Americans as a group have seemed disappointed with themselves through much of the 1960s and 1970s. There has been little celebration of accomplishment. As the country searches for institutions that have the potential to help establish a sense of nationhood, the schools stand out. There probably is a significant cultural memory that helps people appreciate the role of the public schools in helping to unify an extraordinarily varied population in the past. The common schools were an American invention of the nineteenth century. The public was persuaded that they were created to pursue the common good. They are widely credited with helping an emerging people develop a sense of unity and purpose. There is an unarticulated hope, perhaps, that these institutions will be a major force once again in helping the country ascend to its next phase of accomplishment and pride.

Yet the potential of well-intended reform to cripple the system is real. In its impatience for change and in the national preoccupation with faults, the country runs the risk of weakening the very institutions it is trying to strengthen. Schools are more vulnerable than many people seem to think. If changes are imposed that lower morale or have other pronounced negative effects, even if unintended, the system is significantly damaged. It becomes a target for fresh criticism, and a downward spiral can be the result. For this reason, strategies for educational change should be examined with as much care and sensitivity as can be mustered—with a special eye on unintended side effects—even if such a posture means blunting some apparently irresistible reforms. Better to institute changes piecemeal and steadily than to risk large numbers of untested but mammoth perturbations to the system that as a result of unanticipated and undesirable consequences breed counterreaction and overcorrection. No system is infinitely resilient. It is time in American education to consider more conservative and realistic approaches to educational reform, even if they mean reassessment of the goals for public education and somewhat lowered expectations.

PART TWO

Reform and the Curriculum

4

Curriculum in Crisis: Connections between Past and Present

DIANE RAVITCH

With the publication of the report of the National Commission on Excellence in Education in the spring of 1983, and with the near-simultaneous appearance of several other critical studies of the condition of American education, school reform suddenly rose to the top of the domestic policy agenda. Governors, state legislators, professional educators, presidential candidates, and citizen groups debated a wide variety of proposals for improving the schools. Among the proposed reforms, two issues dominated: first, the quality of the teaching staff and, second, the quality of the curriculum. As problems, these issues were closely interrelated, since there would be no point in requiring students to take more science, for example, if the schools were unable to hire sufficient numbers of science teachers. The remedies under discussion necessarily differed, with the teacher issue focused on increased incentives and the curriculum issue focused on increased high school graduation requirements. Insofar as it is translated into programs for study, retraining, and compensation, the teacher issue may be characterized as a question of public-sector resource allocation (whether such responses are adequate to provide well-educated teachers in the public's classrooms is by no means clear). The curriculum issue, however, is a question less of how much money is spent than of resolving conflicts among deeply held attitudes about education and building consensus about what studies, if any, are to be required of all students. What the present paper will attempt to do is examine the curricular implications of the educational reform proposals and to set them in the context of the historical development of the high school curriculum.

* * *

In 1975 the public learned that the national average on the Scholastic Aptitude Test, a college entrance examination taken by about one million students annually, had dropped steadily and dramatically for a dozen years. This indication that something might be seriously amiss in the schools—or somewhere—prompted a series of investigations during the next decade. In most of the national educational reports produced in the late 1970s and the early 1980s, the need for curricular reform was a loud refrain. The major problems identified were seen as declining achievement and declining enrollments in academic courses. These phenomena were usually attributed to inadequate instructional time and to a dilution of the curriculum.

The College Board appointed a blue-ribbon panel, chaired by the former secretary of labor Willard Wirtz, to conduct its inquiry. While notably reluctant to pin the blame for the decline in verbal and mathematical skills on the schools during a period that included the Vietnam War, Watergate, and incessant social turmoil, the Wirtz panel found evidence that schools had been requiring fewer basic courses and introducing many new electives. In Massachusetts, for example, the number of schools offering filmmaking increased, while those offering eleventh-grade English and world history decreased. Ater taking note of grade inflation, social promotion, and the lessened quality of reading and writing, the panel agreed that standards had fallen in the schools, but it avoided any indictment of curricular practices: "We do not read the SAT score decline as an instruction that education in this country must or should be more rigid, more selective, more rejective, more uniform. Instead, the instruction is that education, especially secondary education, must become still more diversified, more varied—but without being watered down."[1]

In reaching this conclusion, the Wirtz panel noted but disregarded the research of Harnischfeger and Wiley, whose 1976 study described a sharp falloff of enrollment in academic courses during the period under discussion. They found "a total drop of almost 11 percent in English enrollments" between 1970 and 1972 and called this "a probable and startling cause of verbal score declines." Although they concluded that there was no "sole and solitary cause of declining scores," they nonetheless held that "the strongest explanatory power seems to come from curricular changes. Our gross data indicate a considerable enrollment decline in academic courses. Secondary pupils have been taking fewer courses in general English and mathematics. But also enrollment in typical college preparatory courses, such as Algebra, first-year foreign languages, and physics, is decreasing."[2]

Two reports issued by the Carter administration implied that the trend toward electives had expanded the gap between the academic haves and the have-nots. In 1979, the President's Commission on Foreign Language and International Studies complained, "Americans' incompetence in foreign languages is nothing short of scandalous, and it is becoming worse." The commission pointed out that "only 15 percent of American high school students now study a foreign language—down from 24 percent in 1965." It also noted with concern that only one out of twenty high school students studied a foreign language beyond the second year, even though four years' study was considered necessary for competence. A report in 1980 by the National Science Foundation and the Department of Education warned of "a current trend toward virtual scientific and technological illiteracy." The problem was that "[t]hose who are the best seem to be learning about as much as they ever did, while the majority of students learn less and less."[3]

At the state level, the most common response to this concern about educational quality was the passage of minimum competency tests by state legislatures. For political reasons, the passing level on these tests was set very low; these tests of the most minimal literacy skills had hardly any effect on the curricular problems that the national commissions had begun to identify. In some states, however, the search for educational improvement went beyond minimum competence. In California, for example, a group of business leaders called the California Roundtable commissioned a six-month study of student performance, which found that the school year and day had grown shorter; academic demands on students had been reduced; course content and textbooks had declined in quality; and students were taking fewer academic courses. In 1982, the Roundtable recommended specific changes, among which was an increase in statewide graduation requirements and the adoption of statewide curriculum standards.[4]

The reform activities within the states were accelerated when the report of the National Commission on Excellence appeared in 1983, followed five months later by Ernest Boyer's *High School.* (The fact that Boyer, president of the Carnegie Foundation for the Advancement of Teaching, had been commissioner of education in the Carter administration tended to neutralize partisanship in the discussion of education reform.) Though proceeding from somewhat different philosophical stances, both strongly endorsed a required common curriculum for all students. The National Commission argued that our "nation is at risk" because of mediocre educational performance and that American "prosperity, security, and civility" depended on a well-educated populace. Boyer focused less on the economic implications of school performance and more on the social and civic responsibilities of education. Both criticized the common practice of separating students into academic, vocational, and general curricular tracks.[5]

The National Commission produced a strong indictment of academic performance and current practices. It reported, "Secondary school curricula have been homogenized, diluted, and diffused to the point that they no longer have a central purpose. . . . The proportion of students taking a general program of study has increased from 12 percent in 1964 to 42 percent in 1979. This curricular smorgasbord, combined with extensive student choice, explains a great deal about where we find ourselves today. We offer intermediate algebra, but only 31 percent of our recent high school graduates complete it; we offer French I, but only 13 percent complete it; and we offer geography, but only 16 percent complete it." Boyer cited evidence of rising enrollments in such non-academic courses as driver education, general shop, and home economics; his study found that about 55 percent of the typical student's program was taken up with required courses.[6]

Boyer called his curricular proposal "a core of common learning" for all students. He suggested that the proportion of required courses should be raised from one-half to about two-thirds of the total necessary for graduation. His core included five units (or years) of language (including two of a foreign language), two and one-half units of history (happily, not social studies!), one unit of civics, two units of science, two units of mathematics, plus assorted half-units on technology, health, work, and an independent community service project. In the typical schedule of five courses per year for four years, Boyer's core would take up fourteen and one-half units, leaving five and one-half units for electives.

The National Commission on Excellence recommended what it called "the New Basics": four years of English; three years of mathematics, science, and social studies; one-half year of computer science; and, for the college bound, at least two years of foreign language. Just how far removed American students were from these requirements was revealed in a study by the National Center for Education Statistics, which sampled the transcripts of 1982 high school graduates: only 1.8 percent met all of the commission's requirements; of those who planned to attend college for at least four years, only 3.7 percent did. Excluding the foreign-language and computer science recommendation, one finds that only 13.4 percent of all students and 22.6 percent of the college bound satisfied the remaining requirements.[7]

The consensus in favor of requirements was further strengthened by the report of the National Science Board Commission on Precollege Education in Mathematics, Science and Technology, which joined the crowded field in the fall of 1983. "Simply put," said the panel, "students in our Nation's schools are learning less mathematics, science and technology, particularly in the areas of abstract thinking and problem solving. Since the late 1960s, most students have taken fewer mathematics and science courses. Mathematics and science achievement scores of 17-year-olds have dropped steadily and dramatically during the same period." The bipartisan panel recommended the introduction of a coherent pattern of instruction in these subject areas, beginning in kindergarten and extending through the high school years. At the high school level, the panel recommended that "all secondary school students should be required to take at least three years of mathematics, science and technology."[8]

By late 1983, a national survey found that forty-six states had either raised their graduation requirements recently or were debating proposals to do so. Yet the apparent stampede to require students to study the traditional academic subjects was not unimpeded. A national shortage of teachers of science and mathematics made the imposition of new requirements problematic. There was no similar rush to set requirements for foreign-language instruction, in part because of doubt about its value but also because of the shortage of certified teachers in any non-English language. Other doubts were expressed: How would the states pay for strengthening the curriculum? Would the dropout rate soar if graduation standards were toughened? Would disproportionate numbers of black and Hispanic students fail to meet the higher standards? Would vocational programs be undermined by the new emphasis on academic courses? Would the new requirements stifle the artistically oriented students who dislike mathematics and science, as well as the scientifically gifted students who dislike history and literature? Not far from the surface of the public debate hovered the suspicion that there was something elitist and mean-spirited about the new reforms, that they represented little more than an effort to fit a diversity of children into a Procrustean bed meant only for the college bound.[9]

The struggle over the "right" curriculum for the high school has been nearly continuous ever since there was a significant number of public high schools. The earliest high schools were academies, pay schools that offered a wide variety of courses. To satisfy student demand, academies usually offered both college preparatory courses (consisting primarily of Latin, Greek, and mathematics) and such courses as English grammar, rhetoric, logic, composition, geography, surveying, bookkeeping, navigation, moral philosophy, and astronomy. At their peak, in 1850, there were some 6,000 academies, which enrolled some 260,000 students. Although a number of states subsidized them, the academies in the 1870s and the 1880s were overtaken by the public high schools, which were controlled by public authorities and paid for by public funds. The curriculum of the public high schools tended to follow a two-track pattern: the "classical" curriculum of Greek, Latin, and mathematics for the few who were preparing for college; and the "English" curriculum, which usually included the diverse modern academic and practical courses found in the academy. Some of the larger public high schools offered a third or fourth curriculum, such as "Latin-scientific," which was the classical curriculum with Latin but not Greek, and the modern-language curriculum, in which German or French was taught instead of a classical language.[10]

In the late nineteenth century, the lines separating colleges and high schools were blurred. Admission to college was based on examinations, not on the credits presented, and many colleges contained departments where students prepared for the examinations. By 1890, there were about 200,000 students in public high schools (and almost 100,000 in private high schools); like academy students, all attended voluntarily, and about 10 percent remained to graduate. As the public high school expanded, educators' interest in practical courses grew, as did criticism of Greek and Latin. At professional conferences, there were repeated calls for courses that were better suited to preparing students for the real world than the languages of the ancient world were. The classicists responded to their critics by claiming that their time-honored subjects were superior for disciplining the mind and the will. The boy or girl who mastered Greek, Latin, and higher mathematics, it was said, could do anything else well.

There were four troublesome issues for high schools in the early 1890s. First was the antagonism between the classical curriculum and the modern academic subjects like science, English literature, and modern foreign languages; since only a tiny minority was actually preparing for college, many teachers and principals resented the "tyranny" (and elevated social status) associated with Greek and Latin. (According to Edward A. Krug, even though a reading knowledge of Greek was required by some colleges for admission, in 1889–90 only 3 percent of public high school pupils studied it, and only 7 percent of those in private high schools.) Second was the problem of preparing students to meet college entrance requirements. Each college had its own requirements even for the same subjects: in Greek, one insisted on Homer, another on Xenophon; in English literature (a "modern" subject), one demanded Chaucer and Burke, while another insisted on Milton and Shakespeare;

still other colleges had no specific readings at all. The third issue derived from the increasing pressure by forward-looking educators to include practical courses like manual training, in order to prepare students for the real world. The fourth issue, intimately related to the other three, was whether the high school should have different curricula for those who were college bound and those who were not.[11]

Uncertainty about these issues led the National Education Association, the organizational voice of principals and superintendents, to create what must have been the first national blue-ribbon panel to examine the high school curriculum in 1892. Chaired by Harvard's President Charles W. Eliot, the Committee of Ten on Secondary School Studies organized nine "conferences" of teachers and scholars to consider the school subjects and make recommendations as to how they should be taught and whether it was appropriate to differentiate between the college bound and others. The Committee of Ten surveyed 40 high schools and discovered that thirty-six different subjects were offered, a number that must have suggested the "disorder" and miscellaneousness of the high school curriculum. The thirty-six subjects included five languages (Greek, Latin, French, German, and Spanish); six mathematics courses; four science courses; four history and government courses; English courses; and such miscellany as stenography, penmanship, and music. How astonished Eliot and his colleagues would have been to read a survey of 741 Illinois high schools in 1977, which found 2,100 separate courses, most of them in nonacademic fields![12]

The 1893 report of the Committee of Ten was surprisingly bereft of the rhetorical flights of fancy that for the next ninety years came to be standard in statements on the role of education in American society. In a spare and understated tone, the Ten made several recommendations. First, it came down firmly against differentiation; indeed, all nine subject-matter conferences agreed "that every subject which is taught at all in a secondary school should be taught in the same way and to the same extent to every pupil so long as he pursues it, no matter what the probable destination of the pupil may be, or at what point his education is to cease." Since so small a number of high school graduates went to college, the Ten insisted that "the secondary schools of the United States, taken as a whole, do not exist for the purpose of preparing boys and girls for colleges." Their chief function was to prepare students for "the duties of life." The case against differentiation was best stated by the history conference, which complained that in some institutions "those who are to get most training hereafter [i.e., the college bound] are the only ones who have any training in history in the schools." The history teachers held "that such a distinction, especially in schools provided for the children by public taxation, is bad for all classes of pupils. It is the duty of the schools to furnish a well grounded and complete education. . . ."[13]

The second major recommendation by the Committee of Ten was that the modern academic sbujects should be made equal in status to the classical curriculum and should be equally acceptable for the purposes of college admission. To this end, it proposed four model curricula, all of which should be acceptable to colleges: classical (containing three foreign languages, including Greek and Latin); Latin-scientific (containing two foreign languages, one modern); modern language (containing two modern foreign languages); and English (containing only one foreign language, either ancient or modern). The model curricula offered by the committee implied that neither Latin nor Greek was absolutely necessary for college preparation and that students should be able to choose from among different programs (even within the different curricula, there was a modest degree of choice from among sciences or languages). But all four of the model curricula included courses in English, mathematics, history, science, and foreign language: all were variations of what would today be called a liberal education curriculum.

The report was widely discussed and debated for years after its publication, and it ultimately suffered a curious fate. The progressive educator Francis Parker saluted its stand against "class education," saying, "There is no reason why one child should study Latin and another be limited to the 3 R's." But G. Stanley Hall, the leader of the child study movement, castigated the Ten as elitists who put too much emphasis on preparation for college, instead of for life, and who ignored what he called "the great army of incapables, shading down to those who should be in schools for dullards or subnormal children." Hall complained that the report of the Ten was responsible for rising enrollments in Latin, which he thought decadent. In response to Hall's critique, Eliot said that early division of pupils into "future peasants, mechanics, trades-people, merchants, and professional people" was common in Europe but unsuited to a democratic society. He insisted that there was no conflict between preparing for life and preparing for college, since all good education is good preparation for life. Eliot insisted that there were only a small number of "incapables" in school and "that any school superintendent or principal who should construct his program with the incapables chiefly in mind would be a person professionally demented."[14]

The strange fate of the report of the Committee of Ten was that the critics successfully branded it a reactionary document that ignored individual differences, written by college presidents who wanted to force all children to take a college preparatory curriculum. Edward A. Krug, the historian of the high school, called this reversal a paradox: "The idea of giving early and separate treatment to those who could identify themselves as college-bound pupils became known as a 'liberal' point of view; while the opposite notion, that of providing the broadest possible entry for all pupils to college, became known as 'conservative.'"[15]

The problem with the report of the Ten was that it was out of joint with the times. The influx of millions of immigrants to the nation's cities put new strains on the schools. The fact that most of them came from eastern and southern Europe caused popular and scholarly commentators to bemoan the future of Anglo-Saxon America, deluged as it was by a genetically inferior and culturally backward mass. The gravest social problem, in the eyes of most contemporary observers, was how to assimilate these illiterate hordes. The schools were, of course, expected to play a leading role in the mission of Americanizing the immigrants through their children. This meant not only teaching them English but also assuming a custodial role, which forced the schools to take responsibility for training them as good citizens and to tell them how to prepare for jobs, how to keep clean, and what was expected of them in everyday life. To meet some of these needs, new courses joined the high school curriculum, such as training for specific trades, sewing, cooking, and commercial studies. In response to what were perceived to be the needs of immigrant children, some educators avidly campaigned for vocational education, industrial education, and trade schools. Because these educators based their advocacy on the needs of a changing society and economy as well as on a recognition of the diversity of children, they were clothed in the garb of reformers; those who resisted the onslaught and contended that all children should be liberally educated were pigeonholed as conservatives, tied to the academic status quo, indifferent to new educational theories fitting the curriculum to the child, and insensitive to the changing conditions about them.

The Committee of Ten's proposal to permit students to choose from among four different curricula ran afoul of more than the new economic conditions. Within the profession, there was a strong sentiment for flexibility and student choice. In 1899, the NEA appointed a committee, called the Committee on College-Entrance Requirements, which offered a new solution to the problems of the high school curriculum. Instead of parallel courses of study, the new comittee recommended the concept of "constants," studies to be taken by all pupils, leaving the rest of their program for free electives. The committee recommended that all students take four years of foreign language, two of mathematics, two of English, one of history, and one of science. This simple suggestion seemed a brilliant stroke, suddenly freeing the high schools of the legacy of discrete courses of study ("classical," "English," and so on).

Yet even the turn to "constants" was for some a transitory expedient: the chairman of the Committee on College-Entrance Requirements declared less than a year after presenting his report that he personally did not believe there should be any constants and that the high school diploma should go to any students who had persisted for four years, regardless of whether they had studied any foreign language, science, mathematics, or history. "It is not what our young people study," he said, "but how they study and how they are taught, that gives them power." High schools in five large cities experimented with the free-elective system at the turn of the century, and the principal of a Boston high school explained that the ideal high school was one with a pleasant room for study, a good library, and helpful teachers. The high school, he said, was the people's college, and the school "must not prescribe to the people what the people shall study." [17]

However, the interest in an elective system organized around certain "constants" or even a totally free elective system was not nearly as persistent as the practice of directing students into separate courses. As more and more practical subjects entered the high school curriculum, new courses of study appeared: a manual training course, a vocational course, a commercial course, and—of course—a college preparatory course. With the arrival of the new practical subjects, the distinction between the classical curriculum and the modern academic subjects disappeared. Progressive reformers lumped the two together as the college preparatory curriculum. And what had once been a contest between the classical curriculum and the modern subjects became converted in a short space of years into a rivalry between a traditional curriculum and a practical curriculum. School leaders insisted that it was inappropriate to force students to take college prep courses if they intended to go directly to work, that what they needed were the skills to prepare for life. The development of separate curricula was inevitably based on presumptions about students' future occupations, as Charles Eliot had feared. It was odd that less than fifteen years after the Committee of Ten had inveighed against differentiating on the grounds of students' occupational destination, the practice was not only widespread but also seemed progressive and liberal.

In the decade before World War I, industrial education was the wave of the future. The growth of American industry, the worldwide competition for markets, the need to train immigrants to be good workers—all presented compelling arguments for making the work of the schools more practical. Critics complained that the schools' stubborn adherence to abstract and academic studies was failing to meet either the needs of modern society or the needs of children. What was required was more job training, more preparation for specific occupations. Poor people, said the social reformers, didn't need to learn history and mathematics and literature; they needed the skills to be farmers and homemakers. Caught up in the new enthusiasm for industrial education, President Theodore Roosevelt declared in 1907, "Our school system is gravely defective in so far as it puts a premium upon mere literacy training and tends therefore to train the boy away from the farm and the workshop. Nothing is more needed than the best type of industrial school, the school for mechanical industries in the city, the school for practically teaching agriculture in the country."[18]

Industrial education had a certain appeal to educators, especially to those who felt besieged by the children of immigrants. Many of them were illiterate and overage; the spectacle of twelve-year-old boys sitting in first-grade classes did not please principals. Among the children of poverty, there were inevitably large numbers who had difficulty learning, which was hardly surprising, since so many urban classes had more than fifty pupils. It must have been easy to conclude that the children of poor immigrants needed an education to fit them quickly for the job market; not much more rationalization was needed to reach the view that an academic preparation should be reserved for the few who planned to go to college. Schools around the country introduced different curricula based on their pupils' probable occupations, and in 1915 the NEA's Department of Superintendence passed a resolution approving "the increasing tendency to establish, beginning with the seventh grade, differentiated courses of study aimed more effectively to prepare the child for his probable future activities."[19]

There was another element in the emerging pattern, stemming from the progressive spirit of social uplift. Social and political reformers ousted corrupt machine politicians, provided medical and social services for the poor, built playgrounds, improved working conditions, established settlement houses in the slums, and battled slum landlords. Naturally, the schools attracted the interest of progressive reformers, because the children of the next generation were gathered there, offering a splendid opportunity to contribute to social improvement. The sociologist Albion W. Small told a general meeting of the NEA in 1896; "Sociology demands of educators, finally, that they shall not rate themselves as leaders of children, but as makers of society." In an era when social reform was ascendant, educators too had a vital role as agents of social improvement, as soon as they recognized that the real purpose of the schools in a democracy was not simply to empower individuals but also to meet the needs of the society. As one school superintendent put it in 1913, "In a political and social democracy such as ours, children must be taught to live and to work together co-operatively; to submit their individual wills to the will of the majority; and to conform to social requirements whether they approve of them or not."[20]

The concept of social efficiency, which was popular among progressive reformers, put education into a new context. It informed educators that they had a critical role to play in shaping society, a far more exciting prospect than merely teaching children about literature or history or science. The possibility of not just serving society but of actually directing its destiny was irresistible, or at least more interesting. The traditional curriculum was inefficient; under its sway, children were taught history, literature, mathematics, and foreign language even though they were not going to college; it was not only wasteful of the children's time but also served no useful social purpose. It became conventional in educational meetings to assert that the traditional curriculum, everything associated with a liberal education, was designed for an aristocratic class and was therefore unsuited to schools in a democracy. When a group of high school English teachers defined the purposes of their subject as the development of the ability to write and speak, the knowledge of the best literature, the cultivation of a sense of style, and the inculcation of love for literature, a professional journal complained that they were too intellectual: "Where does trigonometry apply in a good woman's life? Will it contribute anything toward peace, happiness and contentment in the home? Will it bake any bread, sew on any buttons or rock any cradles?" Then there was the educational writer who read a story about Lady Jane Grey, who had preferred to read Plato rather than to go hunting with her friends in the park. The writer said, "If such a child were found to-day, I dare say she would be hurried off to a physician or a brain specialist."[21]

By the time of the First World War, a strong consensus had formed around social efficiency as the goal of education, and this consensus undergirded the report of the NEA's Commission on the Reorganization of Secondary Education. The commission organized subject-matter groups, as the earlier Committee of Ten had. The committee on ancient languages lamely tried to make a case for the utility of Latin; the committee on modern languages talked of stimulating interest in other nations. The committee on mathematics proposed dividing mathematics courses on the basis of the subject's probable utility to students in their future occupations. The committee on social studies held that the aim of their subject was good citizenship. "Facts, conditions, theories, and activities that do not contribute rather directly to the appreciation of methods of human betterment have no claim," it held, thus effectively disposing of ancient and medieval history and putting current events on a higher plane than history. The science committee tried to show the relevance of biology and chemistry to everyday living, but it was difficult to make a case for physics. As Krug observed, the effect of the emphasis on social utility was to put each subject into the docket to prove its value. The burden of proof was on those who believed in the liberating qualities of the academic studies; those who challenged them had to prove nothing.[22]

The Commission on the Reorganization of Secondary Education issued its report in 1918, which went down in educational history as the "Cardinal Principles of Secondary Education." The main objectives of high school education, said the commission, were "1. Health. 2. Command of fundamental processes. 3. Worthy home-membership. 4. Vocation. 5. Citizenship. 6. Worthy use of leisure. 7. Ethical character." It is noteworthy that the single reference to intellectual development, called "command of fundamental processes," did not appear in the early drafts of the report. Not surprisingly, the report endorsed differentiated curricula, based on future vocational interests, such as agricultural, business, clerical, industrial, fine arts, and household arts. Almost as an aside, the report added, "Provision should be made also for those having distinctively academic interests and needs."[23]

The committee did not intend to limit access to higher education; on the contrary, it believed that those who took a vocational curriculum should also be eligible for college admission. The vocational and anti-academic bent of the "Cardinal Principles" was not lost on high school officials. An NEA survey in 1928 of some 1,200 high school principals revealed that more than half had reorganized their curriculum as a result of the 1918 report. The subjects most often added were commercial studies, home economics, sciences, industrial arts, and social studies; the subjects most often dropped were Latin, French, ancient history, and advanced mathematics.[24]

The "Cardinal Principles" crystallized the new canon of professional educators. It was by no means innovative; it brought together a variety of complementary strands of the progressive era that merged into an ideology in which the schools were society's instrument for guiding the rising generation into socially useful roles. Anyone who protested that the schools were supposed to give children intellectual power, to transmit the accumulated wisdom of the past, and to empower young people to make their own decisions about how to be socially useful was apt to be dismissed as a conservative, imbued with reactionary and individualistic ideas. In order for schools to take their place as agencies of social change, educators had to shed antiquated views about the transmission of knowledge. To be a good teacher was well and good, but it could scarcely compare to the power that flowed to those who took responsibility for shaping and sorting the youth of the nation. No more would educators be "only" teachers, the somewhat impractical and underpaid Ichabod Cranes and schoolmasters to an ungrateful and uncultured people. With the "Cardinal Principles" as their banner, they had the satisfaction of seeing themselves as engineers of social change, marching in the forefront of reform.[25]

The education profession was not uniquely responsible for this new view of its historic mission: it was pushed, pulled, and prodded by reformers, economists, sociologists, even university presidents who believed that it was wasteful to give an academic education to those who were not planning to go to college. It was accepted as incontrovertible truth that an academic curriculum was appropriate only for those who needed it to get into college—that it was both inappropriate and distasteful for the overwhelming majority who would not go to college. What possible reason would a future farmer or machinist have for learning history or science or literature? Educators believed as a matter of faith that the failure to introduce vocational courses would cause students to drop out in droves, especially students from poor and minority backgrounds. The odd thing was that they continued to voice this fear even as enrollments spiraled upward. In 1890, there were about 200,000 students in public high schools; in 1900, there were 519,000; high school enrollment passed the one million mark in 1912, and reached 2.2 million in 1920. As it happened, this growth occurred without the assistance of compulsory education laws. But it was not enough, for there continued to be millions who were not in high school. High school leaders kept rediscovering the dropout problem, even though high school graduation rates remained the same from 1890 to 1910, and they continued to deplore their failure to draw all in. Despite the rapid growth of high school enrollments, educational thinkers insisted that the curriculum was keeping potential students away and driving out others.

Curiously, educators seemed more certain of the irrelevance of the academic studies than did students or parents. Not more than 12 to 13 percent of the high school enrollment graduated from high school in 1910, but fully 49 percent studied Latin, to the despair and disapproval of enlightened schoolmen. By 1915, Latin still enrolled 37 percent of high school students, even though most educational leaders believed that it was inappropriate for any but the college bound. Indeed, many educators doubted that even the college bound should study Latin or any other foreign language. In 1910, 84 percent of all high school stu-

dents studied some foreign language, a figure that dropped to 73.2 percent in 1915. The "Cardinal Principles," which contained no
encouragement for the study of any foreign language, supported the
trend away from language study, and the world war decimated enrollments in the German language, which fell from 24.4 percent of all students before the war to 1 percent in 1922.[26]

Much of the rhetoric in behalf of the introduction of vocational curricula centered on the supposed needs of the children of immigrants. It
was they, said the educators, who needed to be gathered in, and it was
they who needed vocational skills, courses that were immediately practical, studies that had direct utility in the job market; the academic curriculum would never do for children with their special needs. But the
parents of these children were never surveyed about what they wanted,
for the judgment was based on the educators' understanding of society's
needs, not on the parents' or students' idea of their own needs. An
interesting illustration of these different perceptions occurred in 1917,
when progressive reformers in New York City tried to install the "Gary
plan," in which students alternated between academic and prevoca-
tional activities during the school day. The Gary plan, also called "the
platoon system," had won national acclaim from Randolph Bourne,
John Dewey, and others, but its intended beneficiaries were not impressed. Immigrant parents and students demonstrated noisily for three
weeks to protest the plan, which they believed would close the doors of
opportunity to their children. A Tammany candidate for mayor was
elected, having pledged to prevent the introduction of the Gary plan
into the public schools.[27]

This history is relevant to the extent that it identifies the origins of
present-day debates about the curriculum. In the early 1980s, some educators and national commissions argued that all students should be enrolled in an academic curriculum, that certain subjects (like English,
science, mathematics, and history) should be "constants" in everyone's
high school program, and that requirements were necessary to ensure
that all students take the necessary courses. These recommendations
were criticized for ignoring the differences among children; for posing a
special threat to minority children, who needed job training; for placing
too much emphasis on academic subjects; for risking an increase in the
number of dropouts by raising academic requirements; for neglecting
the need for courses that are immediately practical in the job market.

There is some irony in the fact that the case for the academic subjects
was made in the early 1980s on grounds of social utility: it was said, for
example, that students should learn foreign languages because of job

opportunities in international trade or because of the importance of understanding other nations and cultures, and that students should study mathematics and science because of the nation's need for engineers and scientists. Advocates of literature and history struggled with little success to find the appropriate justification that might commend their studies to the near-instinctive demand for social utility.

The argument that students should be well educated because education is a good in itself was rarely heard, least of all from educators. Perhaps they feared that no one would believe them. Or perhaps their own unexamined intellectual heritage inclined them not to believe it themselves.

PART THREE
The Family

5

The Fourth R:
The Repatriation of the School

BRIGITTE BERGER

It is an undeniable fact that parents all over the world, regardless of race, ethnicity, religion and social class, are concerned with the well-being and progress of their children. No other social concern activates and, at times, even enrages people more than this. Across all cultures and throughout history parents have gone to great and extraordinary length to search for what they deem to be optimal or, at least, tolerable situations for their children to grow up and prosper in. American parents are no exception to this rule. In twentieth-century America parental preoccupations with the welfare and advancement of their children have been linked in a singularly close, albeit ambivalent, way to schools as the most decisive instrument for the realization of these expectations and hopes.

For this reason the short shrift given to the role of the family in the most recent commotion over the dismal state of the nation's schools is a puzzling omission in the rousing call for the reform of schools, the reaffirmation of excellence, and the restoration of discipline. To be sure, amid the outpouring of reports, books, and articles on the current crisis in American education, one still comes across the customary genuflection before this much abused social institution. Supreme Court pronouncements, presidential speeches, and sundry statements from the nonelite press of the nation are replete with declarations about the primary role of parents in the upbringing of their children. Yet to the powerful axis of educators, policymakers, and pundits of the media—a formidable political-education establishment, by any measure—the affirmation of the family's role in the education of its children is more of an embarrassment than a serious recommendation. Although more conservative groups are straining to revive the role of parents in education, they have little to offer beyond attempts to resurrect a more pragmatic education ideology and to channel negligible tax sums in their direction.

In this case as in others, it seems sufficient for those who dominate the public discourse to pay ritualistic obeisance to a dimly remembered ideal. To the "real" task at hand, however, the family is held to be largely inadequate and irrelevant. The insistence upon the pivotal role of families in the education of their children—a view maintained by a minuscule group of public individuals, in any event—is quickly shunted aside, ridiculed, and conveniently labeled hopelessly reactionary, if not worse. This contradiction between paying lip service to the importance of the family and the continued disregard of its role in education runs through most of the current publications and discussions. The national attention is fixated on forces active in the system of public education. Reform is firmly linked to visible, clearly identifiable educational measures that, it is hoped, will make a difference: curricular reform, length of school periods, teacher competence, and the means to be provided by the government to finance all of this. The customary politicalization of any and all issues of critical importance has served to polarize the discussion of these measures as well. In the public debate the battlelines have been drawn between the education establishment, on the one hand, and a loose, not fully crystallized coalition of more conservative groups, on the other. They are interlocked in constant battles over education ideology, jurisdiction, legislation, and public funding. In such a struggle the family figures only marginally. This may be partly due to dismal experiences in recent attempts to use or, sometimes, to circumvent or replace the family in public policy efforts. It may also be partly due to the intractable nature of the family. Hence, it typically serves as a convenient legitimation for whatever point happens to be on the political agenda. The situation created in this manner, however, tends to obfuscate what has always moved and continues to move the large majority of Americans to whom the education of their children is neither a liberal nor a conservative issue.

In what follows, I shall argue that the role of the family has been sorely misunderstood and misinterpreted. What has been misconstrued in particular is the past and present role of the middle-class—or, in the European use of the term, bourgeois—family. Variously described as a victim as well as a culprit, it has been deplored and vilified. The middle-class family is neither victim nor culprit. More than any other social institution, it has been the carrier of modernization. Insofar as modern industrial, democratic society is inextricably entwined with this kind of family, a convincing argument can be made that the perpetuation of our free and active society requires its persistence. It has been accepted that education, and a particular kind of education to boot, plays a vital role in all of this. It has yet to be more adequately recognized that education in and for our kind of society is peculiarly dependent upon those sentiments, behaviors, and values that typically arise and are fostered in the cultural milieu of the middle-class family.

I shall argue, too, that this kind of family has persisted despite the many attempts to weaken and to dismantle it. In fact, the middle-class family today continues to thrive in all walks of life, albeit in a more or less unofficial fashion. Its ethos, its practices, and its values are recognized to be beneficial, and they remain the norm for the great majority of Americans—ethnic, black, "old stock," and immigrant. They are certainly appreciated by those disgruntled and despondent parents who are alienated from the wasteland of the public schools. There are persuasive reasons why this is so.

Finally, I shall try to show that there exists good evidence that the link between educational success and the values and practices characteristic of middle-class family life has already been made by the many parents who try either to gain greater control over what goes on in public education today or to seek refuge in private schools. The increased attractiveness of private schools to the affluent sector of America's cities and suburbs, the continued, though troubled, allegiance of ethnic Americans to parochial schools, the attraction of parochial schools for non-Catholic inner-city minorities, the mushrooming of Christian "alternative" schools in various regions of the country, and the not-to-be-underestimated and growing number of "survival" and "grass-roots" schools in the minority sector of American society are all symptoms of this trend. It may well be that a parental revolt against proposals of school reform that disregard parents' role is not merely a fantasy of pessimists.

Recent scholarly research examining the vast transformations that have taken place in the societies of the West has illuminated the degree to which these cataclysmic changes in the economy, polity, and social structure are rooted in the life of the Western nuclear family.[1] Comprising only parents and their children, it was small and mobile enough to allow individuals to participate in the modernization process; at the same time, it was tightly knit enough to make this participation humanly tolerable. Amid a general separation between the public sphere of work and politics and the private sphere of the family, a domestic life of the family was invented in which concern for individual members, and in particular for children, moved into the foreground. A socialization pattern emerged that is characterized by a close relationship between parents and children, greater parental influence, and a greater emphasis upon individualization. Long before the enthronement of modern society, the Western nuclear family fostered mind-sets and values that were instrumental in bringing about the modernization of economic, political, and social institutions. Above all, it fostered far-reaching changes in human consciousness. So, for instance, "rationalization," one of modernization's driving forces, may be sought in the patterns of socialization of such a family.

This process occurred in western Europe over a period of a few hundred years.[2] It has by now become part and parcel of the history of modernization. It can show how the family and the economy changed in tandem and how the individual was liberated from traditional confines inside and outside of the family. This kind of historical scholarship can further demonstrate how the new family sensibilities and values merged with new ideas of property in the rise and eventual domination of the middle class as a new social stratum. It should be noted that during the period of consolidation of the middle-class structure, the new family ethos was often linked to religion: to Puritanism, Presbyterianism, and, later, Methodism in England and in the American colonies; to Calvinism and Jansenism in France; to Pietism in Germany.

At least since the late eighteenth century, the history of the West is, in a very basic sense, the history of the middle classes and its culture. The great historical transformations of the subsequent two centuries, which, in aggregate, have produced what we call modernity, have been overwhelmingly the product of this class. Since the triumph of the middle class (in the major countries of the West, that is), this class and its culture have been identified with the status quo, against which any rebel worth his salt tried to define himself. It is therefore important to understand the revolutionary character of this class and of the type of family that is its carrier.

The middle-class family was an institution—in the nineteenth century as well as in subsequent years—uniquely suited both to providing a "haven" and sustenance for its members and to socializing and motivating them for participation in the many activities in the larger society. Linked to this was the concern for education, both as a general social value and as something for one's own children. It should be added that the effective raising and educating of children became *the* great mission of this type of family. Everything had to be organized, planned, and executed in accordance with this mission. Since the "bourgeois virtues" originating in the middle-class household are also central to education, a few words may be necessary here. It can be agreed that hard work, discipline, diligence, attention to detail, and a systematic cultivation of willpower are core elements of middle-class culture. Others are decency, reliability, politeness, respect, and fairness. Some of these virtues appear maudlin to the modern mind. Perhaps they should not.

Since all of these elements of this new sensibility are based upon a pronounced individualism, there always exists the potential for their distortion or radicalization once the constraining and balancing influences of family and religion are removed. As the many opponents of the middle class never cease to point out, the same traits described here in positive and beneficial terms may well turn into something very different: selfishness, pettiness, narrowness, avarice, competitiveness, bigotry, oppressiveness, and philistinism. Such an escalation, as I have argued in a different context, is precisely what happened in recent decades.[3] What previously was held in balance now appear to be sets of irreconcilable alternatives: rigid stability against mindless innovation, crass egotism against self-abandonment to a community, adventurism without moral constraint (taking *all* risks against fearful passivity legitimated by an absolutist morality (willing to take *no* risks at all) and so on. With this loss of balance, the enormous civilization-building power of the middle classes is undermined and threatened, and the very notion of a middle-class society is thrown into question.

At the same time, in spite of these ever-present dangers, it should also be recognized that the middle-class family has a unique potential to provide the social context for the formation of stable personalities ("strong characters") and autonomous individuals, who are ready for innovation and risk taking in a society undergoing historically unprecedented transformations. It also has the potential to provide a balance between individualism and social responsibility, between "liberation" and strong communal ties, between acquisitiveness and altruism.

There is one further dimension that has to be emphasized here: these middle-class virtues are, in principle, accessible to everyone. No one social class or group can be the sole proprietor of hard work, discipline, frugality, and willpower. The opposite vices—idleness, intemperance, and self-indulgence—can also be avoided by anyone who sets his mind to it. In other words, the bourgeois ethos, reinforced by strong religious morality, was from the beginning a democratic and egalitarian one. These were precisely the virtues that the middle-class family sought to inculcate forcefully in its children, and it is a peculiarly shortsighted vision that perceives the forcefulness of this socialization as "authoritarian" or "repressive."

A good argument can be made that the acceptance of the middle-class ethos by large numbers of people was crucial to their move up the social ladder. The social mobility patterns of the industrial societies of the West during the past one hundred years give further evidence to the legitimacy of this claim. It is not surprising, therefore, that those today who are concerned with the future of their children continue to abide by the middle-class ethos, in spite of the many countervailing trends. It may also not be accidental that this ethos finds particular resonance among the working class, among the lower-middle class and immigrants, and, of late, among a sizable segment of America's minorities as well. Convinced that social mobility is won through personal efforts, the great majority of Americans today cite parental encouragement, a good education, ambition, and plain hard work as keys to success.[4] Most ordinary Americans are still convinced that the traditional middle-class family life provides the best context for the development of the desired personality traits. The middle-class family and its values are still perceived as an important and necessary precondition for success in education and life.

It is important to understand that many of the forces of modernization have been particularly unkind to the family. Gradually at first, yet with increasing rapidity in the course of the twentieth century, the family was removed from the central position it had once held, and was demoted to an ever-more subordinate place. This demotion process becomes dramatically visible in the area of education. To be sure, the transformation of the economy robbed the family household of its traditional integrative basis; and urbanization, the apogee of the modernizing process, had lasting consequences for the patterns of human habitation and interaction as well. But the growing process of institutional differentiation that stripped the family of its earlier unchallenged functions in the nurture, care, and socialization of its individual members, and the concomitant transfer of ever-larger chunks of its socializing and educational tasks to institutions outside of it as well as increasingly beyond its control, presented the family with the most massive challenge yet.

It may well be argued that the expansion and eventual autonomy of the educational system is part and parcel of the modernizing process. The increasing sophistication of the core elements of modern society demand a high level of preparation and education on the part of its citizens. In view of the family's limitations in meeting these essential tasks, a highly specialized and professionalized educational system becomes necessary. However, the complexities of the American situation, accentuated by the great variety of cultural, ethnic, racial, and religious groupings, determined this process to a considerable degree. The real and assumed needs of the children of immigrant families and groups held to be "marginal" to American society have always been the special focus of American schools, be they public, parochial, or private. Above all, the emphasis on equality that is deeply ingrained in the American experience charges education and the schools with becoming, in Horace Mann's words, "the great equalizers of the conditions of man." The paramount purpose of American schools, and of the public schools in particular, many contend, is to liberate children from the emotional, intellectual, and moral confines of their family background. It may thus be argued that an increase in equality of opportunity is directly related to a decrease in the power of the family over its members.

This is not the place to recapitulate the philosophy and history of the American public schools.[5] In the context of the argument pursued here, it need only be observed that as the twentieth century unfolded, the antifamily thrust in education became more and more pronounced. No later than the early 1960s, this thrust received powerful reinforcements from a variety of concerns about the ability of an open society like ours to raise its children for today and for the future. It was argued that in an ever-more industrialized and specialized American society the family had fewer and fewer chances to socialize and prepare its children and adolescents. In particular, as they found themselves spending larger chunks of their days and longer periods of their lives in educational institutions with other youngsters of the same age, they became increasingly susceptible to the actions and approval of other youngsters of the same age with whom they shared life in this separate social structure, cut off from adult society and far removed from adult responsibilities. At the same time, it became evident that this peer society was dominated by a distinct culture, characterized by its own norms and expectations. As a consequence, many observers agreed, the home receded in importance in the life of the young. Parents were diagnosed to have fewer abilities to mold their children. In this socialization vacuum, in which children were largely left to be brought up by their peers in an atmosphere pervaded by subtle opposition to the norms of adult society, the process of "making human beings human" was held to be on the verge of breakdown. The need to counter these destructive tendencies became a priority on the national agenda of the early 1960s. The proposals that emerged varied in their emphases.

Educators felt increasingly inclined to take adolescent society as a given and use it to further the ends of education. This soon extended to younger children as well. Since children and adolescents spent much of their time in educational institutions anyway, the locale of the school and a school curriculum constructed around a "society of peers" was considered by many to be a fortunate instrument. Some thought it still worthwhile to involve parents in a yet-to-be-constructed socialization model for America's children.[6] The Head Start program, initiated at about that period, may serve as a case in point. Regardless of emphasis, however, a general turning away from the family became a widely accepted reality, if not among parents, then at least among the intellectual elite of the country. For a while it seemed as though American schools were turned into immense laboratories. The result of all these activities in behalf of the nation's young amounted to nothing less than an all-out attack against the family's socialization activities.

The factors determining the success or failure of a family in the socialization of its children are so subtle and intangible that they become practically indiscernible. One difficulty in assessing the family's role in education arises from the existence of a voluminous and controversial body of literature, which makes it almost impossible to arrive at unequivocal answers. In reviewing some of this literature, one is struck by the vagueness about the process by which parental behavior is linked to educational effects in even the best of research.[7] When it comes to the bulk of the literature, one is inclined to observe that measures to get at the "intangibles" in parental behavior are often crude and unsophisticated. Furthermore, it is frequently unclear what precisely is being measured. In this case as in others, fuzzy studies, unsecured theories, and competing and contradictory intellectual frames of reference make for a confusing situation. This is not to say that there has been some sort of conspiracy against the family on the part of researchers. But as hosts of researchers began to put the many socialization functions of the family under close scrutiny, it was found to be wanting in virtually every respect. The family now was questioned in the totality of its functions in general, and in its formal as well as informal ones in particular.

Formal functions are those that include the physical protection of children, their feeding, clothing, and supervision. Of the many informal functions, ranging from emotional solace and sustenance to mutual affection, sympathetic understanding, and similarly benign sentiments, the most important ones within this context are those discussed earlier: the inculcation of cognitive propensities, and of all those emotions and motivations that are customarily linked to success in school and beyond. Ethnic and racial minorities and "the poor" in particular, with their distinct family arrangements and pronounced cultural milieus, were soon declared to be defective and in need of intervention. But middle-class families, too, were examined and found to be inadequate and, in some instances, even destructive of their children. There soon emerged a general public perception that in a rapidly changing world the American family was no longer able to protect and socialize its children. In a society like America that is propelled by strong impulses toward doing good, particularly when the welfare of children is at stake, public per-

ceptions are soon translated into policy. Whereas in earlier decades social policies related to poor and weak families had been aimed at
assisting them to care for their children, now the family as an institution
became the target. Programs originally designed to aid families were
increasingly replaced by ones that sought to find substitutes for the family and finally to replace it. To be sure, there were many other forces
working against the family as well. For example, the liberating feminism
turned women away from home and children, and the shift in sentiments within the intellectual elite and America's suburban upper-
middle class significantly added to the attack against the family.

It is very difficult to identify those aspects of family life and family
practices that make a difference in the socialization of a child and to
estimate the extent of the difference. Many claims made in one frame of
analysis are put into doubt, if not directly contradicted, in another.
Moreover, what was frequently thought to be at issue at one point,
ceases to be so at another. For instance, the small family, which had for
many years been advocated and marketed by powerful agencies and
programs as crucial for educational achievement, was later held responsible in the predicted rise of an increasingly "narcissistic" American personality type, one unable to relate, share, and cooperate. The discussion
over the importance of a stable family underwent a similar shift. As
ever-more homes were found to be unstable, broken, or in the process of
breaking up, the "disastrous effects" of this situation upon children
stirred the nation at midcentury. More recently, however, arguments—
and, of course, data—have replaced the earlier discussion that now support the trend of "going it alone." And as befits such a shift in perception, there was a linguistic shift as well: debates over the "broken home"
were conveniently reformulated into debates over the needs of "single
parents." As questions about the implications of working mothers for
their children moved into the forefront of public attention, as debates
over "favorable" parental attitudes ("child-centered" or "disci-
plinarian") proliferated, as disputes over "proper" paternal roles ("com-
panionable" or "authoritarian") became commonplace, and as, finally,
issues over children's rights versus parental responsibility became a
legal concern, the problematization and the politicalization of all aspects
of family life reached a degree not previously known in American history. The very different political alignments that have emerged in America can marshal evidence in support of each issue on their distinct
sociopolitical agendas.

Regarding "effective" parenting as a necessary preparation for success in school, it is quite clear by now that one should be very cautious
about identifying effective parenting with kindly, understanding at-

titudes and practices that indulge the child. In so far as "effectiveness" has to do with educational achievement, ample data indicate that "good" students often come from demanding, rigid, and unreasoning homes! One might object at this point that parents have always known that home discipline and parental demands have something to do with a child's success in school and in life in general. They have applied all the methods available to them to socialize their children for what they think is appropriate behavior to this end. They have tried to be firm, shouted at them, cajoled them; they have applied "positive" as well as "negative" sanctions, to use Skinnerian terms, by withdrawing their allowance, by grounding them; and, yes, they have even spanked them. In this, families have often resembled a battlefield. But what are parents to make of research that demonstrates that disapproval tends to increase the likelihood that a child will show hostile behavior and that physical punishment increases the likelihood of social aggression? Moreover, what are parents to do when they are confronted by "experts" of child rearing with arguments that their customary methods are detrimental to their children and their future?

If it is already difficult for sophisticated researchers to sort out the many contradictory claims made, it certainly goes beyond the capacity of most parents to do so. In any event, the problematization of every family practice in the socialization of its young contributed in no small measure to a general public perception that the contemporary family was unable and unfit to carry out its important social task. It added fuel to the turmoil surrounding the "death of the family" debate flaunted by the ever-eager media from every newsstand. It also gave momentum to the rise and growth of the child care establishment conceived in a therapeutic mode—the legions of social workers, counselors, psychologists, and therapists that have become a part of every American school today. Intimating that schools and child care specialists know how to carry out the necessary socializing tasks and that families do not, that establishment transferred ever more of the traditional family functions to schools and child care specialists. The convenient alliance of therapists and educators that rapidly developed at this point soon began to confront the family as a massive hostile reality. All of these activities ultimately led to a diminution of the family's role and responsibility in the education of its children.

Together, these developments created havoc for the self-understanding of the family. Parents became increasingly uncertain about their child-rearing ability and their socializing practices; they lost self-confidence and became disoriented. As might have been expected, it was the child-centered middle-class family that became the principal captive of the educational-therapeutic complex, as a number of studies clearly demonstrate.[8] Anyone who has raised a child in the ghetto of America's suburbs can easily supplement academic findings with personal experience. The lower-class, inner-city family, on the other hand, tended to close itself off against the massive intrusion into its life. To the bafflement of teachers and the many "friendly intruders" alike, these families developed into reluctant, commandeered consumers of those efforts and programs that went beyond the supply of direct material and financial aid. Parents and children felt disrespected, humiliated, and increasingly hostile toward all these efforts in their behalf.

The attack against the family's socializing and educational roles received an additional blow with the emergence of a variety of more overtly critical positions and radical movements in the late 1960s and early 1970s. Now it was no longer enough merely to uncover and illuminate the shortcomings of the family—and, by extension, those of the educational practices of American schools. Now the goals and values, the fundamental structure of modern Western society in general and of American society in particular became the primary issue. In other words, the problem was no longer a particular type of family—or educational system—held to be inadequate and malfunctioning; it was rather a "sick society," of which the "sick family" and an "ailing school" were integral parts. As the growing critique of Western industrial society sharpened into a critique of capitalism, the middle-class or bourgeois family and, by extension, a "bourgeois education" became primary objects of critical attention.

The policy positions emerging at this juncture focused on the fundamental reorganization of the larger structures of society. In the main they largely sought to bypass the family, just as they sought to bypass education when the failure to realize the increased expectations for education became obvious. Any attempt to reform or improve either was held to be futile as long as the system that had produced both remained in place.[9] The family policy proposals, like the education policy proposals, inspired by this vision sought to use the family and education as instruments for the fundamental reconstitution of Western capitalist society.

On the other hand, those critical policy positions that aimed at revolutionizing the institutions of the family and school concentrated on the transformation of the content as well as the style of socialization carried out within either institution. At issue here are the familiar bourgeois virtues that emphasize the acquisition of formal cognitive skills, that stress structure and discipline, and that seek to encourage achievement and success. Taken together, these virtues were thought to be "one-

dimensional" deformations of what it means to be human. In a manner
reminiscent of earlier criticisms of the estrangement of the school from
the life of the working classes, it was now argued that schools that reflect the ethos of the dominant middle classes essentially serve to stifle
and suppress the educational aspirations and achievement potential of
lower-class children. Locked into the "culture of poverty" of their families and ethnic groups, the children of America's poor were held to be
neglected and forgotten by an ignorant and hostile school system. Experts, among whom the noted British scholar Basil Bernstein figured
most prominently, proposed that if schools wished to be of use to the
lower-class child, they would have to adapt to his particular mentality.
The critique from within did not stop here. Inadvertently it became all-
inclusive, a logical step, considering its revolutionary program. Family
and school in capitalist society were declared to be destructive of all
children, middle class as well as non–middle class. Powerful "saner"
and "more human" countervisions of socialization and education soon
became fashionable. The influential writings of A. S. Neill, particularly
his book *Summerhill*, are perhaps the best-known, though by no means
the only, all-inclusive critiques of the organization of personal life in
capitalist society.

It is important to realize that the critical positions were verbalized in
the main by a small coterie of intellectuals located in academe and in
social policy institutions like the Carnegie Council. It gained momentum
when the failure of the public schools became dramatically visible. As
study after study was released and evidence accumulated, it became
increasingly evident that schools—no matter how hardworking and
dedicated the teachers, no matter how adequate the physical facilities,
no matter how well designed the curriculum, and no matter how much
money spent to advance these aspects—failed to have substantial impact upon the performance and achievement of children. It became clear
in particular that programs to bypass family disadvantages and to make
a child's cultural background irrelevant, could not measure up to this
task, and perhaps never would. It also became evident that the many
attempts to reach this end had created havoc in the life of poor inner-city
families—that is, precisely those people for whose benefit the interventionist programs had been developed in the first place. Targeted problems continued to persist, to multiply, and even to become magnified.
The spreading dismay among many responsible educators over the failure of massive interventionist programs and attempts slowly gave way
to what has been called a "post-reformist" stance of taking-inventory
and realistically rethinking the possibilities to reform American educa-

tion. In this manner, the stage for rethinking the family's role in education had been set as well.

Taking stock of the realities that have emerged in what, in retrospect, amounted to a war of official society against the family's role in education, we today have the advantage of the larger view. The upheavals of the past decades can now be elucidated in a manner that escaped those who were actors in the events. We shall thus refrain from presenting a petty calculation of the costs of good intentions. In any event, the realities that have emerged stand in stark contrast to the beneficial rhetoric accompanying many of the efforts in behalf of children. Not only have many of the attempts to invest the therapeutically defined school with enormous tasks for which it seemed to be distinctly unsuited resulted in failure, but in the process of the transformation of their functions, schools have been diverted from their essential tasks. At the same time, efforts to take away from the family what is the family's have, in large measure, contributed to a dangerous weakening and, in some cases, an actual breakdown of the family. In the final analysis, we are confronted with the paradox that schools, in attempting to bypass and supplant the family, have robbed themselves of their essential basis.

The inability of educators to accept the role of parents as an indispensable element in education may be the greatest obstacle to a more realistic assessment of what is possible and desirable. It has often been said that old dreams take long to die, particularly if material interests are vested in these dreams. The dream of equal opportunity for all Americans is a noble one. There is good evidence available today that many American parents have already taken steps to make equal educational opportunity more of a reality and less of a dream. Parents may go about it in different ways than educators and social planners, but they are not idle when it comes to the future of their children.

All through the war against the family, ordinary people continued to believe that the small, tightly knit, nuclear family unit, caring and mindful of children, was still the best guarantor of their children's future. They have struggled along unrecognized and largely unsupported. To be sure, the contemporary American family is no longer as stable and secure as it used to be. A considerable variety of arrangements—single parents, to-be-divorced parents, remarried, foster, and adoptive parents, and grandparents—coexist with the more prevalent "typical" family of father and mother, well known to us. More often than not, these arrangements are dictated by necessity. All of these parents recognize that the student who fails in school often comes from a stressful home.[10] The normative value of the middle-class ethos is still accepted by the great majority of parents. In some cases, it has been *re*accepted, though somewhat belatedly. The sizable number of American women who support families on their own are no exception to this rule. Any researcher who cares to make the effort to ask "female heads of households" in the inner city about their aspirations for their children will be surprised by the degree of commitment to norms and standards associated with the old middle-class ethos.[11] Most parents agree on the value and the importance of their involvement in their children's education. Most of them regard schools as necessary, though inadequate. They also know that the real crisis in education lies in the abdication of parental responsibility. Different cultural, ethnic, and religious groups have different ways of coping with this essential task. Some try to establish greater control over what goes on in public schools; others may seek to take refuge in parochial and private educational institutions.

Parental influence on the education of a child in public schools can be more readily achieved in America's suburbs and small towns. Of late, American middle-class parents have become extraordinarily active when it comes to the educational advancement of their children. Looking after what they perceive to be in the best interests of their children, highly verbal middle-class parents, knowledgeable about their children's legal rights and skilled in using them to their advantage, have become the bane of many a small-sized school system. The battles of parents with school boards and administrators in small-town settings have by now taken on legendary proportions.[12]

Further evidence is beginning to accumulate on the progress of children in the public schools of America's inner cities. Black parents who believe that there is such a thing as a "good" school have begun to make enormous efforts to assure that their children can attend one.[13] The same evidence also shows that in the growing number of cases where parents have shifted their initial emphasis on racial balance to one on the quality of education and their ability to produce it, they have been strikingly successful in rehabilitating whole schools—and whole neighborhoods along with them.[14]

Other groups have turned to private schools that seem to be more adequately suited for the realization of their expectations for their children's education. The increased attractiveness of private schools to the affluent sector of America's cities and suburbs is a case in point.[15] Although parochial schools have recently encountered a number of problems (many flowing from demographic changes), none is due to a decline in the belief in the importance of the middle-class ethos of parochial schools—witness the attractiveness of parochial schools to non-Catholic inner-city minorities.[16] The mushrooming of Christian "alternative" schools, on the other hand, is propelled by more than just parental concern about the decline in learning. As Peter Skerry has cogently argued, these schools are based on the voluntarism that springs from deeply held religious beliefs. Their advocates protest the notion that a child is a mere creature of the state. These schools constitute about one-fifth of the total non-public-school enrollment today and are largely composed of working- and lower-middle-class families. They are, perhaps, the most loyal adherents of the old middle-class ethos, which they perceive to be vital in the education of their children.[17]

Finally, there is the growing number of "survival" and "grass-roots" schools in the minority sector of American society. As the data gathered by the National Center for Neighborhood Enterprise suggest, these small independent schools—whose representatives first gathered in Washington, D.C., in 1983—claim to meet the academic and social needs of black, Hispanic, American Indian, and Asian American children, primarily in urban settings.[18] They all share the belief that they can do something better than the public schools. Each one of the roughly three hundred schools represented at the Washington meeting can point to a massive parental involvement as well as the development of strong academic curricula as their most distinctive features. Leery of public funding, they often struggle against enormous odds. But, as one participant observed, "that has never clouded the main issue of self-determination for our children."

There are clear signs that we are about to begin to form a better understanding of what aspects of schooling make a difference. At the same time, we are learning that those things that make a difference are the hardest to measure and manipulate. In *Fifteen Thousand Hours*, the British researcher Michael Rutter and his associates have provided us with some pointers.[19] Above all, they demonstrate beyond any doubt what many people have known for some time: schooling alone is just one of several factors in a pupil's performance. "The child's own characteristics, his family, circumstances and home background, and his peer group also constitute substantial influences."[20] They emphasize the need for consistency between the values and practices of the home and those of the school. They show that discipline, standards, and the acceptance of norms originating in the family, when reinforced by a similar ethos in the school, make the best formula for an individual child's success.

By the same token, we are about to learn that children continue to model their behavior on that of "significant" adults and that the influence of peer groups has perhaps been overestimated.[21] And a new breed of teachers and administrators on the local level is about to rediscover what an earlier generation of educators took for granted: a positive home environment that emphasizes parental understanding, parental control, and involvement is still the best precondition for a child's successful performance in school and life.

Amid the public dismay over the crisis in American education, there is reason to hope that the pattern of incremental change spearheaded by parents today in many small locales may eventually lead to necessary reforms. Admittedly, these efforts on the part of parents will be insufficient to be translated immediately and directly into a national groundswell. Lower-class parents will still have to learn how to become the best mediators for their children. They will still have to find the language and the method for exercising the responsibility they feel for their children. Those parents who already have started this trend may serve as an inspiration here.

The shared meanings of getting ahead and the vision of what is a good life in our pluralistic, open society are still firmly anchored in the social milieu of a family that, to a surprising degree, revolves around the old middle-class ethos. The vast majority of Americans, it would now seem, did not lose faith in the middle-class family and its ethos, but the American intellectual leadership did. And those who were confused and disheartened by the proliferation of attempts and programs that, perhaps inadvertently, weakened the family's role and responsibility in the socialization of children are beginning to realize that parents can and do make a difference in their children's prospects. Middle-American families—unfashionable, patriotic, industrious, and family-loving—may soon add the fourth R to education: The Repatriation of the School.

PART FOUR

The Unions

6

Teacher Unions and School Quality: Potential Allies or Inevitable Foes?

CHESTER E. FINN, JR.

Teacher unions are here to stay. That much is clear. But it remains to be seen whether they will turn out to be beneficial, harmful, or irrelevant to the quality of education in the nation's public schools in an era when quality matters more to more Americans than at any other time in modern history.

Nearly 90 percent of the 2.1 million public school teachers in the United States today belong to the giant National Education Association (NEA), the fast-growing American Federation of Teachers (AFT), and the handful of independent unions to be found in some communities.[1] Teaching is now one of the most heavily unionized occupations in the society, certainly *the* most unionized white-collar occupation, and there is no reason at all to expect this to change.[2]

Not all teacher union members, however, engage in the central—some would say the defining—activity of trade unionism, namely, collective bargaining. Probably only about three public school teachers in four are employed under the terms of union-negotiated contracts, "meet and confer" arrangements, or "memoranda of understanding."

Whether public employees are able to bargain collectively depends, first, on state law and, second, on the ability of a particular union local to win recognition as the bargaining agent for its members.[3] Thirty-eight states now permit teacher collective bargaining, but the other twelve do not, and even in those that do, the normal arrangement is a "local option" whereby teachers in some school systems end up bargaining as a group while others do not.

In private industry, it would be virtually meaningless to talk of the

role of unions that do not bargain collectively. In the public sector, however, salary levels, working conditions, and other terms of employment
that hold intense importance for workers are established through the
machinery of public policy-making and are thus susceptible to political
influence and activity. A public employees' union that does not bargain
collectively may nonetheless obtain significant benefits for its members
by persuading the governor and legislature (or mayor and town council)
to do its bidding. Even the protection of individual workers' rights can
be achieved through political action, such as the enactment of tenure
laws.

For teachers, union membership—with or without collective bargaining—ordinarily brings an entire additional set of benefits, those historically conferred by participation in a "professional association." For
more than a century after its founding in 1857, the NEA (originally the
National Teachers' Association) was a professional association for teachers—and, until fairly recently, for other educators such as principals and
superintendents.[4] Although the AFT has always styled itself a union, it
did not really succeed in acting like one on a large scale until the early
1960s when, first in New York and then in one city after another, it won
the right to represent sizable groups of teachers in collective bargaining
negotiations that produced contracts. In the ensuing two decades, AFT
membership grew tenfold. But throughout its history, the AFT has also
provided its members the services and benefits of a professional
association.

These take many forms. Some are subtle: a sense of fraternity and
fellowship with one's colleagues and peers. Others are mundane but
important: inexpensive group insurance policies and similar cushions
against misfortune and hard times. Still others are frivolous but attractive: cut-rate tours and excursions, for example. But perhaps the most
valuable services are the enhancement of the profession itself and the
development of one's own role within it. Thus, much like the bar and
medical associations, teacher unions have supplied advanced education
(through journals, workshops, institutes, and conventions); codes of
ethics and behavior concerning how members of the profession should
act and, especially, how they should expect others to act toward them;
norms and qualifications for membership in the profession itself (often
made binding by incorporation into state licensure requirements); and
leadership, representation, and "voice" in the innumerable gatherings,
events, and decisions of the larger society that bear on the profession
and its work.

Inasmuch as the working conditions, prosperity, and status of any
profession are inextricably linked to the (real and perceived) quality of

the enterprise in which its members serve, the teachers' unions have generally displayed an interest in the scope, reputation, and efficacy (and, of course, the financing) of public education.

One need not dwell on the *motives* that led teachers to form associations and unions, for though scholars disagree on the exact proportions, it is reasonably clear that such motivation was—and is—compounded of three elements: the desire to improve one's own material well-being, job security, and working conditions; the desire to associate with one's peers for companionship, shared knowledge, and vocational betterment; and the desire to strengthen the enterprise of public education itself, both for reasons of self-interest and for the benefit of the children one teaches and the society one inhabits.[5] The NEA's federal charter asserts that "the purpose and objects of the said corporation shall be to elevate the character and advance the interests of the profession of teaching and to promote the cause of education in the United States."

In seeking to fulfill those multiple expectations, teacher unions have faced a dilemma. Like other public employees, but unlike most other professionals, teachers do not set the essential policies or make the key decisions affecting the organizations in which they work. The public schools are government agencies, and teachers are civil servants, organizationally subordinate both to other civil servants and to myriad elected and appointed policymakers. Thus, whatever a teacher's personal reasons for joining the union, as organizations the unions have needed to attend to more than the traditional triumvirate of "wages, hours, and working conditions." They have had to recognize that the perceived quality of public education bears heavily on the public's willingness to invest in it, to trust the judgments of the professionals working in it, and to establish policies by which it can flourish. Yet even as the collective action made possible through unionism has empowered teachers to improve their material circumstances and the conditions of their schools, the low esteem in which the public holds unions in general and public employee unions in particular has created an additional stimulus for the teachers' unions visibly and shrewdly to engage the large issues that the public in any given era associates with the improvement of education.

It is against this backdrop that one should view the four major genres of teacher union activity. The first, which is useful to teachers but which can speedily be placed outside the bounds of this discussion because it is apt to have little impact on government policies and public perceptions, is the array of membership benefits and services that the unions supply to teachers, much as any professional association would.

The second genre, direct political activity by the unions and overt efforts by them to influence government policies, is plainly relevant. It ranges from endorsements, campaign contributions, phone banks, and doorbell ringing on behalf of individual candidates for public office to lobbying in the committee rooms of Congress, the corridors of state legislatures, and the clamorous meeting halls of local school boards.

The third genre, collective bargaining between groups of teachers and their employers, and the techniques employed outside the negotiating room to influence and enforce the agreements reached within it, is laden with potential for good and for ill. If a union is—or is thought to be—oblivious to student learning and educational quality, interested only in short-run material gains for its members, and willing to use high-pressure tactics (including strikes) to secure those gains, then the immediate contractual "pay-off" for teachers may be considerable, but the long-term public reaction is liable to be detrimental to their interests. This is no trivial matter: in the fall of 1983, there were seventy-one teacher union strikes, affecting ten states and 1.3 million schoolchildren and involving 67,000 teachers. If, on the other hand, the union uses the bargaining process to bring about changes in the schools themselves that the public regards as desirable, benefits may accrue to students as well as to teachers.

The fourth and subtlest but most pervasive mode of union activity we may think of as the *public values* projected by the teachers' organizations, not only implicitly through their actions in the first three genres but also through their convention resolutions, the statements of their leaders, their involvements with noneducational matters foreign and domestic, their alliances with other organizations and causes, the cultural and political emphases in their publications, and so on through the innumerable ways by which any large organization signals to its society what it stands for, what it deems important, what its values are.

With that background, I propose to sketch briefly the ways the NEA and AFT conducted themselves and the signals they sent in the period immediately preceding the recent surge of national concern about educational quality; then to outline some of their responses to the dramatic developments of the past two years; and, finally, to describe a set of circumstances that creates an extraordinary—if fragile and perhaps fleeting—opportunity both for the unions and for a society now deeply interested in the quality of its schools.

Over the decades, the NEA and AFT accumulated quite a lot of political power and economic influence, and a measure of moral authority as well. They claimed to represent both what was good for schoolchildren and what was good for teachers and insisted that the two were compatible. Though not everyone accepted that premise, there can be little doubt that the unions became extremely influential participants in thousands of decisions by local, state, and national governments that affected education. In fact, they probably wielded more influence over such large policy decisions than over the actions of the principals and supervisors with whom their members worked on a daily basis.

The NEA and AFT, often working in concert with other education organizations, have shaped federal school aid policies, have leveraged appropriations for favored programs from Congress, have blocked proposals (such as tuition tax credits) that they found abhorrent, and have acquired genuine power within the political councils of the Democratic party (though steadily less within the Republican party), and their support is now eagerly sought by individual candidates for Congress and the presidency. The AFT has had the institutional versatility and political savvy to function sometimes as an education organization, at other times as a branch of organized labor. (It is one of the largest international unions in the AFL-CIO, and the AFT president, Albert Shanker, is a member of the federation's executive council.) With its larger staff and budget, and its chameleonlike ability to take on the coloration of a "professional association" when that serves its ends, the NEA, too, has shrewdly built up its influence on national politics and policies. Its members composed one of the largest identifiable blocks of delegates to the two most recent Democratic national conventions—302 of them in 1980, compared with 306 for the entire state of California—and its efforts in behalf of Jimmy Carter's election in 1976 were rewarded by the establishment (over the misgivings of many and the outright opposition of the AFT) of the Cabinet-level Department of Education.

Though the NEA and AFT often join forces on such tactical matters as the level of federal education spending—and in opposition to perceived threats to public education—they have generally projected distinctive ideological images, especially on broad issues of domestic and foreign policy. Particularly in the decade from 1973 to 1983, when Terry Herndon served as executive director and shaped the association's politics, the NEA became ever more closely identified with left-wing positions on matters ranging from civil rights (where the association embraced quotas) to foreign affairs (where it helped launch, lead, and underwrite the nuclear "freeze" movement). The AFT, on the other hand, maintained the political coloration of what are sometimes called "Kennedy-Humphrey Democrats," favoring extensive social welfare programs at home but without racial preferences, and seeing a necessary relationship between the love of peace and the maintenance of adequate means to deter the warlike tendencies of others.[6]

The philosophical gap between the two unions also widened with respect to fundamental issues of educational values and standards. The NEA came out in strong and steadfast opposition to standardized testing of children—and to any kind of testing of teachers—whereas the AFT endorsed this means of monitoring pupil performance and insisted also that new teachers not be hired unless they could pass appropriate tests of intelligence and knowledge. The AFT was skeptical of policies, such as bilingual education, that tend to segregate youngsters according to group characteristics and to retard their amalgamation into the larger society, whereas NEA convention resolutions called for all manner of special (and usually separate) treatments of various ethnic and linguistic groups within the schools. Not surprisingly, NEA publications lauded cultural relativism in the curriculum and the approach to values education that encourages children to invent, examine, and criticize their own values (all values, presumably, being equally valuable), while AFT journals showed teachers how they could more effectively impart to their students such traditional virtues as honesty, compassion, courage, and integrity. (The differences remain striking. As I write, the latest issue of *NEA Today* contains a serious pro-con "debate" on the question "Is it time to give up on grammar?")

The same educational priorities animated AFT and NEA actions at the state level, though the decentralized character of the unions also yielded much variation from one jurisdiction to the next. The most striking fact about education policy-making in the state capitals through the 1970s and into the 1980s, however, is how little of it dealt with the quality of teaching and learning, with the content and rigor of the curriculum, or with the effectiveness of school performance. Instead, state education boards and legislative committees concentrated on matters of finance and management, on compliance with externally generated obligations (such as federal laws and court orders), and on appeasement of the innumerable interest groups that sought within the schools favorable treatment of concerns ranging from migratory birds to handicapped children, from drug abuse prevention to the United Nations.

State education policy in this period became a playground for special interests. Seldom was the "general public" heard from. So rarely were legislative leaders and governors seen to deal with large issues of educational standards and direction that when one took a visible interest—as Terry Sanford did in North Carolina and Tom McCall in Oregon—he could quickly be labeled an educational statesman. The media did not pay much attention to school quality, nor did business leaders or other influential groups and opinion shapers. Absent their participation and scrutiny, education policy at the state level naturally followed the path of least resistance, which was the path into a low-visibility "brokering" mode wherein officials accommodated as best they could the demands and desires of those groups that *were* keenly interested, that *did* have precise agendas, and that were increasingly able to reward officials who succored them and to make political life less pleasant for any who resisted.

The teacher unions adapted readily to this mode, both to advance the interests of their members (and of themselves as organizations) and to retard the efforts of those with conflicting aims. Indeed, the unions were remarkably effective, being generally the largest, best-staffed, shrewdest, and best-financed of all the interest groups regularly engaged with education issues. This enabled them to prevent (or modify) a number of unwanted developments, to win some benefits for their members in almost every year's cycle of legislation and appropriations, and to reduce barriers to union expansion. This era thus saw a steady expansion of collective bargaining laws (often permitting "agency shops," in which teachers not wanting to join are nonetheless obliged to pay union dues for "representational" services they would rather not have), the strengthening of tenure laws, and the creation of cumbersome and costly procedures for dismissing incompetent teachers. The unions were not oblivious to issues of educational quality, nor timid about involving themselves on one side or the other. Such issues simply did not loom large on the policy agenda at the state level.

By the late 1970s, however, mounting public dismay that "Johnny still can't read," the onset of popular awareness that standardized test scores were declining, and a few celebrated cases of illiterate high school "graduates" were beginning to spark a move for "minimum competency testing" and statewide "proficiency exams," typically intended to ensure that no one would in the future be awarded a high school diploma who could not handle the "three R's" at a sixth- or seventh-grade level of performance. The back-to-basics movement was beginning, and it was beginning at the state level.

The NEA, characteristically, scoffed at this reactionary folly. The AFT, also characteristically, pondered the underlying problems and concerns. It had never opposed student testing or scorned "the basics." If this new movement actually signaled a large change in the nature and extent of the public's interest in education, and in the concerns of policymakers, it might well redound to the benefit of the AFT as well as of the schools. The "traditionalist" positions that the union's leaders had consistently espoused with respect to such matters as curriculum, discipline, and standards had long clashed with much of what passed for conventional wisdom in the education profession. The back-to-basics movement meant that the AFT's views might no longer seem so eccentric. Moreover, the union had an image problem caused by its record of militant labor tactics, notably the protracted, acrimonious, and much publicized New York City strikes of the sixties and seventies. Careful observers understood that some of the issues that had led the AFT to the picket line involved high principle (such as racially neutral treatment of teachers), while the NEA had contributed more than its share to the decay of the culture and the erosion of democratic principle. Still, the NEA continued to benefit from its lingering aura of "professionalism" and its earlier aversion to labor militancy. The advent of a genuine public interest in educational essentials was thus as much an opportunity for the AFT to improve its reputation as it would prove to be a source of damage to the image of the NEA.

Before moving into the recent past, we must note some pertinent developments of the sixties and seventies at the *local* level. As unionism spread from one school system to another, a marked change took place in the basic relationship between the teacher and his employer. While indubitably a member of a professional peer group, the individual teacher had traditionally enjoyed—and sometimes been victimized by— a one-to-one relationship with the school system that paid him.

In an exemplary school within a good system, this meant that the teacher was hired, evaluated, and retained according to his ability and performance, that as a respected member of the faculty he participated in decisions about curriculum, standards, and school organization, and that it was thus relatively easy to fuse his interest in a secure job and decent working conditions with the interests he shared with his colleagues in the quality and reputation of the school as a whole.

In a mediocre or bad school, however, the individual teacher could be abused by a capricious or tyrannical principal, his classroom prowess would be irrelevant to the judgments made about him in a highly politicized atmosphere, he might be entirely excluded from important decisions about school content and format, and he would find it impossible to lift his eyes from the harassments of the hour to the overarching goals and performance of the institution.

Thus vulnerable to the circumstances in which he found himself, the lone teacher was also nearly powerless to alter them. Though certain commonalities, such as the uniform salary schedule and the protection of tenure, meant that teachers throughout a system were apt to be treated alike with regard to fundamental bread-and-butter matters, virtually all professional decisions were the prerogative of the school management.

Joining a union was thus a way to bring a semblance of rationality into a world of confusion, to confer stability on an idiosyncratic environment, and to assure teachers some leverage over decisions affecting them, their students, and their schools.

The key was in banding together, and the teachers' strength lay in unity—the customary basis for trade unionism in any occupation or industry. But there was a cost, one well worth paying for teachers in bad situations but more problematic for those in exemplary schools. It lay in submerging the teacher's individuality into the pooled efforts of an organized block of workers, in formalizing many relationships within schools that had previously been informal, and in focusing the attention of the organized teaching force on material issues, yielding the possibility that teachers might find themselves even less involved than before with education policy decisions facing their schools and school systems, less attentive to distinctions of ability and accomplishment among their professional peers, and less able to influence developments outside the four walls of their own classrooms.

In the early years of teacher collective bargaining, according to many studies of the process, most union locals did emphasize bread-and-butter issues, maximizing the material gains for their members and consolidating their own authority as teacher leaders and spokesmen, while school boards did their utmost to retain control over what they deemed "education policy" issues, even as they bargained about salaries, workloads, and working conditions.[7] But as the two sides grew more accustomed to the relationship, as old patterns of "collegial" behavior persisted willy-nilly in the best schools, and as it became clear that one person's notion of a working condition is another's idea of an education policy, more issues began to be thrust into the bargaining process, into the procedures by which contractual provisions are enforced between negotiating sessions, and into consultative arrangements outside the bargaining process.

An AFT "negotiations manual" that was provided to its local affiliates in 1973 urged the establishment by contract of a joint labor-management "educational policies committee" in each community. The list of suggested functions for such a committee contained twenty-five items, ranging from textbook selection to testing and grading. "We have not only the right but also the duty," said the manual, "to represent professional interests as well as economic interests. . . . Accountability can be sanctioned only when its due measure of authority and responsibility has been given to those held accountable."

This was more easily said than accomplished. In many communities, management clung to its prerogatives, perhaps even more tightly now that its hegemony was threatened. Frequently, the state collective bargaining law itself discouraged negotiations on anything *but* the "terms and conditions of employment."[8] Though the enduring professionalism of teachers, now sometimes channeled through their unions, meant that most would still seek to influence education policy decisions through whatever means were available to them, a whole set of new mechanisms had to be created for this purpose, inevitably colored by the basic union-management relationship, though sometimes external to it.

As the collective bargaining process matured, as the terms of the new relationships were better understood and their limits explored, it became easier and more common for the union itself to become involved on the teachers' behalf in issues of education policy at the local level, sometimes even to take the lead in proposing improvements to an unimaginative school system. Naturally, the union could exert more muscle in such encounters than could the individual teacher.

Beginning in the mid-1970s in Dade County, Florida, for example, the teachers' union (an AFT affiliate after 1974) pressed for a series of changes in school policy and procedure. It was at the union's behest—and was then written into the contract—that only master's degrees in teachers' actual subject fields would henceforth bring the salary bonuses that had previously been attached to any advanced degree in any subject. It was the union that pressed the board to reduce the vast smorgasbord of elective courses available to Miami high school students under the "Quinmester Plan" and to introduce more uniformity (and more requirements) into the curriculum. It was through bargaining that the union persuaded the school board to establish "faculty councils" at every school to consult with the principal, to create systemwide union-administration "task forces" to review the content and pedagogy of specific subject areas, and to establish a permanent "joint educational policy oversight council" in which teachers and administrators could work together on matters that either group deemed consequential, much as the 1973 union manual had urged. Though harmony did not prevail on every issue, by decade's end the Dade County teachers' union and the school board were comfortable enough with one another that either's lobbyists in Tallahassee would frequently speak to the legislature on behalf of both.

Elsewhere, many school boards and superintendents resisted such developments—some still do—and many union locals lacked the wisdom or savvy to enlarge their vision beyond standard bread-and-butter issues and grievance resolution. But by the end of the 1970s the potential was clearly there for teacher collective bargaining to incorporate matters bearing directly on the quality of education itself.

*   *   *

Then came the "educational excellence movement," a phrase increasingly used to identify a decentralized but nationwide effort to infuse American schools with higher standards and enhanced effectiveness.

That American education had a "quality problem" had long been obvious to a handful of critics and, evidently, to a widening portion of the general public, including a fair number of teachers themselves. There was, I believe, a growing underground reservoir of dissatisfaction with the educational system, which by the late 1970s was wide, deep, and under considerable pressure. It began to trickle into the political and policy streams with the back-to-basics movement and the rapid spread of competency testing laws, but it did not become a gusher until the early 1980s, when two big drills bored into it.

First, a handful of governors, especially in the South, analyzed the barriers to economic development in their states and found their school systems grievously lacking, even as a handful of business leaders looked into the slackening productivity and international competitiveness of the American economy and discerned that part of the problem was the inadequate development of human capital, due at least in part to the failure of the schools to impart necessary skills and knowledge.

Second, a series of national commissions, blue-ribbon task forces, and foundation-sponsored study teams scrutinized the condition of American education, found it unsatisfactory, and said so in blunt language. The best known of these was the much-quoted report of the National Commission on Excellence in Education, entitled *A Nation at Risk* and released in April 1983.

Rather suddenly, educational quality was a high-priority public concern, a front-burner policy issue, and a topic of intense interest among the very same opinion shapers and public officials who had generally ignored it for most of the preceding two decades. By 1982, this was evident in a number of states, again mostly in the South, including such predictable ones as North Carolina but also such surprises as Mississippi. By 1984, only the rare state was not awash in reform proposals, as commissions and task forces bumped into each other at every intersection, governors made speeches (and, often, bold legislative proposals), major metropolitan newspapers editorialized on the subject every week or so, special sessions of state legislatures convened right and left, "education specials" aired on almost every television station, and pundits and critics declaimed as if they had always cared deeply about such arcana as teacher certification.

The specific proposals that the excellence movement prompted in the several states were numerous and varied. What they had in common

was a heavy emphasis on the attainment of higher standards of cognitive skills and knowledge by students, more exacting high school
graduation and college entrance requirements, firmer discipline and
more homework, greater emphasis on science and the humanities in the
curriculum and a corresponding reduction of nonacademic electives and
extracurricular activities, better teacher training, higher standards of intellectual aptitude and achievement among entering teachers, various
schemes for rewarding "merit" on the part of teachers and for restruc-
turing the teaching "career path" into a "career ladder," restoration of
the principal's role to that of "instructional leader," and far greater performance accountability—to be accomplished mostly through testing—
for individual students, teachers, entire schools, whole school systems,
and even states. In return for such reforms, the excellence movement
was willing to commit more money to the schools, and opinion polls
indicated widespread public support for this approach: additional resources, even additional taxes, provided that large changes were made
in educational policy and sizable gains were demonstrated in pupil
achievement. But not another cent for "more of the same."

By and large, the policy thrust of the excellence movement was compatible with the educational priorities of the AFT's Shanker and his national staff, and support for many of its points could be gleaned from
policy resolutions passed at AFT conventions over the years. Shanker is
also a gifted reader of the political entrails, and he concluded far sooner
than most other educators that a rare window of opportunity had
opened. He thereupon set about to ensure that his union and the public
education enterprise as a whole did not allow it to slam shut.

The NEA, by contrast, was initially blindsided by the excellence
movement, which would lead public education in directions almost precisely opposite to those the NEA had been pulling toward. Moreover,
the NEA's leadership was in a somewhat confused state in 1983. Herndon was stepping down as chief executive, and the terms of several key
elected officials were expiring.

Hence, by mid-1983 the two national teacher unions were again send-
ing very different signals. The NEA said, in effect, that these reforms
were basically wrongheaded, that nonprofessionals had no business
meddling in major educational decisions, that the nation's public
schools were in far better shape than the critics realized, and that the
familiar planks in the NEA's left-leaning platform created a sounder
base for educational (and social) reform than anything the commissions
and governors were proposing.

The message communicated by the AFT leadership, by contrast, was
that the goals of the excellence movement were sound, that they were

indeed virtually identical to the AFT's own objectives, that the entry of powerful new participants into the education policy debate was a welcome development, and that educators should at least be willing to engage in serious conversations with anyone who wanted to improve the schools, who had ideas for doing so, who offered resources with which to do so, and who had the power to deliver.

The specific policy proposals of the excellence movement were so numerous that it does neither the reformers nor the unions justice to concentrate on a few of them, but it is particularly illuminating to examine one that was guaranteed to give any teachers' union great cause for concern: the notion of differential rewards for individual teachers *according* to their classroom effectiveness. Underlying it, of course, was intense concern over the perceived intellectual weakness of new teachers, the tendency of the best and most experienced teachers to abandon the classroom, and the presence of at least a few "incompetents" within the ranks of the profession.

Merit pay was the most controversial notion in American education in 1983 and 1984. As an idea, it took many forms, ranging from the school system counterpart of the corporate "Christmas bonus" (in which all the teachers in a particularly "effective" school might get extra money), to a classroom variant of the old sweatshop practice of "piecework" (in which each teacher's salary would essentially depend on how much his pupils learned), to sophisticated "career ladders" up which a good teacher might climb over the course of many years, attaining added status, responsibility, and remuneration at every level. By the end of 1983, two states (California and Florida) and at least one locality (the Charlotte-Mecklenburg school system in North Carolina) had committed themselves to different models of the career ladder (also known as the master teacher) concept, and a number of local school systems were offering other kinds of merit pay—as some of them had done for years. In early 1984, the Tennessee state legislature approved its version of Gov. Lamar Alexander's "master teacher plan"—the most thoroughgoing statewide teacher career ladder enacted to date—and, as other legislatures reconvened and other governors presented their annual policy packages, it appeared that kindred proposals were being introduced at the rate of about three a week.

All forms of merit pay posed serious problems for teacher unions. All would tend to isolate the individual teacher and compensate him under terms of a series of judgments and agreements that are both unique to him and liable to be changed. Yet the essence of union membership, embodied in a collectively won contract (and in the standard, seniority-based pay scales and tenure laws that antedate and surround the bargaining process), is that teachers are treated by their employers as if they were interchangeable, that individual differences in ability or perform- ance have no bearing on salary or other terms of their employment and that any improvement—or degradation—in status, pay, or working conditions for one will be shared by all.

Public school teaching, to be sure, has never been open to all comers. State certification or licensure is a long-established practice. Nor has the career "path" been completely flat; a teacher can ordinarily get onto a higher salary scale by accumulating additional graduate school credit hours. But while the teacher unions have accommodated themselves to these practices, they have also striven to influence the policies by which exceptions are made, to dominate the procedures by which individual performance judgments are conducted, and to defend individual teach- ers against any actions that do not hew to those procedures. The union is threatened by any change that would strengthen the hands of state bureaucrats, of lay boards, or of principals and other school "managers" with regard to key determinations about individual reward and progress within the teaching occupation. To oversimplify just a little, the ideal personnel system from the union's standpoint is one that regards teach- ers as a group rather than as individuals, that treats all members of the occupation alike, and that—when exceptions must be made and judg- ments about individuals rendered—gives teachers-as-a-group primary responsibility for determinations about teachers-as-individuals.

Acceptance of this last responsibility by AFT and NEA affiliates has actually been rare. Though it is wholly compatible with the practice of "peer evaluation" that is part of the professional tradition, and with the skilled craft guild's practice of training and evaluating newcomers as they progress through the familiar steps from apprentice to journeyman to master craftsman, it clashes with an important tenet of the industrial union: the presumption that any qualitative appraisal of an individual's work is entirely the duty of management. This is, of course, a common presumption among industrial managers as well.

Yet, at least in matters of professional competence (not the same thing as differential pay), there are scattered instances of teacher union as- sumption of substantial responsibility for hard judgments. Perhaps the most interesting and sophisticated of these is the arrangement that one AFT local has painstakingly worked out with the Toledo school system, whereby a labor-management review panel (with a majority of teacher members) identifies teachers with serious shortcomings for an "in- tervention" program. The intent of such intervention is, of course, to rehabilitate the teacher, but—though the union disavows direct respon- sibility for this outcome—a teacher who cannot (or does not want to) be rehabilitated clearly becomes a candidate for dismissal proceedings by the school system.[9]

The unions' responses to the merit pay and master teacher ideas are especially interesting, for here there was no pre-existing policy gap between the AFT and the NEA. And, indeed, there has been no palpable difference in their reactions to the piecework and Christmas bonus versions of this idea. Notwithstanding very strong public support for the general principle of teacher merit pay, notwithstanding myriad commission reports, legislative proposals, and presidential orations lauding that principle, notwithstanding even some evidence from teacher opinion polls that significant numbers of their members themselves endorse the concept, neither union has eased its opposition to schemes that would link an individual teacher's compensation in a particular year to indicators of how much that teacher's students actually learned that year.

The concept of a career ladder, however, prompted quite divergent reactions. This first became clear in Tennessee, where Governor Alexander's much-publicized master teacher program was unveiled in early 1983. It would have created a career structure for teachers quite similar to the familiar college faculty sequence. After several years of experience at each career level, a teacher who wanted to could seek to be evaluated for promotion to the next level. Beyond the initial apprenticeship, there would be three major stages, each with added status, greater responsibility, and a good deal more pay. All teachers would have to be regularly re-evaluated, but all such performance appraisals would be carried out under the auspices of a new state certification commission comprising largely teachers and other line educators, with the actual field evaluations conducted by panels of master teachers drawn from outside the school systems of the individuals being evaluated.

Tennessee is an "NEA state"—the AFT enrolling only a few hundred members—and so naturally the NEA's state affiliate, the Tennessee Education Association (TEA), reacted first. Despite the very large amounts of money that Alexander proposed to add to the education budget to finance this program, despite heavy editorial support for the proposal, and despite opinion polls showing wide public acceptance, the TEA opted to fight. Tennessee is a state in which the majority teacher union has grown accustomed to wielding much the greatest influence on the legislature with respect to education issues (indeed, several key legislators are former TEA members, lobbyists, and relatives thereof), and the TEA aimed all its accumulated power against the master teacher proposal. This yielded a narrow (and provisional) defeat for the idea in 1983. But the governor also knew how to play political hardball, and he successfully opposed (eventually vetoing) all efforts by the teachers to win the usual cost-of-living increase in their salaries that year.

Meanwhile, Shanker deduced that the Tennessee situation presented an opportunity. The AFT had nothing to lose, and potentially something to gain, within the state itself. More important, Shanker recognized far earlier than the NEA leadership that it was a strategic mistake for a national teacher group blindly to oppose every version of merit pay in a year when the public was intensely interested in improving teacher quality and willing to spend more money for the purpose. Furthermore, Shanker and his lieutenants determined that the Tennessee career ladder plan actually met a number of the objections that the union had historically had to straightforward merit pay schemes. It was a career-minded approach rather than a system of isolated pay bonuses. It was open to participation by practically all teachers and assumed that a very sizable fraction of them would eventually climb the career ladder. It was financed with "new money," not subtracted from current salaries. Perhaps most important, the crucial evaluations of teacher performance were not to be conducted either by laymen or by regular principals and supervisors—who might be motivated by politics, favoritism, or vindictiveness—but by panels of fellow teachers drawn from other school systems.[10]

Accordingly, the AFT began a rather dramatic process of internal reconsideration of the merit concept, and Shanker himself began to make known through speeches and columns that, although the "Tennessee Plan" had some specific provisions that he disliked, it and proposals like it should be regarded by AFT members as a basis for serious discussion rather than outright rejection. Did the teacher's union, he asked rhetorically, want to follow in the wake of the steelworkers and the auto workers, oblivious to the need to reform their troubled industries and ultimately much diminished by the near collapse of those huge enterprises? Or would teachers face up to the public's dissatisfaction with the education industry, would they welcome these new participants in the policy arena, would they recognize that sizable amounts of additional money would be forthcoming only in return for significant quality-related reforms, and would they therefore be willing to enter into serious negotiations even when these might threaten long-established labor principles?

It was a brilliant strategic conception, it was shrewdly carried forward, and—partly because of the recalcitrance of the NEA and the sullenness of the rest of the education profession—it catapulted Albert Shanker into the front ranks of American educational statesmanship.

The AFT never actually endorsed the career ladder concept or any other variation on the merit pay theme (though AFT spokesmen gave partial approval to the Tennessee plan, and the AFT's Florida affiliate, unhappy with the master teacher scheme under consideration by that state's legislature, actually came forth with its own career ladder proposal), but the union's declaration of open-mindedness was a huge public relations coup and a source of intense embarrassment to the NEA. Accordingly, in late 1983, the new NEA leadership (President Mary Futrell and the new executive director, Don Cameron, both having assumed office in July of that year) began to echo the AFT's tone of "open-mindedness" toward school reform in general and even toward the ticklish issue of teacher career ladders in particular. Such daring flirtations ended rather suddenly, however. At its 1984 convention, held in Minneapolis over the Fourth of July weekend, the NEA vowed "unalterable opposition to so-called merit pay plans" and to "any alternative compensation plan" that is not based on "across-the-board salary increases [for] all teachers." The union again condemned teacher testing and peer review. President Mary Futrell insisted, "If you can't pass that test, I don't think you should become a teacher," but conceded that this was her personal view, not the position of her organization.

Although the NEA's brief romance with reform seems already to have ended—at least with regard to reforms affecting teachers directly—the AFT is forging ahead. There is no need to romanticize the reasoning of Shanker and his lieutenants in 1983 and 1984. Enormous amounts of money were being tendered to teachers in return for their willingness to "consider" policy changes. Public opinion was clearly on the side of the reformers, and by margins that even the pollsters regarded as decisive. Rank-and-file opinion within the unions themselves favored the principle of merit being associated in some fashion with teacher compensation.[11] The concept was rapidly gathering momentum in state after state, and a cynic might point out that all the unions had to do was say maybe to a popular idea that would quite likely pass anyway. Even so, assent did not come easily—if it came at all. When the Tennessee legislature resumed consideration of the career ladder proposal in January 1984, the TEA bitterly fought until the union's supporters lost a string of roll-call votes on key amendments in the senate and house education committees—and its eventual acceptance of a "compromise" version was contingent both on a number of policy concessions by the bill's sponsors and on legislative approval of a generous across-the-board raise for all teachers. So the union emerged from the bruising fight with some of the spoils of battle, but it yielded a principle to which for an entire year it had clung so tightly as to endanger the reform initiative as well as the prospects of higher pay for teachers. Alexander later commented, "Most of the year I felt like I was trying to raise money from people who didn't want to pay it and give it to people who didn't want to get it."

Lessons and implications can be drawn on many levels from the teacher unions' responses to the educational excellence movement in 1983 and 1984. Some of these are straightforward. Astute leadership makes a difference. The public's expectations for teacher unions are so low with regard to issues of educational quality that even a hint of open-mindedness can be taken for evidence of large progress. Teachers' twin interests—in their own material well-being and in the efficacy and re-pute of the educational enterprise itself—are keen enough that mossy doctrines which are seen to impede the pursuit of those interests can, under the right circumstances, be suspended or even changed. The pov-erty of policy imagination within the education profession is so severe, at least with regard to issues of quality, that a single person with the acuity, energy, and articulateness of an Albert Shanker can rapidly emerge as a major statesman, influential far beyond the ranks of his own organization's membership.[12] This is made easier by the fact that his larger rival union has vacillated on the issue of educational reform and that it appears, at least in late 1984, to have settled on a strategy of stonewalling all of the changes that the reformers deem most urgent— changes that most classroom teachers actually favor.

As one looks toward the future and ponders the general relationship of the teachers' unions to the attainment of better schools for the na-tion's children, the really interesting possibilities are subtle and rather complex.

Begin with two assumptions. First, as suggested at the outset of this essay, assume that teacher unions are going to endure, that most teach-ers are going to continue to belong to them, and that they are going to continue to carry out their now-familiar functions and to pursue their established goals.[13] Second, assume that most Americans want good schools and that it will be easier to improve the educational system with the cooperation of the teachers' unions than with their enmity.

The near future holds an authentic opportunity to improve the schools on that basis. But this opportunity is the delicate product of a convergence of six circumstances, some of which may themselves prove fragile or transitory. I offer them, therefore, with little confidence that the occasion will prove durable or that we will have the wisdom and fortitude to make the best use of it while the necessary conditions last.

First, the breadth and intensity of today's public dissatisfaction with the quality of American education, together with the energies and attention currently being directed at it by a number of influential groups and individuals that had previously evinced little interest, has plowed the most fertile field for bold education policy innovation that we have seen in many years. No longer are fundamental issues of school performance and direction strangers to the statehouse. No longer are the interests of the "general public" unrepresented. Long-established notions about the content, shape, and dimensions of education policy and school practice are not now taken for granted by the current policy leaders. There may in time emerge a new orthodoxy, fresh constraints, maybe even a pre-mature set of policy panaceas (merit pay is already a candidate), and the present leaders may thereupon lose interest or assume that the problem has been solved. But at the moment, change is in the air and policy is in flux, and there are few ideas for improving the schools that are so hereti-cal or "off-the-wall" as not to command at least a respectful hearing.

Second, the political impulse actually to *make* reforms—not merely to deplore problems and debate solutions—is so strong in many states and localities that significant changes are apt to be made with or without the cooperation of the education profession. For the teacher unions, this situation creates some tactical alternatives. They can let out all the stops, call in various political debts, and successfully stymie educational re-forms that others demand, thereby risking a backlash of public opinion, loss of influence, and perhaps a long-term decline in public confidence in the public schools. They can attempt to block reforms but *fail* in that effort, thereby bringing upon themselves both a loss of esteem (and later influence) and a series of changes in school policy and practice that they will find extremely unpleasant. (Such unwanted reforms will almost cer-tainly include much heavier external regulation of every aspect of the teaching occupation, with little or no added reward for those engaged in it.) Alternatively, teachers can cooperate in the design of reforms di-rected at the same objectives that will lead not to more regulation but to greater professionalization of the teaching occupation: increased status, pay, autonomy, and authority. Sophisticated teachers and union leaders already understand these choices, and some have concluded that the last alternative is better for them as well as for the schools.

Third, many teachers are themselves discontented with their lot. An overwhelming majority of them respond to polls by saying that if they had their lives to live over again they would probably not choose teach-ing as a career. The majority would also advise young people not to pursue teaching careers. Everyone who knows the schools can name able people who have quit the classroom for other lines of work, and others still teaching who wish they were not. The meager intellectual ability and sketchy educational background of the average new entrant into the teaching occupation, and the tendency for the best among the new entrants to be the first to exit, are well documented. These trends also cause understandable anxiety on the part of the best and most dedicated current teachers. Who, after all, wants to be thought part of a deteriorating profession or to have as colleagues people for whom one has little respect? Though some say that low pay and poor working conditions explain the current demoralization of the teaching force (as well as the difficulty of recruiting able newcomers), significant improvements in the material conditions of teaching hinge on policy reforms that will bring higher educational standards and yield better schools. However circular this logic, teachers are coming to understand it and are prepared to support drastic changes in their profession, including some that union leaders oppose. Eighty-seven percent believe that establishing career ladders would improve the quality of teaching, 84 percent would simplify the removal of incompetent teachers, 82 percent would oblige teachers to take competency tests before being certified, and 57 percent would even require experienced teachers to be retested periodically. This suggests that the discontent of today's teachers is matched by their willingness to swallow strong medicine in order to improve educational quality and thereby improve the quality of educators' lives.[14]

Fourth, an accumulating body of research about the characteristics of unusually effective schools indicates that those in which children learn the most usually have a "collegial" staff structure and a strong sense of common purpose among teachers, administrators, and other adults in the school. This is often described in such abstract terms as "shared moral order" or "school ethos," but what it really comes down to is that the school's professional staff functions like a team: it has clear objectives, it works together smoothly, its shared goals transcend those of its individual members, and if problems with one or another member of the team arise there is a sense of mutual responsibility for solving them.

Yet the "school team" model of educational staff organization is significantly different from the classic "labor-management" model of workplace organization. That the team approach can be made compatible with unionism is obvious from the fact that some outstanding schools display both characteristics. This is not easy, and it certainly is not automatic. It can be wrecked by a weak, insecure, or authoritarian principal—but it can also be destroyed by local union leadership that is fundamentally hostile to the school administration, that encourages its members to "work to rule" (for many situations during the school day require improvisation and flexibility), or that regards troubled teachers and unsuccessful curricula as management's problems. It can be further impeded by legal, judicial, or contractual constraints—more often encountered thus far in higher education—that bar union members from taking part in collegial decisions that penetrate traditional management domains, or that bar nonunion faculty members from participating in consultative and policy-making forums established through the bargaining process. Indeed, so many factors can prevent or dissipate the team approach that it is little wonder few schools have developed it to a high level of educational success. That it can exist, however, and that it is almost indispensable for school effectiveness, holds immense significance for the future structure of the educational workplace.[15]

Fifth, a revolution of sorts is under way in the theory of organizational behavior and the practice of labor-management relations in noneducational domains, and this appears to be compatible with school effectiveness research and to have large implications for the ways we run our educational institutions. I refer to the principles of organization and management that Peters and Waterman adduced from their examination of "America's best-run companies," to the conclusions and inferences that many observers have drawn from their study of Japanese management practices, and to the efforts that a number of private employers *and unions* have made to improve the quality of the workplace environment and to boost productivity through such mechanisms as "quality circles."[16]

One must guard against romantic rhapsodies. A lot of today's trendy works on management techniques are celebrations of love and indulgences in antirationalism—the corporate counterpart of "affective education," so to speak. With only a bit of exaggeration, those organizational modes that seem so attractive in Japan and Western Europe can become images of a corporatist society that holds some danger for individualism and possibly even for democracy. Devices such as quality circles look marvelous on paper, but they are vulnerable to exploitation by both management and labor and can end up achieving nothing but deepening cynicism. Finally, we know practically nothing as yet about the feasibility of translating even those approaches that work well in the private sector, with its organizational flexibility, legal independence, and clear "bottom line" output measures, into such public agencies as the schools, with their legislated rigidities, cumbersome procedures, hazy objectives, and susceptibility to political manipulation.

Still, there are lessons lurking in the "new organizational theory" for teacher unions, school administrators, and education policymakers. The heart of that theory is that an enterprise functions more effectively if everyone working in it "is invested" in its goals and subscribes to its central values, takes part in the decisions by which it organizes itself to attain those goals, shares in responsibility fo the successes and failures of the entire enterprise, and in turn can assume that the enterprise as a whole has an authentic interest in the well-being of its individual participants.

Actually, most of these ideas are not new, even in the highly structured world of industrial labor-management relations. In 1942, during World War II and after a decade of strife within the steel industry, Clinton S. Golden and Harold J. Ruttenberg (both key figures in the Steel Workers Organizing Committee) set forth thirty-seven "principles" of union-management relations that foreshadowed much of the modern literature on corporate excellence (at least for unionized companies). "Management's assumption of sole responsibility for productive efficiency actually prevents the attainment of maximum output," they wrote, while "union-management cooperation to reduce costs, eliminate wastes, increase productive efficiency and improve quality represents a practical program that provides workers with effective direct participation in the creative phases of management."[17]

The Golden-Ruttenberg principles have been honored in the breach more often than in practice during the past four decades, and the creators of "modern management theory" would not agree with them that collective bargaining by workers is a necessary precondition for labor-management cooperation. Still, the principles of "industrial democracy" enunciated long ago do appear to be compatible with the latest theories of organizational behavior, and collective bargaining in and of itself neither guarantees nor prevents the establishment of conditions of organizational effectiveness. The essential requisite is keen awareness on the part of both labor and management that the success of the enterprise in which both are engaged depends heavily on their ability to devise and execute strategies through which authority and responsibility are shared with respect to the quality of the organization's product, its competitiveness within the outside environment, *and* the quality of life for those engaged in the enterprise.

There is certainly no necessary contradiction between unionism per se and a manifest concern by workers about the efficiency of the production unit, the competitiveness and reputation of the industry, or even the quality of fellow workers' performances. Unionized airline pilots have a clear interest in the flight-worthiness and safety of their aircraft as well as the competence of their cockpit colleagues. Unionized symphony orchestra musicians regularly participate in auditions of performers who might be added to their ranks as well as in "peer reviews" of any whose work becomes unsatisfactory and thereby diminishes the quality—and value—of a combined product. Even huge national industrial unions such as the United Auto Workers and the Communication

Workers of America have become deeply involved in the quality circles movement because, as the CWA president, Glenn Watts, explained in a 1982 address, "[C]hanges in the economic and social scene challenge us to develop new approaches. Collective bargaining, in its plain vanilla version, is not enough to keep pace. . . . The Labor Movement must add new skills and strategies to affect the planning of the future."

Sixth, although labor-management relations in public school systems today do not routinely achieve the level of mutuality implied in the preceding paragraphs, there is some evidence that the collective bargaining process in education is maturing to the point where that level is at least visible and thus presumably attainable. Perhaps the clearest scholarly exposition of this point is contained in a 1981 study by Charles T. Kerchner and Douglas E. Mitchell. Their research, conducted well before the excellence movement arrived, indicated that labor relations in public education have "generations," two of which are clearly visible to date and the third of which can be glimpsed. The first, "the rise of teacher voice," is the initial coalescing of a group of angry and unhappy teachers around potential leaders. This phase "draws to a close when teachers break a cultural taboo about the way 'in which teachers ought to act'" and is followed by an "inter-generational" period in which teachers engage in militant activity—often but not always centering on a newly recognized union—to improve their situation. In the ensuing second generation, teacher organizations have become legitimate and "good-faith bargaining" occurs between union and school board, but it is confined to a relatively narrow set of issues concerning teacher pay and working conditions.

This outwardly pacific arrangement is disrupted by an "unexpected revolution" in which a discontented public, unhappy about the overall condition and performance of the schools and feeling excluded from the "bargaining" process, begins to hold the teacher organization responsible for such things as declining pupil achievement, "inefficient" schools, and other symptoms of educational decay. This leads to public agitation for school reform and, sometimes, a "public drubbing" of the teacher union that is deemed to be the villain.[18]

At this stage in the "generational" sequence, which roughly corresponds to the conditions that most of American education had reached by 1983, there is an opportunity to emerge from conflict into "the era of negotiated policy." This "Third Generation comes about," according to Kerchner and Mitchell, "when the teachers for their part agree on a need to support the general good of education and of the enterprise" and "when they understand that what the public thinks counts, and the public is ready to accept them when they believe that 'teachers want

what kids need.'" Management "enters the Third Generation when it
realizes that important school policies are made through collective bargaining, . . . that bargaining in public education fundamentally involves
political exchanges rather than economic ones, and that in order to
maintain political support, the enterprise of education must appear
robust and effective." [19]

For anyone with a traditional view of labor management relations, the
Third Generation is full of ironies. "It begins with the allegation of low
productivity or improper self-interest on the part of teachers and a politically generated movement to back management in regaining control,"
but it leads to the "legitimization of the teacher organization's role as a
representative of the teacher interest in *representing the clients of education*"—which in turn recalls the image of "the professional" and the
vastly greater moral authority and cultural status associated therewith.
In the Third Generation, we also find "an explicit joining of bargaining
and policy." The scope of negotiations is widened. Management may
even become "the aggressive party at the bargaining table," seeking
from teachers agreement to an array of changes in policy and practice
intended to yield more effective education, thus placing into negotiation
a number of issues that in earlier generations it would have preferred to
handle outside the bargaining process. [20]

Whether specific issues are dealt with inside or outside the bargaining
process itself, the Third Generation describes a mature relationship between teacher union and school leadership wherein the overall quality
and credibility of the educational enterprise are matters of intense mutual interest and in which action designed to enhance them are taken
jointly—if not always amicably—with each participant in the enterprise
keenly aware of a vigilant and none-too-pleased public monitoring his
every action.

Is such a Third Generation relationship dream or reality? So far as I
can tell, relationships of this kind—albeit in different degrees and with
various idiosyncrasies—are emerging in a handful of school systems,
especially those where teachers are represented by some of the more
visionary AFT locals. [21]

The "Toledo Plan" has already been noted, as have a number of developments in Dade County. Also worth consideration are "Dial-a-
teacher" systems operated by the union in New York and a number of
other communities, whereby a youngster needing help with his homework can obtain it over the phone; the continuing refinement of school
discipline procedures (including the teacher's right to exclude any dis-
ruptive student from his classroom) in the contract of the St. Louis
teachers and kindred policies in other systems; and a summer program

for strengthening the knowledge of science and math teachers, a program led by the Robinsdale (Minnesota) Federation of Teachers and co-sponsored (and partly financed) by the school system and by the 3M Corporation.

In other communities, the union may work for educational quality improvement outside the bargaining process, and may even achieve its results by publicly embarrassing the school system. Public "hearings" conducted by the AFT affiliate in Oklahoma City in 1983 and extensively reported by the media led the school board to adopt an "assertive discipline" program. In early 1984, the Cincinnati local sponsored a series of radio commercials calling attention to the continuing practice of "social promotion" by the school system. The unions, it may be recalled, have four established genres of activity and can avail themselves of whichever seems best suited to the task at hand. Bargaining is only one option, and not always the most efficacious.

Are the foregoing examples just pebbles in the sea, or do they denote a larger and more durable shoreline shift? All that is clear is that some educationally sound policies and practices are now in place in some communities primarily because the teachers' unions invented them, pressed for them, in some cases provided the leadership and resources needed to carry them out—and in other cases merely concurred in them, possibly suggesting refinements along the way. One cannot assume that, in the handling of issues bearing on educational quality, management is invariably the "reformer" and the union routinely a source of resistance. Some union leaders are braver, smarter, more imaginative, and more knowledgeable about the sources and manifestations of educational inadequacy than some American school administrators and board members. On the other hand, it would be a mistake to suppose that all union locals routinely place the quality of the child's education at the top of their list of priorities, that they set and enforce high standards of pedagogical practice, that they initiate school reform ideas, or that they always respond warmly when someone else does. All I am sure of is that in those instances—too few, alas—where strength, confidence, and imagination characterize all the key participants, a Third Generation relationship can develop through which children are better served.

American public education is currently going through trying but exhilarating times that appear to be accompanied by an extraordinary level of public concern, the participation of many new political and policy actors, and the opportunity for epochal changes in school organization, educational standards, and classroom practices.

It so happens that organized labor in the United States is also under-going a period of intense self-scrutiny, bold experimentation, and deep anxiety about its own future.[22] Not only has union membership been declining, both absolutely and as a proportion of the work force, but public esteem for organized labor is very low. According to a December 1983 ABC News–*Washington Post* survey, only 18 percent of the public has much "confidence" in labor unions; banks, by contrast, enjoyed a 46 percent and the military a 66 percent rating, and even the Congress received 24 percent. (The public schools, incidentally, had a confidence rating of 40 percent in the same survey.) It is scarcely surprising that the leaders of the AFL-CIO are alarmed.

The teachers' unions are caught up in education as well as labor reforms.[23] Though they dominate neither, they are influential in both and are in turn profoundly influenced by events in both. What events in the two spheres appear to have in common is the widening realization that the lasting interests of the working person—as breadwinner, union member, consumer, and citizen—oblige him and his fellow workers to manifest a keen interest in the long-term viability of the enterprises for which they work, even as the analogous interests of those who own or manage the same enterprises oblige them to reciprocate. This heightening sense of mutuality of interests is a sufficient basis for changing some assumptions, modifying some practices, and altering some familiar dogmas. Intersecting private interests do not make for an especially noble framework in which to consider something as inherently public-regarding as excellence in public education.[24] But I believe they are an adequate pragmatic foundation to sustain my own conclusion: under the circumstances that exist today, and that have been (briefly) set forth in the preceding pages, teacher unionism can be compatible with high-quality public education, can even be a positive force for achieving it. But whether this will in fact happen in most American schools depends on both the perspicacity of the union members (and leaders) and the wisdom of those with whom they must contend—and neither of these attributes can be taken for granted. The problems of American education include, but do not consist primarily of, the teacher unions; so, too, must the solutions.

PART FIVE
School Climates

7

Schools That Make an Imprint: Creating a Strong Positive Ethos

GERALD GRANT

In a delightful essay in *Harper's* several years ago, Frances Taliaferro pointed out that fictional literature about education can be divided into proschool and antischool novels. It is a bald distinction, but it works:

> In proschool novels, school is the seat of order and civilization, the clean well-lighted place where conventions are learned and value accepted. It is the cradle of hierarchy and the nursery of striving; prizes and demerits are justly given, the class has a top and a bottom, and the Head, in his (or her) wisdom, separates the sheep from the goats.
>
> Antischool novels assume that school is the place where we learn the conventions of oppression and hypocrisy. Here, as elsewhere, the best lack all conviction: management is in hands of oafs and bores. Survival requires conformity, or even submission. The trophies are brummagem, the Head is a fraud, and all right-thinking readers must find the goats far more interesting than the sheep.[1]

Tom Brown's School Days is the classic representative of the proschool novel in which the hero defeats the loutish bully and slowly demonstrates the strength of character that wins the true friendship of honorable peers. After depositing his eleven-year-old boy at the school, Tom's father reflects on his hopes for the outcome of Christian nurture at Rugby: "If he'll only turn out a brave, helpful, truth-telling Englishman, and a gentleman, and a Christian, that's all I want."[2] In the antischool novel, anarchy defeats a corrupt old order. The hollow sentiments of character training turn to ashes in the mouths of those seeking to preserve venal privileges. We are prepared to view the teacher as anything but moral, as in the porter's comment about Paul Pennyfeather in

Evelyn Waugh's *Decline and Fall*. After Pennyfeather has been convicted of indecent behavior and "sent down" from his Oxford college, the porter observes, "I expect you'll be becoming a schoolmaster, sir. That's what most of the gentlemen does, sir, that gets sent down for indecent behavior."[3]

Although Taliaferro's essay, inspired by Elizabeth Bowen's introduction to one of the great proschool novels, Antonia White's *Frost in May*, drew mostly on British precedent, we can think of American equivalents: *The Rector of Justin* dealt with a representative of the good school and just Head, and *Catcher in the Rye* aimed at the hypocrisy of the school society. Even more interesting to a social scientist is the way that this distinction captures stereotypical views about private and public schools in America. The analogy is inexact, but some interesting patterns and reversals of patterns can be discerned in both the stereotypes and the data about private and public schooling.

In the latter nineteenth century and for much of the twentieth, the American public school was seen as the virtuous source of democratic character, whereas the private school was treated as the antischool, a breeder of class privilege and of an antidemocratic spirit. In their aptly named *Managers of Virtue*, David Tyack and Elisabeth Hansot argue that the consensus animating the creation of public education in the nineteenth century was not unlike a moral crusade. The common school movement was led by citizens of Horace Mann's generation

> who both shaped and represented a widespread ideology that stressed civic and moral values that they claimed could only be maintained through public education. The nation could fulfill its destiny only if each rising generation learned those values together in a common institution. This was the dominant theme in the rhetoric of consensual persuasion.[4]

The Protestant-republican ideology that Tyack and Hansot saw undergirding the founding of the public schools was also evident to the Lynds in their study of Middletown in 1929. Although the public schools do not teach religious beliefs directly, the Lynds observed, "these beliefs tacitly underlie much that goes on in the classroom."[5] The discussion of John Dewey and the Progressives linked the success of public education with the survival of democracy itself. Lester Ward, one of the founders of American sociology, argued for exclusive state control of education on the grounds that private education tends to increase inequality and that "the less society has of it the better."[6] In *Philadelphia Gentlemen*, E. Digby Baltzell saw the development of private boarding schools as the means of shaping a distinctive upper class: "These fashionable family surrogates taught the sons of the new and old rich . . . the subtle nuances of an upper class way of life."[7] Catholic schools were often seen as serving another kind of class interests: a narrow and sectarian set of beliefs taught in a rigidly authoritarian atmosphere that was inimical to democratic beliefs. When large-scale racial desegregation programs were begun in the 1960s, it was charged that private schools, especially the Roman Catholic parochial schools, further offended democratic aims by providing a refuge for those who wanted to avoid attending school with blacks.

Thus the broad stereotypes served to reinforce the notion that public education was the good school of the democratic social order, whereas private education meant basically either schools for snobbery or bastions of Catholicism indoctrinating immigrants with the formulas of the Baltimore Catechism. The real moral vision was held to be that espoused by the common school reformers. The public school opened its doors to all comers and classes while the private schools preserved the divisions of class, race, and religion.

Now these stereotypes have given way, if they have not been smashed altogether. The public school seems to have lost its sense of a moral crusade as it grew bureaucratized and became more officially value neutral. The growth of metropolitan areas after World War II also resulted in an expansion of urban and suburban public school systems highly stratified by race and social class, sometimes maintained by gerrymandering school boundaries. A few years ago, at a time when the average tuition for members of the National Association of Independent Schools was $3,700, the Greenwich, Connecticut, public school system decided to open its doors to nonresidents to fill empty classrooms. The tuition would be that of the average per-pupil expenditure—$4,000.

Meanwhile, in the private sector, many of the old elite schools had democratized and were sponsoring scholarships for blacks and urban poor. The most impressive shift had occurred in the Roman Catholic schools, which were most heavily concentrated in urban areas and which account for two-thirds of all students enrolled in the non-public schools. While some parochial schools closed as upwardly mobile Catholics moved to the suburbs, many parish schools remained open and served the new urban poor, including non-Catholic blacks as well as the new Hispanic immigrants. About a fifth of those attending Catholic schools are officially defined as minority students, according to a 1983 survey. Of these, 8.8 percent are black, 9.1 percent Hispanic, 2.1 percent Asian, and 0.04 percent Native American.[8]

This reversal of the conventional wisdom was demonstrated most dramatically by James Coleman in the wake of his 1981 study of public and private schools.[9] Coleman surveyed 58,000 students and their teachers in 1,015 public and private high schools and concluded that it was the Catholic schools that now most nearly fit the ideal of the American common school. Although Catholic schools draw fewer blacks than the public schools (about 6 percent by Coleman's estimate in 1981 and 8 percent in two 1983 surveys, as contrasted with about 14 percent in public schools), there is less internal segregation in Catholic schools in either racial or economic terms. That is, within the Catholic sector black and poor students are distributed more randomly, whereas in the public sector suburban schools tend to be predominantly white and urban schools heavily black. Coleman also found that student aspirations in Catholic schools were less class based, that Catholic students are more likely to say that discipline is fair in their schools, and that poor black students appear to learn more in Catholic than in public schools (a finding that has been challenged by critics of Coleman's report).[10] Coleman traces the differences in school policies that he believes undergird the higher achievement—policies to require homework, to establish good discipline, and to reduce absences. His report says much less about how one achieves the consensus within the school that is reflected in consistent policies.

While Coleman was surveying a large sample of schools, my colleagues and I were intensively studying a small number of public and private schools through participant observation methods. Our findings are congruent with his, and we paid special attention to the question of how good climates are formed, or what I would like to address in this article as the elements of a strong positive ethos.[11]

First, let us look at some of Coleman's data. Listed in Table 1 are responses by students to questions that reveal broad differences in disciplinary climates, or ethos, between several types of schools. From left to right, the first three columns report results from public, Catholic, and other private schools that are non-Catholic (including Lutheran, Christian, Jewish, and nondenominational schools). The last two columns refer to high-performing public and private schools. Each of these two represents about a dozen schools with the highest proportions of their graduating classes listed as semifinalists in the 1978 National Merit Scholarship competition. The high-performing public schools tend to be affluent suburban schools, and the private schools are weighted toward elite boarding schools.

Although the public schools have experienced an enormous growth in guarantees of student rights and in new legal procedures to back them up, it is interesting to note that students in these schools are much less likely to feel that discipline is effective. More important, significantly smaller percentages of public school pupils feel that discipline is fair or that their teachers care about them. Compared with students in Catholic schools, those in public schools report that they do about two hours' less homework a week, watch more television, skip classes more frequently, and witness more than twice as much back talk and fighting in school. One should not overinterpret the data from the small samples represented by the high-performing schools, yet the differences are striking. Essentially, students in high-performing private schools look like enhanced versions of those in Catholic schools, with particularly impressive percentages reporting that discipline is effective and fair and that their teachers take an interest in them. The high-performing public schools show a sharp distinction in one way that we would expect, equaling the Catholic schools in hours of homework per week. However, discipline is seen as much less effective than in the Catholic schools, and the report on fairness and teacher interest is nearly as low as for all public schools in general.

Table 1. High school student responses to questions on discipline, fairness, and average hours of homework in public, Catholic, other private, and "high-performing" public and private schools*

	Public	Catholic	Other private	"H-P" public	"H-P" private
Effectiveness of discipline is excellent/good[a]	42	72	58	52	79
Fairness of discipline is excellent/good[a]	36	47	46	40	62
Teacher interest is excellent or good[a]	12	25	41	15	64
Average hours of homework per week	3.7	5.6	6.0	5.6	9.1
Average hours of watching TV per week	4.2	3.7	3.2	3.2	2.2
Students often don't attend school	46	8	16	28	3
Students often talk back to teacher	42	23	22	26	9
Students often get into fights with others	27	9	6	15	3

* This table was constructed from data in James Coleman et al., *Public and Private Schools* (Washington, D.C.: National Center for Education Statistics, 1981), 119–35. Responses noted "a" are seniors; all others, sophomores. Responses are given in percentages, with the exception of hours of homework and television watching.

If we let the reported hours of homework represent the norm for an intellectual climate of the school, and the response to questions about discipline stand for the moral or social norms within the school, then it would seem that the average public school is weakly normed with respect to both intellectual and social climates and that the Catholic schools are strongly normed on both. The high-performing private schools would be exceptionally strongly normed on both. However, the high-performing public schools are strongly normed on the intellectual but weakly normed on the moral or social dimensions.

Recognizing that these are very gross interpretations of the data—interpretations with which Coleman himself might not agreee—we must ask what produces schools with strong intellectual and moral climates. My colleagues and I were granted a year's access to two private schools that were strongly normed on Coleman's measures. The Sturgis School, an upper-middle-class nondenominational school for girls, covering kindergarten through grade twelve, would qualify as a high-performing private school in Coleman's categories. St. Teresa's, an inner-city parochial school, would fit the profile for Catholic schools, although it spans kindergarten through grade eight. In both schools, we were given extraordinary freedom to visit classes, to examine files and student records, to sit in on discussions and evaluations of students, and to interview teachers, students, and staff. We attended social events, parent meetings, and school plays and in some cases were invited to student and teacher homes. Sturgis, located in an eastern seaboard city, was originally founded to prepare girls for entrance to highly selected colleges and continues to serve families whose median income exceeds $50,000 a year. St. Teresa's, on the other hand, draws families whose median income is less than $15,000 a year, two-thirds of whom are black and most of whom are Protestant. About a third of St. Teresa's families are on welfare, but all make at least a token payment on the $350-a-year tuition ("There's dignity in that," the principal explains). Tuition at Sturgis is more than ten times that amount, but we were struck by many of the similarities in the ethos of the two schools despite class difference.

It can never be settled definitely whether Coleman's findings are school effects or are the results of collecting like-minded children who come to school disposed to behave and to achieve. In looking at the ethos of the school, we shall in effect be asking, If it is something that the school does, what is that something? Our answer is that the school does indeed do something but that it does it in interaction with parents, and in part because it is a collection agency. But it does not only collect: it collects and educates and enhances.

The Greek root of *ethos* means the habits of the animals in a place. Joan and Erik Erikson describe it as "the organizing power of the social processes. . . . [I]t is a certain spirit. . . . It is almost like what the community is for." [12] The ethos is what people in a community share that makes of them a community rather than a group of disparate individuals. It is the configuration of attitudes, values, and beliefs that members of the community share. For a private school, it is the values represented by the parents and founders of the school or of the agency, such as a church that took the leading role in its founding. In some instances, as Burton Clark has shown, the ethos is reshaped or restated in more powerful ways by second founders, who assume the leadership later in the life of the institution and elaborate a new saga or life history of the school. [13] In that sense, the ethos of the school is personalized by references to those founders or second founders who represent the revered values of the institution.

Schools with a strong positive ethos are led by those who clearly enunciate a character ideal. Judith Smilg Kleinfeld was struck by the way Eskimo students from a particular Catholic boarding school stood out in her classes at the University of Alaska at Fairbanks. When she went to the school to observe, she found that the leaders repeatedly enunciated an ideal of responsibility to others and stressed the development of character and intellect in a caring community. [14] As in the urban Catholic school we studied, this was emphasized not only in its catalog rhetoric but at every important juncture in the life of the school. Much of the effort of the school is spent in communicating the ideals for which the school stands and in encouraging a dialogue with a public about those ideals. There is a deeply embedded belief that education is inseparable from a concept of what constitutes a good life and a good community. These ideals are sometimes embodied in a formal statement of aims, such as this declaration by the faculty of Phillips Academy:

> In a community such as Andover, all must commit themselves to the goals of the community and to loyalty to each other. Since education at Phillips Academy is both intellectual and humane, the students and faculty derive mutual support from sharing of themselves and their ideals. . . . Yet the happiness of everyone in the community depends on consideration and awareness, restraint and candor, discretion and shared joy. Collaboration toward these imprecise but worthwhile ends is an expectation which all in the academy hold. [15]

But ideals are most often conveyed in less formal ways, by example and by story, especially stories of exemplary students, founders, patron saints, formal heads, or beloved teachers. For instance, a typical article in the newsletter of a Quaker school we visited celebrated the retirement of a respected teacher, Palmer Sharpless:

> Palmer came to George School with a good sense of who he was and what he wanted to accomplish. This frame of reference was nowhere

more evident than on his application for employment: "I believe in frankness, earnest effort, honesty, daily reference to ideals, constant and unselfish devotion to the common weal. I plan to fight with every ounce of my strength any graft, injustice, discrimination, or foul play that I meet in my daily community contacts. Only through endeavoring to better our own community will brotherhood and peaceful living ever be realized for mankind." [16]

Intellectual and moral virtue are seen as inseparable. The aim is harmony. A good school is not one that is merely "effective" in raising test scores. Although intellect is important, one does not assume that the maximization of test scores is the highest aim; rather one wants a harmonious development of character. There is a concern for rigorous academic education but also for the qualities of endurance, resilience, responsibility, resourcefulness, and social concern. Teachers must have equal concern for mind and for character; schools should be neither morally neutral factories for increasing cognitive output nor witless producers of obedient "well-adjusted" youngsters. There must be a balance in both the life of the student and the life of the school. Like a good parent, the school does not want to squeeze a student too hard to raise his or her grade average at the expense of other aspects of development. Publications often feature craftspeople—artists, musicians, carpenters, excellent cooks, mechanics, or gardeners—because this is a concrete way of talking about intellectual and moral virtues. As my colleague Thomas Green has pointed out, "to possess a conscience of craft is to have cultivated the capacity for self-congratulation or deep satisfaction at something well done, shame at slovenly work, and even embarrassment at carelessness." This sense of craft shapes our concern for excellence. "It is what impels us to lay aside slovenly and sloppy work simply because of what it is—slovenly and sloppy." [17]

References to the spirit of the place were made frequently in both of the private schools that we studied. Teachers expressed a belief in the saving power of the community and exhibited great reluctance to expel or give up on a difficult student. As one teacher noted, "I can't let go of our 'rescue fantasy,'" At the same time, teachers recognize that it takes time for the ethos to make its imprint on the student. As a nun remarked of a recalcitrant younger pupil, "it takes a few years to make a St. Teresa's student." And older students recognize that it has formed them. "They've done so much for me; they molded me," said one Sturgis junior. "They want us to do something important, to make some impact, to do our best." Evidence that the ethos "takes" shows up in surprising ways—for example, in a classroom discussion of Walden that brought forth the criticism that Thoreau shouldn't have isolated himself at Walden Pond, because "it was his duty to do something for another, to serve other people."

Adults make plain that they are responsible for shaping and maintaining that ethos and that it makes a difference in the lives of all in the community. That sense of responsibility is fostered by detachment from bureauracy. Teachers are not waiting for curricular guides, nor are principals reading "directives." They are mutually creating and sustaining a world. Principals also teach, and may return to full-time teaching after being a principal. Teaching is more likely to be regarded as a vocation than as a step in a bureaucratic career.

The ethos is also evident in the high expectations that teachers have for students. A first-grade teacher told us, "Each day we make a point of asking them, 'What did you read last night?'" Another teacher who was trying to describe her first year at the school explained, "You always felt you had to give your best; there was an expectation that you would never slack off. I can't pin it down. It was just there." In one class we visited, a nun told a student, "Now that you've gotten 82 on this test, I'll never accept anything less than that again." In discussing a troublesome child, another nun told us that the girl's mother had committed suicide, then said, "I can point to any child in this room and give you a sad, if not tragic, story. But they still have to be educated."

There was a reluctance to accept excuses, and an expectation that people would get down to work. Teachers are role models for students and create expectations by the way they approach their own job, by how quickly they get down to work, and by how seriously they take their work. Absenteeism was extremely low at both schools. A nun who was ill insisted on reporting to work; when the principal saw her, she sent her home. After two hours' rest at the convent, she returned to class, saying, "I'm well enough to teach now."

The foregoing also makes plain that the ethos is reflected as much by what people do as by what they say. Teachers are expected to be available beyond the usual office hours and to be scrupulous in writing letters of recommendation. Students in both schools are taught not only to be sensitive to the needs of others but also to serve others in volunteer projects in nursing homes and hospitals. Even in difficult situations, deadlines are to be met; students who were up most of the night getting ready for a play are not excused from handing in their history paper, and they are told that tiredness is no excuse for sloppiness. Both schools emphasized schoolwide rules of behavior and standards of conduct. As the principal of the Catholic school put it, "the rules of the game should not change from grade to grade." Order should not be a result of obtaining compliance at the cost of crushing spontaneity; it should be the expression of freely chosen good ends. Students are aided in acquiring those norms when reasons are frequently given for observing rules: you should not be late to class, because you are disturbing the learning of others; you have an obligation to do your homework and be prepared for class for your own benefit and because it's part of your obligation to your classmates and to the progress of the whole class; courtesy to others consists not only in remaining quiet but also in actively listening to what is being said. The degree to which norms have been internalized is evident when children are left to their own devices. When a class of Sturgis second-graders was told they would have twenty minutes to wait in the hall before they could use the gym, one girl turned to the others and said, "Let's tell stories." They then formed into a group, sitting on the floor, and without any prompting from the teacher the first girl began to tell a story.

The ethos is also expressed in judgments about whether norms are met, and in the kinds of sanctions attached to those judgments. We paid special attention to those times when teachers were making judgments. At both Sturgis and St. Teresa's, the faculty spent hours discussing individual pupils. At St. Teresa's, problems that particular students were encountering were often introduced for discussion in faculty meetings by the principal. At Sturgis, all the teachers responsible for teaching a particular grade gathered twice a year to evaluate the progress of pupils in that grade. In these reviews, each pupil was discussed for ten or fifteen minutes. It is important to note that every pupil was discussed. One of the characteristics of these schools was that they paid equal attention to the average student, whereas in many large public schools today the average student is likely to be more invisible. In such schools handicapped students may have individually prescribed programs, tabs are kept on troublemakers, and teachers may notice that a student in the top, college bound track has taken a nosedive, but the broad middle mass is likely to be faceless. If one's aim, though, is to save a soul or imprint a character ideal, then every soul is equally worth saving and each imprint deserves close inspection.

At Sturgis, the inspection began with a report on a student's scores on standardized tests, but the discussion rapidly evolved into a general appraisal of the character of the child, in which the grades achieved were but one indicator. The discussions were parentlike in their concern as noted above, in that higher achieved scores were regarded not as an unalloyed good but as something to be considered in relation to the optimal development of the child as a whole. Here are some excerpts from our field notes on a review conducted by the tenth-grade teachers:

The art teacher gave her a 92. She said, "Sandra is very unusual. She does beautiful detail work and knows what she is doing. She's naïve but has a lot of style. Her personality really disturbs me. She gets so negative if you give her a suggestion. And then afterward I find she doesn't want me to come near her work, which is limiting for her if I can't help her out. It limits her possibilities. Sometimes this almost borders on rudeness. She has a rare talent, but somehow she just puts you off." Then others nod in agreement, and the biology teacher said, "Yes, that's true. She's very defensive and really shy. She does respond well to humor, and if you can kid her about her work, she loosens up a bit."

We were impressed with how carefully teachers prepared for the reviews, making written comments about each child. They knew an amazing number of details about each child, in class and out.

Teachers did not always agree in their remarks. In fact, they felt free to express their disagreement, to admit their preferences and biases. It was taken for granted that only if the teachers themselves were honest in their reactions to a child would they be able to learn much from this discussion. Putting one's assessment in writing before the meeting encouraged this diversity. For example, this exchange occurred among sixth-grade teachers:

"She can be so unpleasant and inconsiderate of other people's feelings," said the homeroom teacher. "It's not that she's inconsiderate," another teacher replied. "She considers it carefully. She *intends* to wound them." The others laughed and then the math teacher commented, "That must be why I like her. She can be very enchanting. Of course, she's just passing in my class." Then the homeroom teacher brought the discussion to a close, "Well, so much for being enchanting."

The teachers were interested in the emotional and mental development of the child and in a wide range of qualities and virtues, including honesty and courage. The judgments they made applied to both the individual and the community: the student was expected to meet the standards of the community, but the community was also responsible for meeting the needs of the child. A troubled girl was described as an anguished complainer who was growing increasingly self-absorbed and isolated. A teacher responded, "Let's break this thing if we can. Why is she so miserable? We really need to talk to her. We need to get her to believe that she's a serious, capable, worthwhile person." The assistant head of the school, who had discussed some of the family problems the girl was having, summed up with a plea: "Please watch out for her— help her balance her life, help her in that fragile balance."

In these schools, the adults stand unambivalently in loco parentis, and, like good parents, the teachers and staff exercise a caring watchfulness, concerned with all aspects of a child's development. Cooperation between parents and teachers is evident at every turn as parents help to paint the walls (at St. Teresa's) or redecorate the teachers' lounge (at Sturgis). At Sturgis, parents are members of the board of trustees; at St. Teresa's, pupils may not be expelled without the consent of the parent advisory board. Such parent representation in formal governance arrangements is an outward sign of the trust teachers and staff feel that parents have placed in them. They act with an easy confidence that parents have faith in them and in the ends they are trying to achieve. As the admissions director at Sturgis said, "If we feel we can't work with the parents, it's no go." However, that trust also means tht parents are not supposed to bargain or negotiate for their child to obtain preferred teachers in the way that is fairly common in public schools. As the head of the middle school at Sturgis put it:

> Parents aren't that directly involved in the educational program of their child, but they must be in agreement with us, or there is no point in their child coming here. It does no one any good to have tugs of war over a child's program. Parents have to understand what this school is all about and trust that we want good things for their child.

The ethos forms the ground on which all stand in a relation of trust, and that ethos constitutes the ends of education. In this context, the task of the leaders is to choose the best means to those ends. With agreement about ends, the role of the leaders is to remind others of those ends, to keep them vivid in the life of the school. The critical responsibility of the leaders is to ground the daily decisions in an interpretation of that shared ethos—to choose the best means to the agreed upon ends. The leaders of such schools are chosen because they exemplify those values; they are "the best of us," persons capable of symbolizing the tradition and of drawing others into it. Leaders are supposed to have the wisdom to choose teachers who represent the tradition. They must be able to evoke commitments and to guide others to a fuller realization of the valued goods of the community.

Briefly, then, we have sketched the elements of a strong positive ethos in schools where parents voluntarily join together in a mutual orientation toward valued intellectual and moral virtues. Now we can state a question that has never been far below the surface. Is it possible to create schools with such an ethos in places where there is less agreement about ends, where a substantial proportion of students and even many teachers did not choose that school, and where some may be attending against their will? In such instances, must we settle for weakly normed schools tied together by a system of rules and procedures that at best can only ensure that no one of the disparate elements within the school gains an edge or a preference on the others? Or is it possible to create public schools with a strong ethos in both intellectual and moral terms?

Certainly, as Tyack and Hansot have shown, there was once widespread agreement on the ends of public schooling The Protestant-republican ideology that provided the social cement for public schooling in its founding period was a powerful character ideal. A somewhat secularized version of that ideology, what Robert Bellah has called the civic religion, provided the moral consensus for public schooling through the middle of the twentieth century. In the last two decades, the consensus underlying the moral authority of the school has come apart because of strains from within and without. Again, Tyack and Hansot furnish a good capsule history of the period:

> New York, with its baroque bureaucracy of 110 Livingston Street and its bitter and violent conflicts over community control was an exaggerated version of the disintegration of earlier forms of governance and the demolition of consensus on education. . . . Decisions by federal and state courts set limits on religious ceremony and instruction, prescribed how students could be suspended and assigned to special classes, required help for limited-English-speaking pupils, guaranteed freedom of expression for teachers and students, revised school finance, proscribed sexual inequities, and ordered desegregation. State governments demanded new forms of "accountability," including tests of minimum competence for promotion and graduation. Federal and state governments created dozens of new categorical programs, each with complex guidelines and reporting requirements. Pressures from local protest groups and mandates from higher governments increased citizen participation in decision making. . . . Often protesters and their supporters—popular writers, social scientists, foundation and government officers—portrayed local educators as unjust or ineffectual foot-draggers. On educational leaders, it seemed, rested the burden of remaking society, and the inevitable failure to do so undermined their authority.[18]

The effects of the series of overlapping social revolutions just described were evident in the urban public school that we studied intensively. Hamilton High had been the leading academic high school in the city. By the early 1970s, a third of the city's high schools had been closed as part of a desegregation plan, and racial balance was achieved in all the remaining high schools, including Hamilton. In less than a decade, it went from being a school that was predominantly white and middle and upper middle class to one that is 46 percent minority, now including a significant number of Asians and Hispanics in addition to working-class and ethnic whites. In the early years of the transformation, a number of

the teachers who had functioned well under the old academic ethos simply could not cope with the new clientele and left. New teachers and a
liberal principal were brought in at a time when civil rights protests were
escalating. Teachers from that era who remain feel that his compassion
for minority students overruled good disciplinary policy. A modular
curriculum with elective courses on topics ranging from "revolution" to
"paramedics" replaced much of the old standard fare. Skateboards appeared, and students began to play radios in classrooms and to "party"
(i.e., smoke dope) in the halls. Buses sent by organizers of civil rights
demonstrations would show up at school during school hours, and students would freely leave classes to board them.

    After a few years, complaints—many of them from black parents who
did not feel that their children were learning much in the new curriculum—led to the replacement of the liberal principal with a get-tough
administration. Police and hall guard monitors were brought into the
school. "Sweeps" were ordered to clear the halls of students who came
to school to do in the hallways those things that students had once
dropped out of school to do on the corner. In fact, school life for them
was not too different from life on the corner. New disciplinary codes
were published, and efforts were made to expel some students. But students had also discovered new rights and new due process procedures
that made expulsion increasingly difficult. Adults became reluctant to
press a point if it meant the hassle of litigation. A teacher who had been
subject to extreme verbal abuse in our hearing was asked why she did
not report the students. "Well, it wouldn't have done any good," she
replied. "Why not?" we inquired. "I didn't have any witnesses," she
explained. Increasingly, adult authority was being defined in terms of
what would stand up in court, and a new standard of behavior was
being shaped—namely, that which is not illegal is expressly permitted.
This, of course, is the negative of a standard represented by a character
ideal. The school handbook stipulates what penalties will be levied for
defacing or stealing property. It says virtually nothing of altruism, nothing that would encourage students to pick up trash that they didn't
throw or to improve what they've inherited. In the face of new diversity,
many adults have given up hope that any consensus can be achieved
with respect to a moral standard. Others are no longer sure that they
know what is right or, if they do, that they have any right to impose it.
When we asked the school's drug counselor, who dealt primarily with
students assigned to her by the courts or referral systems, whether she
would take the initiative to approach a student whom she knew to be a
heavy drug user, she replied:

> Let's face it. It's not a problem if there is no effect on the kid's perform-
> ance. I mean, who are we to say what's right or wrong? A kid could
> always turn around and say to you, "How many of the faculty have an
> alcohol problem or a drinking problem? And yet their job goes on, they
> continue to teach"—they can point that out to you. So who are we to
> say what's right or wrong?

When she says there's no problem if there is no effect on performance,
she is also indicating that it is only the technical performance, the end
product, that matters. Her view rules out questions of character, of responsible and desirable conduct.

By the end of the decade, order had been restored. Although some
tensions remain between blacks and Asians in the school, an easier ca-
maraderie now exists, and a dozen interracial couples came to the 1984
senior prom. The current principal has been concentrating on strengthening the curriculum, and the school has returned to its premodular
outlines, with less tracking by ability group than occurred in the earlier
era. Students are assigned to most classes randomly by computer, and
the college bound curriculum now includes a much broader group of
students. The real top track is now reserved for a handful of students
who take calculus and Advanced Placement courses and who are aiming
at the most selective colleges. A laissez-faire attitude characterizes relations in the school, which can be aptly described as an educational shop-
ping mall, with about as wide a tolerance for dress, behavior, and casual
purchase of goods. A few boutiques or specialty shops are more engag-
ing; in them relations between teachers and their customers may be
quite special, and a high price in student effort will have to be paid. For
most of the students, however, school is an undemanding and fairly
pleasant custodial institution. Teachers do not complain about students
who habitually drift into class ten minutes after the bell. Students acknowledge that cheating is widespread; even the best students are
cynical about it. As polls have indicated about students elsewhere, students feel that too little is asked of them, and many are yearning for
adults who have the courage to expect altruism of them. Earlier tensions
over new rules have settled into routine compliance, and students are
treated more as adult clients in a bureaucratic system than as adolescents who are being encouraged to live by a worthy set of ideals. It is,
rather, a form of socialization that teaches the young to ask, "How do I
manipulate this rule system to maximize my self-interest?"

Students are often at a loss when you ask them what they feel proud
of at school. It may come down to something like tolerance for diversity,
or a sense of freedom, neither of which is unimportant. Certainly

schools could be worse. But could they be better? Does a more pluralistic and admittedly fairer world mean that we must give up any hope of stating positive ideals in public schools? Is school the place where we treat the young as if they were already adults because we dare not suggest to them what a good adult or citizen ought to be?

Serious reflection leads to the realization that there is no real forum for the discussion of such questions in most public schools. Schools are the major links in a chain of social revolutions that are essentially moral in their intentions—to break down age-old racial prejudice through a program of desegregation; to mainstream disabled and severely handicapped children who have been treated as pariahs in the past; to end sexual discrimination. Students of the current generation have been expected to be the midwives of this new world, but without the benefit of any guiding ethic. Do it, but don't expect us to talk about it, the adults seem to say. The heart of the problem is that the adults fear they no longer have a common language or a moral consensus about the way to address such questions. Programs of racial desegregation rose out of the moral appeals of black ministers in small churches in the South, but they are being carried out in schools in an increasingly bureaucratic context. Bureaucracies are better at generating rules than dialogue. Janet Ward Schofield has shown, in her three-year study of racially desegregated middle schools, the ironies that abound when teachers and staff do not address the moral implications of desegregation.[19]

Private schools have a genuine public because their existence depends upon developing a continual dialogue with those who share their orientation toward a character ideal, and the values behind that orientation provide the language in which to discuss how students ought to act toward one another, in ways that transcend rights or legal obligations. The voluntarism that underlies that dialogue is a great advantage, and more voluntarism is needed in public schools through open enrollment plans that give parents wider choices within the public sector. But it is wrong to assume that a character ideal can be achieved only at the expense of reduced racial or ethnic diversity within the school. Agreement on broad principles can encompass great diversity on other grounds, as Coleman's data show with respect to contemporary Catholic schools.

The critical problem for public school leadership is to regenerate a dialogue about the nature of moral community in the school—to recreate a sense of the public good for which public education exists. The reformers of Horace Mann's generation did have a notion of a character ideal, and they drew on the examples of the founders of the Republic and on McGuffey's readers to express those ideals in ways that made a strong imprint. We cannot put McGuffey's readers back on the shelves, nor can we return to a supposed golden age. But we must have the courage to reinvent a modern equivalent of McGuffey's readers, a moral basis for the common beliefs of a democratic pluralist society, or what R. S. Peters has called a provisional morality.[20] By provisional, Peters means that teachers initiate children into such beliefs or broad principles guiding conduct in a nonbehaviorist way, not stamping or "fixing" a particular moral content for life, but teaching in such a way that the children recognize that as adults they will have the responsibility and freedom to reevaluate those beliefs. This means that although we respect differences of opinion on many issues, there are some salient or core beliefs to which we all subscribe. Pluralism is in fact not possible without agreement on some kinds of values: decency, fairness, the minimal order required for dialogue, the willingness to listen to one another, the rejection of racism (or openness to participation in the dialogue), honesty and respect for truth, recognition of merit and excellence, as well as those transcendent values that shore up the whole society—a sense of altruism and service to others and respect for personal effort and hard work. Without such agreement one has not a public but a kind of radical relativism—not pluralism but mere coexistence.

PART SIX
Private Education

8

The Storm before the Lull:
The Future of Private Schooling
in America

DENIS P. DOYLE

This essay builds and elaborates on an earlier essay on private schooling in America, "A Din of Inequity? Private Schools Reconsidered."[1] That essay was widely reprinted not because of its penetrating insights but because of its novelty—in 1979 there was little or no research or policy analysis concerned with private schools. Indeed, it was this striking omission that had attracted my attention to the subject. As an assistant director of the National Institute of Education, the U.S. government's education research arm, I discovered that research into private school questions was virtually off limits. The prohibition was neither formal nor conspiratorial, except in the loosest sense of that term. It was simply that the liberal culture of education research did not incline toward examining questions that private schools might help answer.

In raising an altogether different question—the likely impact of impending enrollment declines—I had the idea of including a research section on the anticipated enrollment changes in private schools.[2] After all, about 10 percent of the nation's children attend private school, and about 10 percent of all the things education researchers like to count—dollars, the number of teachers, and the like—appear in the private sector. As much to my surprise as anyone else's, it emerged that private schools were not losing enrollments as their public analogues were: it was true that Catholic school enrollments were declining, but wholly unnoticed by the research community or public school interest groups was the reality that non-Catholic private school enrollments were increasing. An extraordinarily interesting development was unfolding, and no one was aware of it or its significance. It is important to remember that at this time the work of Virgil Blum was not available, nor was the more widely reported work of Coleman and Greeley completed.[3] Similarly, the work of Rutter and his colleagues in England was not seen as having any bearing on the private school question, because Coleman's collateral work had not been published.[4]

Since that time, private school research and private school research findings have achieved some attention; they are at least controversial and are now reported in the daily newspapers. But the impact of this modest research actively has not yet penetrated to the American consciousness. Today most Americans still believe that private schools occupy a small and marginally important part of the education system. They exist as an option for the well-to-do, the devout, and the discriminatory. Private school enrollments, both as a fraction of total public school enrollments and as an absolute number, are declining, and private schools are of only secondary importance in the educational life of the nation. Such is the stuff of the conventional wisdom. And the conventional wisdom is not just the province of the man in the street; it is shared—indeed, it is shaped—by the educator, foundation executive, policymaker, member of the press, education professional association, and dean.

This is in large part caused by Americans' ambivalence about the place of private schools in a democracy. Is the notion of a selective institution, particularly the elementary and secondary school, consistent with the American vision? About this matter Americans have mixed feelings, and separate, distinct messages are revealed in American practice. We have the most extensive and robust system of public education in the world; we have the world's most robust private schools as well. The most telling part of the American scene, however, is that while private elementary and secondary scools are permitted, they are not extolled. Their critical role is acted out in virtual anonymity. They are phantom schools. True, many Americans recognize the names of a few of the most distinguished private schools—Choate or Exeter, for example—but that name recognition bespeaks the American fascination with wealth and power rather than with education.

Perhaps the most authoritative evidence for this assertion is to be found in the world of education research. Private school research is virtually nonexistent—it is not just limited, or modest; it barely exists. Take, for example, the National Institute of Education. Since its inception NIE has had available to it more than one billion dollars in research, policy analysis, and dissemination funds. Of that amount it would be difficult to identify a quarter of a million dollars that has been targeted to private education questions. Similarly, private foundations, particularly such giants as Ford and Carnegie, have invested almost nothing in private school research. Now, how is it possible that so few people are interested in learning about private schools? Do we know so much about them that we have nothing else to learn? Of course we do not.

The problem does not end there. It is more subtle. Because of the sheer size and scope of the public school exercise—90 percent of the nation's children attend public school—and because of the rhetoric that surrounds the public schools in this country, one can understand that the incentive to study private schools for their own sake is not great. In addition, since America—alone among the industrialized democracies—does not make available public funds for private schooling, there is no immediate public policy pressure to study private schools. For these reasons, modest levels of public or foundation research funding to study private schools would not be surprising.

But the virtual absence of research funding for private schooling is genuinely puzzling for two additional reasons. The first is simple intellectual curiosity: Why do so few academic researchers and policy analysts find private school questions interesting? The second is considerably more important, for, to use the jargon of the trade, the very existence of private schooling represents a "naturally occurring experiment." The great expense and difficulty associated with launching large-scale controlled experiments is widely known, and something so desirable as the random assignment of subjects and treatments is almost impossible to achieve. That reality, and the difficulty of securing funds for large-scale experiments or demonstration projects, makes the neglect of the opportunities inherent in studying private schools all the more stark.

The conclusion one draws from this set of observations is hardly novel or surprising. There is a strong liberal antipathy to private schooling in America, and that antipathy extends to learning about them.[5] But why, one must ask, would there be any reluctance to learn about them? Because there is apprehension about what one might learn. As it happens, such apprehension may have been well placed, for as we find out more about private schools, we discover that they are not only different from public schools but in many important respects better.

That this should be so is itself a curiosity, because the contemporary public school owed its very existence to the nation's private schools. As in other areas of public life, the public sector grew organically from the private sector, and today the two exist side by side, their relation to each other uncertain and ambiguous. This uncertainty is revealed in what we know about the two sectors and how we compare them. Do we compare them routinely and regularly, using the one to measure the other? Or do we examine only one? And why do we examine one set of schools rather than another? The answers to these questions reveal much about American attitudes toward the private sector and toward education. Our conventional wisdom speaks volumes.

The conventional wisdom, in education and in other areas of national life, is both a cause and a consequence of the way in which data are collected and displayed. For example, for many years the collection and display of private school data were designed to be opaque, and it is not surprising that the effect has been to mislead. The gathering of national education data is the responsibility of the National Center for Education Statistics (NCES), an arm of the U.S. Department of Education. (Indeed, it is of some interest to note that the historical reason for the existence of a federal presence in education has been precisely to gather and report national education data.)[6]

Given the size of the data bases involved and the limited resources of the National Center for Education Statistics, it comes as no surprise to learn that many of the data that are collected are aggregated into large blocks of information—so many high school graduates by race, gender, and state, for example. Frequently, these aggregations are sensible and useful, but, as any amateur statistician knows, data aggregation often obscures as much as it reveals. The most important example of this phenomenon has been the long-standing practice of aggregating private school data into one data set, without discriminating among different types of private schools.

Thus, Catholic schools, which even today account for more than two-thirds of private school enrollment, simply swamp total enrollment figures. Any sharp change, up or down, in the numbers for Catholic schools causes corresponding changes in the total. Ordinarily, this was not a problem, because Catholic school enrollments were steady, growing at an even pace for more than a century. But in the late 1960s and the 1970s Catholic schools began to experience an unprecedented enrollment decline. And this led observers to conclude that private schools in general were declining. No less important a public figure than Daniel Patrick Moynihan became concerned, and in 1978 he wrote a stirring defense of private schools entitled "Government and the Ruin of Private Education."[7] He believed, as did many in the late 1970s, that the private school was an endangered species, threatened with destruction by profound social and political changes.

The dilemma is manifest in the changes that Catholic schools were undergoing. Although government financial support—or lack thereof—clearly affected Catholic school enrollments, that was only part of the story. Catholic schools were losing students for reasons not widely understood at the time. Most dramatic was the decline in live births among Catholics. Like people of other religions who had no prohibition against birth control, Catholics were having fewer children. Moreover, they were bearing that smaller number of children later in life and were spacing them farther apart. These microchanges had a major system impact, because the population of Catholics began to look just like the population of the nation as a whole. The baby boom was replaced by the birth dearth, a phenomenon that did not respect religious proclivities. But Catholic school enrollments fell for two other reasons as well.

The most obvious had to do with the decisions made by the Catholic bishops in the 1950s regarding the construction of new Catholic schools in the suburbs. The issue was critical because Catholics were sharing in the general prosperity of the postwar period and, like other Americans, were moving to the suburbs in large numbers. The decision not to build new suburban Catholic schools thus exacerbated "natural" Catholic school enrollment declines. At the same time a more subtle but no less important event unfolded. One of the principal reasons that Catholic schools had been vigorous for more than a century was the need for Catholics to have their own institutions, their own sense of identity.

For Catholic Americans, the church and the ancillary services it provided were critical to self-esteem, dignity, and even economic success. But the election of John F. Kennedy changed all that. They were still Catholic and still American, but the order was reversed: they were now Americans first and Catholics second. This development, too, reduced the pressure to attend Catholic school. In particular, it lessened the incentive to commute from the new suburb to the old inner-city Catholic school that the parents of the baby boom generation had left behind.

The move to the suburbs had other effects that seemed minor at the time but that in retrospect were enormously important. The construction of the new churches (sans schools) in the suburbs meant major fund-raising drives among suburban Catholics, redirecting funds that might otherwise have gone to school operations. It also meant that the remaining Catholic schools in the urban core became the responsibility of less affluent parishioners, precisely those who could not afford to move to the suburbs. As a consequence, the urban collection plate had heavier and heavier demands made upon it, the religious analogue of what public finance economists call "municipal overburden."

More services were to be provided from more meager resources. It is an old dilemma: those who most need help are least able to finance it. Because of the collection plate shortfalls, then, the urban Catholic school found itself compelled to turn to tuition. Although the tuition was modest, at least initially, this superficially small change raised a major issue of law and social policy. So long as Catholic schools had operated out of the proceeds of the collection plate, they had represented a sort of do-it-yourself tuition tax credit system, because voluntary contributions to church schools were tax deductible. But the Internal Revenue Service ruled, early on, that compulsory payments—tuition, fees, and other charges—were not tax deductible. Thus, the emergence of fee-charging Catholic schools produced some severe financial hardship for low-income Catholic parents. It was for this reason that they began to look to the state for some relief, in the form of tax forgiveness or of direct aid to either families or church schools.

The idea of aid to church schools, or to the families that patronize them, is not as farfetched as the typical American might think. There is ample historical precedent for public aid schemes, the most important being the Lowell Plan of the early and middle nineteenth century. Public funds were provided for what were euphemistically called Irish schools. The practice, once widespread, was discontinued by Protestant-dominated state legislatures in state after state. It was a systematic form of disestablishment of religious school.

To complete the work so successfully begun by the Protestant legislatures of the 1840s and 1850s, the Know-Nothings of the 1870s and 1880s attempted to enact the national Blaine amendment (named for its fiercely anti-Catholic author, James G. Blaine, Speaker of the House, and friend and confidant of Ulysses S. Grant).[8] The Blaine amendment was actively supported by so many because of the widespread belief that it was constitutional to provide public funds for private schools; if a legislature could by fiat cut them off, it could as easily reinstate them. Although the Blaine amendment failed enactment at the national level, numerous states enacted Blaine amendments precisely to eliminate the future possibility of aid to Catholic schools. The language of the California state constitution is typical:

> No public money shall ever be appropriated for the support of any sectarian or denominational school, or any school not under the exclusive control of the officers of the public schools; nor shall any sectarian or denominational doctrine be taught directly or indirectly, in any of the common schools of this State.[9]

The demographic and economic developments that had propelled large numbers of Catholics into the suburbs also carried many non-Catholics into the old Catholic schools of the central city. In Washington, D.C., for example, 76 percent of the children enrolled in Catholic elementary schools are black.[10] Nationwide, about 7 percent of all blacks are Catholic, and though that number is undoubtedly higher in Washington, it is still not nearly as high as Catholic school enrollment might suggest. What is happening? Large numbers of inner-city black families see Catholic schools as affordable alternatives to the public schools— indeed, they are virtually an alternative public school system, for this is precisely the role they play. Their doors are open to all. One's religious affiliation or denomination is neither a condition of admission nor a barrier to matriculation.

The data for minority Catholic school enrollments over time are quite remarkable, displaying a significant shift in minority attendance without parallel in American history. (The one parallel is the behavior of Catholic immigrants themselves, not so long ago a minority.) The work of Cooper, Ericson, and Nault, published in 1978, was the first of its kind to display this significant change, and it is confirmed by the ongoing data collection activities of the National Catholic Education Association and the Council for American Private Education.[11] Indeed, it is a matter of pride among the nation's traditional private schools that they are today fully integrated. The staff and student profiles characteristic of many, if not most, of the nation's elite suburban school districts would be unacceptable to most of the nation's established private schools.

But all of this was obscured by the way data were collected. The lumping together of all non-public schools made it virtually impossible for analysts to see what was happening in what had historically been the most important part of the private school world.

An extraordinary transformation was going on, and it was hidden from view. A few prescient observers—notably, Virgil Blum, Don Ericson, and Bruce Cooper—had the knowledge and insight to pursue these developments, but their work was not widely known. Blum's important examination of inner-city Catholic schools, for example, *Inner City Private Education: A Study*, stood as a solitary and neglected contribution to scholarship.[12] Unfortunately but not surprisingly, Blum's work was viewed by most liberal education researchers as suspect because Blum was a "party at interest"; that is, researchers saw his work as "advocacy" because Blum is a priest. (The irony is consummate: although American education researchers are almost without exception unabashedly supporters of public schools their work suffers no opprobrium for lack of "detachment.")

These commonplace observations are important in a context of research, data collection, and policy analysis. It is one thing to note that political antipathy to Catholic schools in America led to their disenfranchisement; it is another to cite the old saw that "anti-Catholicism is the anti-Semitism of intellectuals." But when a discipline, however young and however weak, simply refuses to acknowledge a whole body of relevant information, it is profoundly anti-intellectual.

The failure to disaggregate private school data, however, did more than hide the changes in the Catholic school world. It also hid the steady increase at the same time in the size of non-Catholic private school enrollment. Taken alone, these developments might not have been particularly significant, just a normal part of the ebb and flow of public and private school enrollment. But there was more to it than met the eye, as this essay will try to demonstrate. Fundamental changes are under way, and their downstream consequences are likely to be profound.

As Bruce Cooper writes, "Private education in the United States has become a topic of great interest and controversy. . . . Despite this increased interest, [however,] little basic, reliable information exists on the size and growth trends in private elementary and secondary schools."[13]

(The data for Catholic schools are very good. Thanks to the unstinting efforts of the National Catholic Education Association, we know with precision what is happening in the world of Catholic schools.)

Christian schools, counterculture alternative schools, and the schools of small religious sects are very hard to identify, however. The federal government has no way to do so, and state governments do very little. Accordingly, Cooper undertook the straightforward task of actually counting them. In the twenty-one counties studied, Cooper found that "NCES listings included only about 75 percent of the non-Catholic private schools in these countries. . . . Based on these data, the overall national estimated numbers of non-Catholic private schools totaled 13,700 in 1979, not 10,248 as previously believed."[14] This represents an annual rate of growth of 8.2 percent. Cooper estimated that between 1956–66 and 1981–82 the growth of non-Catholic private schools was a remarkable 212 percent.[15]

A variety of interpretations of this growth are possible, but it is hard to improve upon Cooper's:

> Clearly, the growth in the non-Catholic private sector is a sign of real entrepreneurship at the local level, for most of these new schools were opened through local, separate efforts, not a coordinated national push by large associations or churches. This growth pattern seems to indicate a broad-based, energetic, grass-roots attempt by families, religious congregations, and individuals to provide a special kind of schooling for children—much the same localist impulse, it seems, that built the American public school system in the nineteenth century.[16]

Blum's "micro" findings are as interesting as Cooper's "macro" findings. Whereas Cooper looks to the private school universe as a whole,

Blum has carefully studied fifty-four inner-city Catholic schools, all of which are at least 70 percent minority.[17]

His research and the findings based on it are too rich and varied to be fully reported here. Suffice it to say that he has identified families and schools that are making enormous sacrifices to provide quality education to poor and minority youngsters, and they do so side by side with failing or indifferent public schools. Consider what the loss of such schools would mean. Blum observes:

> Such a result would be tragic in many ways; especially when one considers the impact such a loss would have on the lives of the children in these schools, on the dreams of parents who are already making immense sacrifices to better the future of their children, on the missionary-like lives of principals and teachers in these schools, indeed, on the very quality of life in the neighborhoods of America's inner cities.[18]

If information about the quantity of private schooling is provisional and difficult to confirm, information about its quality is even more elusive. Indeed, until the recent publication of *High School Achievement: Public, Catholic, and Private Schools Compared,* by James Coleman and his colleagues, there was very little systematic information about the quality of private schools. (There was—and is—very little information about the quality of public schools, for until recently it was a taboo subject in America.)

In many respects, Coleman's most recent work is more interesting for the reaction it provoked than for the findings it contained. To most readers (excepting only educators or social scientists), the principal finding was thoroughly unsurprising: all things being equal, it makes a difference which school a child attends. The idea that some schools are better than others is hardly startling; the assumption that a student is better off at a good school than at a poor one is deeply rooted in experience and convention.

Why, then, must one prove such a proposition? And what accounts for the ferocious response to the Coleman study? The answers are not reassuring to those who like to think that the social sciences are mature disciplines.

First, why must one prove the obvious? Because for the past decade or so it has become intellectually fashionable to assert how little we "really" know (about crime, housing, juvenile delinquency, prison reform, drug addiction, or education). Second, counterintuitive explanations of the world around us, ideas that pull the rug from under the conventional wisdom, at once demonstrate the cleverness of social science and its importance to public policy. If common sense tells us the world is flat, what guidance will it provide policymakers? God forbid that they should make decisions without proper study and scholarly inquiry.

Indeed, a number of social scientists, policymakers, and analysts made their reputations by defending ideas that run against the tide of conventional wisdom. First among them has been James Coleman—for example, when he asserted, in what is now called Coleman I, that what goes into a school in the form of bricks and mortar, teacher salaries, and the like, seems to have little influence on what comes out in terms of student accomplishment. To an intellectual, a counterintuitive conclusion is heady wine: it brings pure pleasure. To activists, the "right" counterintuitive conclusion is a sort of aphrodisiac, because it reinforces an ideological stance, and Coleman I became the school busers' bible. Coleman II (as his most recent study is known by the cognoscenti of such things) appears more than a decade later, and now we find that schools matter after all. This is a bit disorienting because it suggests that it might make a difference *where* one is bused: all destinations are not equal. Indeed, in some instances, it might be better not to board the bus at all. Had Coleman's report stopped here, it would have elicited little reaction (except perhaps a sigh of relief).

But Coleman's research did something genuinely novel in the annals of American education: it compared private with public schools. Before we turn to his findings, try to imagine the reception he would have received had he discovered that private schools were simply bastions of well-to-do white privilege, antiblack rednecks, and ethnic Catholics escaping their larger obligation to support public schools. Would the establishment have attacked his methodology?

In fact, Coleman found something quite different: private schools are meeting their social responsibilities to poor and minority youngsters, and, other things being equal, these children do measurably better in private than in public schools. Not content just to present findings, Coleman went on to suggest that the historical exclusion of private schools from public funding might not be a sensible public policy.

Once one cuts through the rhetorical thicket of outraged indignation produced by Coleman's study, one finds two important issues: Should social science be useful, and is it appropriate for social scientists to have opinions about the meaning of their work? Coleman's critics clearly thought not—at least not for Coleman—because they felt no sense of restraint in arguing that his report was counterproductive, that it was improper for him to support positions that were "detrimental" to the public schools. No disinterested social scientists they, nor endowed with any sense of irony or humor. The paradoxical nature of their criticism was lost upon them.[19]

The paradox flows from a peculiarly modern conceit that itself cannot withstand scrutiny: that scientific inquiry is disinterested and objective. It is not. Objectivity is an element of methodology; it does not determine the purposes or objects of scientific inquiry, nor does it provide much guidance as to the application of findings. In terms of methodology, in reporting procedures, in susceptibility to replication and independent verification, scientific inquiry strives mightily for objectivity, as it should. But the purposes of social science are no more objective than those of any other discipline. Medical practice and research strive for "cures," not because of some objective "scientific" imperative, but because health is better than illness. The object of scientific inquiry is not selected at random. As Santayana observed, "something not chosen must choose, something not desired must desire."

In the final analysis, Coleman and his colleagues proved what the public has really known for a very long time: that some schools are better than others, that frequently the better schools are private schools, and that if money were no object, many more children would attend private schools than now do so. The 1983 Gallup poll for the first time found that a simple majority of parents prefer private to public schools.[20]

There is, however, no sensible or responsible way to turn education back to the private market in toto. If that were to happen, the most serious problems would ensue: the poor and the dispossessed would find themselves altogether at the mercy of a system that did not serve their interests. But the issue need not be cast in those terms.

The role of government does not have to be viewed in the stark "either-or" of the radical: the government provides education or it does not. This apocalyptic vision of government obscures the subtlety with which government intervention strategies may be designed. For example, government may provide goods or services directly, or it may provide for them by transfer payment or indirect incentives or disincentives, such as tax credits. Indeed, there is no a priori reason to think that government must do one or the other—the decision as to which strategy to pursue is appropriately a public policy decision.

Catholic school parents in particular think that history provides a precedent for direct government aid (even though the American precedent of much of the preceding century was largely negative). Nevertheless, what had been undone by political pressure could be redone by political pressure. In addition, the rest of the world provides interesting precedents and examples. Only the totalitarian countries of the Eastern bloc lack private schools, religious or secular, and in the developed democracies, apart from America, public aid for private schools is the rule rather than the exception. Indeed, the conceptual and philosophical framework for such aid has been fully developed by diverse authors.

The classic expression of government aid to private education is typically ascribed to Adam Smith, who argued that the state had an interest in providing limited aid to the poor so that they might attend school. In the nineteenth century, John Stuart Mill insisted that state-sponsored education is

> a mere contrivance for moulding people to be exactly like one another: and as the mould in which it casts them is that which pleases the predominant power in the government, whether this be a monarch, a priesthood, an aristocracy, or the majority of the existing generation, in proportion as it is efficient and successful, it establishes a despotism over the mind. . . .[21]

More recently, Albert O. Hirschman's *Exit, Voice, and Loyalty*, Charles Schultz's *The Public Use of Private Interest* and John Coons and Stephen Sugarman's *Family Choice in Education* make the case with great power that public "provision" and public support are not synonymous.[22] Indeed, there is no a priori reason to think that the state must own and operate the means of production just because it has a substantive interest in the issue at hand. The state's interest in health and safety does not lead to state ownership of hotels, restaurants, and airlines; rather, it leads to a body of public interest regulations designed, in so far as possible, to be neutral as regards the market in which these private enterprises exist.

It is especially interesting that our nomenclature for activities in this sphere is the language of the "public sector": restaurants are "public," hotels are "public accommodations," and airlines are "public carriers." Their "publicness" derives not from who owns them but from whom they serve. And this is not an argument lost on "private" schools.[23]

We have before us, then, a variety of models based on experience that reveal alternatives to an exclusive reliance on government ownership and operation of the means of production. These models become more important with increasing dismay about the quality of public schools. The "rising tide" of education reports that issued forth in 1983 were symptoms, not causes. They revealed rather than shaped the depth and intensity of public concern about the quality of the schools. For years, citizen complaints about the quality of schools fell on deaf ears, but the reports in 1983 legitimized and validated the free-floating anxiety that many Americans felt about their public schools.[24] Interestingly, the evidence to support this view has been available for more than a decade. Since 1970, the Gallup organization, with the support and cooperation of the *Phi Delta Kappan*, has published the results of one of its national polls on public attitudes toward education.[25] The findings have been consistent and strong. Certain issues, such as school discipline, have figured prominently in each poll since its first administration. The evidence that the public was worried about discipline should have been treated with more seriousness by the education community; to fail to do so was to invite the contempt of the public.

Equally interesting have been public attitudes toward the question of school quality. Asked to assign a letter grade to the schools—A through F—the number of Americans who give their schools an A has been steadily declining, while the number of those who give F's has been increasing. Even more revealing is the distribution of respondents: those who consistently give the schools their lowest marks are inner-city blacks in the Northeast, precisely the population that has the most riding on school quality.

The most striking finding, however, is in some respects the least surprising—namely, the change over time in attitudes toward public support for private schools. In 1983, for the first time since the poll was begun, a simple majority of the public supported public aid to private education.[26]

These various issues are important to public policy analysis and public policy makers because of the new synergy they suggest. Not since the mid-nineteenth century has there been serious public funding of private elementary and secondary schools. The nativism that was then sweeping the country led to the wholesale disestablishment of private school support systems. In the nineteenth century, however, the disestablishment of private schools was the work of state legislatures, not the Supreme Court. Today, however, the roles are reversed. A number of state legislatures, particularly in states with large Catholic populations, are now interested in enacting aid schemes that will help parents enroll their children in non-public schools.[27]

By the mid-twentieth century, however, the fate of public support schemes for private schools had been sealed by U.S. Supreme Court decisions. A series of rulings beginning in the late 1940s found that public aid represented an unconstitutional breach of the wall separating church and state. These decisions effectively closed off debate about the relation of the state to the private school, a debate that had proceeded vigorously and constructively in all other advanced democracies.[28] The issue is deceptively simple, and has to do with the locus of control. Who should decide what is best for the child—parent, child, teacher, state, or some combination of these? In all the democracies save only America, the decision has been made to provide for some mix of control over where the child goes to school and what the child studies. As a practical matter, this means state financial support for private schools. The range is truly remarkable: the Dutch send 70 percent of their school age population to private elementary and secondary schools at state expense, while the Danes send less than 8 percent to private schools.

In Denmark, for example, the state religion is quite naturally included in the curriculum of government schools—to preserve the religious freedom of nonevangelical Lutherans, provision is made for them to start their own schools at government expense. The Danish government is explicit about this:

> The principle behind . . . large subsidies [for private schools] is that although Denmark has an efficient education system providing educational opportunities for all, it should be possible for people to choose an alternative kind of education for their children should they wish, whether their reasons for this are ideological, political, educational, or religious.[29]

What has occurred in Denmark, Holland, Australia, and the rest of the free world is an orderly and responsible debate about the philosophy of enlarging the government sphere of education interest to include public funding of private schools. The conviction that government must own and operate the means of production has been characteristic of totalitarian states, no matter how idealistic they may at first blush appear. The most elegant expression of this view comes from Simon Bolivar:

> Let us give to our republic a fourth power with authority over the youth, the hearts of men, public spirit, habits, and republican morality. Let us establish this Areopagus to watch over the education of the children, to supervise national education, to purify whatever may be corrupt in the republic, to denounce ingratitude, coldness in the country's service, egotism, sloth, idleness, and to pass judgment upon the first signs of corruption and pernicious example.[30]

In most other areas of public life, government ownership of the means of production is tempered by common sense. Public highways, tunnels, and bridges, for example, are built by the private sector for the public sector not because the public sector could not do it but because the private sector can do it better. Similarly, the government issues food stamps rather than running soup kitchens or opening government commissaries for the poor. Indeed, on those rare occasions on which the government reverses the order of things and actually owns and operates the means of production, it frequently finds itself in a muddle. Public housing is only the most notorious example.

A most interesting recent example was of a scale so small as to not be worthy of national attention, except that the issue it raised was symbolically important. In California in the fall of 1983, the Sacramento County Welfare Department stopped cash grants for the indigent; in their place, a county facility with free beds, meals, and bathing facilities was opened. For his pains, the welfare administrator was sued. The allegation? He was stripping indigents of their dignity by forcing them to accept services (or go without) in a government-owned and -operated facility. Thus, in this area and in areas like it, we are still able to debate the philosophical merits of who should provide what for whom under what circumstances. Not so with schooling. The philosophical debate has been smothered by a judiciary that has effectively foreclosed all but the most arcane means of aiding private schools. Direct transfer payments to private schools are prohibited if those schools are religiously affiliated.

It is possible that a future Court will reverse the decisions of the past thirty years, just as the *Plessy* decision supporting segregation of the races was reversed, but to await such an eventuality requires great patience. More important, it means that except for reasons of academic and intellectual interest there is no profit in exploring the philosophical and political merits of fundamentally altering the relation of the state to religious schools. And there is no mistaking that religious, not private, schools are the issue. (Strictly speaking, they are not identical, because the universe of "private schools" is slightly larger than the universe of religious schools.) Although there are a small number of private, secular schools, the lion's share—more than 95 percent—have religious affiliations. To talk about government aid to private schools without including religious schools is either meaningless or disingenuous. But if debate and discussion about public sector support of private schools will not be conducted on philosophical grounds, are there practical reasons to do so? There are: if private schools "work" better than public schools, they will gain public support, just as they now enjoy public support at the level of higher education.

There are, then, two major trends unfolding in American elementary and secondary education. As Coleman shows us (and by all accounts will continue to show us), private schools do a "better job" than public schools, particularly with those populations most in need of help—poor and minority youngsters.[31] Furthermore, as Cooper points out, private school enrollments continue to grow and give every indication of further growth. The reasons for this are only surprising in the context of liberal antipathy to private schooling. The myth does die hard, but when it dies it may do so with a vengeance. What is the public to make of the fact that the children of public school teachers are overrepresented in private schools? According to a recent *Detroit Free Press* poll, 20 percent of all Michigan teachers enroll their children in private school, twice the state average.[32] There is no conspiracy at work here: the reason is at once more prosaic and important. Disproportionately high numbers of public school teachers enroll their children in private schools because they know what they are doing. They care about education, considering it important enough for them to invest in it.

Moreover, significant demographic, sociological, and economic developments explain why there will be a continued shift in the larger population toward private education. Americans as a people value education: they are proud of the accomplishments of the public school system, they have invested heavily in it, and they see the fruits of their investment. That ours is the richest society in the history of the world is not sheer accident. It is in large measure a function of our "human capital," the acquired skills, knowledge, and abilities of our people. The principal source of human capital is still the schools. To most Americans it is self-evident that the high standard of living we enjoy is the product, not of rents collected, coupons clipped, or money inherited, but earned income, based on what one knows. Similarly, the inheritance one may extend to a child is today found not in the security of physical capital but in human capital. The best gift a parent can give a child is a sound education, one thing that cannot be taken away.

These free-floating ideas, though rarely stated in explicit terms, are nevertheless revealed in behavior and are made possible by a set of collateral changes that are of the utmost importance. The smaller family of today makes many things possible that were only dreamed of in earlier days. Moreover, the delayed onset of childbearing means more disposable family income because of its principal consequence—the impact of which is only dimly understood today—the higher incidence of two-income families. Women's entry into the labor force will probably emerge as the single most important domestic development of the second half of the twentieth century. Its impact is being felt in a number of ways, but none more important than the opportunity it presents to enroll children in fee-charging schools. (The other development of equal import is the emergence of virtual income parity as between intact black and white families. In light of this, it is not surprising to learn that middle-class black children are slightly overrepresented in private schools.) As mystery story fans well know, the solution to a crime is to be found in the convergence of motive and opportunity. So it is in the larger world of human behavior generally. Many parents who want to enroll their children in private school are now able to do so: in fact, it is clear that their numbers are increasing.

Is there a larger theory to explain this change? There is, and it owes a debt to the theory offered in behalf of public schools in the days of their creation. In short form, the explanation is this: the well-to-do have always had easy access to private schools of high quality, whereas the poor, excepting only those in the most unusual circumstances, never do. The American public school, then, was first created as a school for paupers, children who could not buy in the marketplace the education they needed. Indeed, the creation of our public school system was an explicit recognition that the market did not work for the poor. The poor individual had only the most limited capacity to improve his own human capital through education. Enter public schools—they serve the interests of the individual as they serve those of the larger society. And as ever-larger numbers of children are educated in them, they lose their character as "paupers' schools" and emerge as public schools.

But today it is precisely that label that public schools in the inner city begin to wear. And they are becoming "paupers' schools" for the identical reason—market failure. Today, however, it is not the private market that is failing but the public market. Indeed, it is for reasons of public sector market failure, both real and anticipated, that a shift to the private sector is occurring. Given the size and expertise of the modern education bureaucracy, there is little choice available to the student who is interested in quality education. As Hirschman points out in his elegant and prophetic book *Exit, Voice, and Loyalty*, if "voice" is not heard, "loyalty" is exhausted, and "exit" occurs. Thus, the unresponsive public school invites quality-conscious families to leave. And leave they did in the early 1980s.

What does all this suggest for the midterm future? What is likely to happen by the early 1990s as regards private schools and public policy toward them? First, they are almost certain to continue to increase their enrollments, as larger numbers of quality-conscious consumers decide that "good" education is both desirable and affordable. The "natural" enrollment increase that will occur, will, by definition, be heavily inclined toward those who can pay their own way. (It is worth noting that private sector scholarships will be important as a means of entry for a small but important number of poor youngsters. No similar opportunity is available in the public sector.)

What we will witness, then, is an increasing movement of the middle class—black, white, Hispanic, and oriental—into private schools, at least in our central cities. And if past is prologue, what the middle class does sets our social policy agenda. If its members want tax relief or education vouchers, they will eventually get them. Who is to gainsay them? They not only vote but form the social and economic engine of modern society.

We will also witness the appointment of a new Supreme Court. Whoever is elected in November 1984 is almost certain to have five Court appointments at his disposal, and it seems reasonably clear that the law and legal scholarship are now leaning toward more generous constitutional interpretations of what may be done concerning the public funding of children who attend schools with religious affiliations. *Mueller* v. *Allen* makes the straightforward point that, so long as the child is the primary beneficiary and as public and private schools both are objects of government solicitude, aid schemes that permit children to attend private sectarian and nonsectarian schools, as well as government schools, will be upheld.[33] Thus, together with an increased interest on the part of the middle class in private options, there is likely to occur a greater liberality in court interpretation about the appropriateness of the public support of private education.

Given the prospect of an increasingly vigorous private sector, peopled by the more affluent and ambitious, what should the principal public policy concern of the 1980s be? It should be the design and implementation of public support systems to expand the opportunities of the poor. The benefits of liberty should be extended to them; today they enjoy only the benefits of equality. And it is no longer a secret that equality in a public school setting, particularly the urban public school, is the equality of mediocrity. A low-income voucher system poses no great conceptual or administrative problems. It is easy to design, easy to implement. It need not be restricted to private schools. In fact, such a voucher system would be strengthened if it were available for public and private schools both. It would be a welcome sight to watch well-to-do suburban enclaves deal with the prospect of receiving low-income inner-city children, who equipped with vouchers, could consider enrolling outside of their neighborhood.

What, finally, are we to say about the storm of controversy that will surely break as the debate over public aid to private schooling becomes more serious and as the approval of such aid grows more likely? Simply that it is the storm before the lull. Such debate marked the development of public aid schemes in Australia and Holland, and their outcomes are now widely accepted in both countries. The fact is that major social change is always accompanied by strong reaction, because real issues and real interests are at stake. There will be winners and losers, and the actors in the present scene know that only too well. As things now stand, the constituency groups for the potential losers are very well organized, and they enjoy a position of tactical advantage by virtue of numbers, formal organization, and intensity of interest. The NEA, for example, sees itself as having the most to lose in any major reconfiguration of Amerian education, and it is well positioned to slow the rate of change. But, in the final analysis, the victory will go to whoever holds the strategic rather than the tactical high ground, and that is clearly the larger public that pays the bills and enjoys the benefits of the current or prospective system. In fact, the very nature of the embrace with which the NEA grasps the system may accelerate the movement out of it by quality-conscious families.

This is especially important in an American context; of the industrialized nations, free and totalitarian, America is least guided by abstract ideas and is most the product of a vigorous pragmatism. The test of an idea in America is "Does it work?" Indeed, it is now an old story that the job of the policy analyst is to "examine the world of practice to see if it will work in theory". Whatever humor attaches to this anecdote does so because it captures the American spirit. In America, ideas achieve importance as they produce concrete results; they achieve mythic status as a consequence of performance. In Europe and the East, ideas first seize men's minds and are then applied to the world around them. That is why American soil has been so inhospitable to ideology. Americans have no patience with failed ideas. The American inclination to pragmatism is graced by a retrospective mythology: if it works, it is not only valid, it is noble. So it was with the myth of the public schools—the very embodiment of democracy. Through them and with them, we civilized the savage, tamed the ignorant, Americanized the immigrant, democratized the larger society. It is a grand and exciting vision. That it is no longer true only makes its demise the more likely and complete.

PART SEVEN

The Courts

9
Our Black-Robed School Board:
A Report Card

BARBARA LERNER

On April 26, 1983, I testified as an expert witness for the defense in the case of *Debra P.* v. *Turlington*[1] before Judge George C. Carr of the federal district court in Tampa, Florida. Four years earlier in the same case,[2] the same judge had issued an injunction against the state defendants, forbidding them to deny high school diplomas to Florida students who failed to meet minimum competence standards for graduation. The question before the court in 1983 was whether to make that injunction permanent or to lift it. During my cross-examination, toward the end of a long day on the stand, opposition counsel asked a long question, and the following exchanges took place:

Q.—Now in your *Public Interest* article on "The War on Testing: David, Goliath and Gallup,"[3] which was written after Judge Carr's 1979 opinion, you detail to some extent your disagreement with the theory of law which has—law based on the social science which has become known as the perpetuation-of-past-discrimination theory. Again, this was a little while back. And I want to focus your attention on your writings in—*The Public Interest* writing.

You began to focus on what you describe as "a key educational testing case, *Debra P.* v. *Turlington.*" And you stated, "Judge Carr was not only expansive in his definition of the notice requirements of the Due Process clause, he was inventive as well. . . . Judge Carr had to make some rather remarkable rulings of law before proceeding to issue his decision, but he did not shrink from the task. . . .

Judge Carr's treatment of the Equal Protection clause was equally
expansive. . . ."

And, passing on, on page 145 of that article, "Still in need of a
clincher for technical-legal reasons, Judge Carr fell back on the ubiq-
uitous perpetuation-of-past-discrimination line, a handy-dandy all-
purpose legal cement used to prop up any equal protection argument, no matter how weak."

You go on, "The decision is remarkable, not only because it turns
the traditional standard of judicial restraint in constitutional cases
on its head but because it reflects an even greater disrespect for
education and educators, and for reality itself."

You then gave your medical analogy of issuing certificates of
health to sick people. And concluded, "Activist judges, and the
self-proclaimed public interest spokespersons who applaud their increasingly frequent usurpations of the policy-making powers our
Constitution reserves for representative assemblies, may be blind to
absurdities like that, but ordinary Americans are not."

Now, what is it precisely that you take issue with in terms of, first
of all, the social science data, and secondly the legal inferences that
are drawn from the data in terms of the perpetuation-of-past-
discrimination theory?

A.—I do not, Your Honor, believe that any of us have a property interest in claiming abilities or skills that we do not possess. And I do,
Your Honor, very respectfully, but very strongly, disagree with
that, sir. That's my legal—

THE COURT: You are not the first.

THE WITNESS: Thank you, sir.

THE COURT: And I am sure you will not be the last.

THE WITNESS: Thank you, Your Honor.

Judge Carr's kindness in reassuring me that he was neither shocked
nor angered by my characterization of his 1979 decision did not change
my opinion of that decision. It did help to change my opinion of him and
of the factors that led him to make such a decision. And it set me to
wondering how many other federal judges make similar decisions for
similar reasons with similarly profound consequences for American
education.

Before 1983, I had assumed that the educational policy preferences
that federal judges were imposing on American schools and enshrining
into constitutional law were their own personal preferences. For that
reason, I had also assumed that arrogance and zealotry played a role in
all such decisions. In my experience, arrogant zealotry is highly corre-

lated with petty and vindictive behavior. Judge Carr's response to the
excerpts from my prior writings that opposition counsel selected to read
aloud to him in open court was not petty, and no vindictiveness was
evident in his decision. On May 5, 1983, he lifted the injunction, permitting the implementation of Florida's minimum competence requirements for high school graduation.

With this act, he also lifted the imminent threat of judicial invalidation
of similar requirements in some three dozen other states. Thus, when
Florida school officials sighed with relief, they were echoed by their
counterparts across the nation. At the state and local level, the abolition
of minimum competence requirements would have been no easy task.
In all but one state, these requirements had only recently been adopted,
most of them between 1976 and 1979, and, unlike other educational innovations of the 1960s and 1970s, they were adopted in response to popular demand.

That demand was an outgrowth of the anguish millions of American
parents experienced over the fact that their children—some 20 to 25 percent of all American seventeen-year-olds between 1970 and 1975—were
functionally illiterate. Some 50 to 60 percent were, at best, semiliterate.[4]
The widespread anguish this created was expressed in a massive grass-
roots movement demanding an end to the social promotion policies of
the 1960s and 1970s and a return to essential standards enforced by
meaningful sanctions. Public opinion poll results show that the movement had overwhelming support from American parents of all races and
classes. It also had the support of a clear majority of America's classroom
teachers. Elected officials responded appropriately, for the most part,
enacting minimum competence laws in state after state in a few years.

Judge Carr's 1979 decision brought this mighty ground swell of desperately needed reform activity to an abrupt halt, immobilizing school
officials in Florida and elsewhere for a period of four years, and threat-
ening to make their paralysis permanent thereafter. It was, perhaps, the
most dramatic single clash between the federal judiciary and the American public over educational policy in recent years, but it was hardly the
first. Again and again, throughout the 1970s, the efforts of American
parents, teachers, and state and local officials to raise public school standards—for discipline as well as for achievement—were frustrated by the
actions of federal judges.

If Judge Carr and an unknown but potentially substantial number of
other federal judges were not imposing their personal policy preferences
on American education during those years, a reasonable reader might
ask, what in God's name were they doing? My own conclusion, based
on my experience in the *Debra P.* case and subsequent ones, is that at

least some of them were making a conscientious good-faith effort to do exactly what they are supposed to do: guarantee equality of educational opportunity.

How, then, did things go so awry? One obvious problem is that definitions of equality vary. That is an important problem, and it has received and is receiving some of the attention due it, but in this area it is, at best, half the problem. The other, larger "half" has to do with the definition of educational opportunity, a problem that has not received broad scrutiny. That is unfortunate, because it is the key to many disastrous recent decisions in court cases involving schools and because the usual criticism of these decisions—criticism focusing on the threat posed by the innovations of activist judges—may miss the point entirely.

In a number of these cases, the trial court judges were not being innovative at all. They were doing what Anglo-American courts traditionally did when they needed a standard to apply in any specialized area of life: they accepted the definitions of experts in that area. In the area of education, this time-honored approach has been disastrous, first, because the educational theories fashionable with experts in recent decades have been thoroughly discredited by empirical evidence and, second, because the legal dynamics of these cases virtually ensure the incorporation of these discredited theories into the fabric of constitutional law.

The educational experts who defined educational opportunity for federal judges in the 1970s were not classroom teachers, for the most part. Nor were they local school officials. When ordinary classroom teachers or local school officials testify in court, they are usually there not as experts but as defendants, persons who stand accused of having acted to the detriment of hapless schoolchildren—because they are poor or because they are black, or simply because they are children with limited powers of self-defense.

Morally, this is no better than appearing before the court as a criminal defendant. Procedurally, it is much worse. In a criminal case, the defendant's innocence is presumed; he does not have to prove it. The prosecutor must prove his guilt. In education cases, the burden of proof is on the defendants. They must prove their innocence by convincing the court that their definitions of educational opportunity and of the practices that promote it are the correct ones, and that they have acted in strict accordance with them on all possible occasions.

Obviously, educators who offer definitions under these circumstances cannot be disinterested. They have a strong personal stake in definitions that would serve to exonerate them. For that reason, courts are understandably reluctant to place too much weight on their testimony on these key questions, even when it is offered in some detail. Often, it is not. Defendants are too busy struggling to produce the evidence that plaintiffs' attorneys routinely demand of them—truckloads, literal truckloads of minutely detailed data on every action they ever took with regard to every child who ever passed through their schools—to have much time and energy to spare for theoretical arguments.

The theories the courts hear at length and, in most cases, accept and enforce, are those of the plaintiffs' witnesses. Plaintiffs' witnesses are almost always all experts—outsiders with no immediately apparent self-interest in the outcome of the case—and their credentials are almost always more impressive appearing than those of the defendants. They are more likely to come from places like Harvard than from ones like Ben Franklin Primary School or West Everywhere Junior High. Usually, they are people with Ph.D.'s in education or in related fields like psychology and sociology, people who earn their livings as college or university professors or as directors of various sorts of advanced specialized centers for educational research and training. Most of them are at least as comfortable in the courtroom as they are in life. After all, they are there because they chose to be there. Defendants did not choose to come. Most are uncomfortable in court and eager to be done. Many are scared to death.

The essence of the theories their adversaries present to the courts is that educational achievement is facilitated by three major factors: (1) school resources, (2) student self-esteem, and (3) student freedom. Insufficient amounts of each are described as the cause of poor educational performance by students; court action to force schools to increase each, or to compensate students for past insufficiencies, is presented as the cure.

Faith in the importance of school resources and self-esteem was widespread among experts in education in the 1950s; belief in the importance of freedom from external limits and constraints became widespread in the 1960s. All three beliefs had a major, transforming impact on American schools in the 1960s and 1970s, making them very different places from the schools of the 1950s, and the role of the federal courts in this transformation was a large one. In the 1970s, it was rare to find a court decision in an education case that was not based, in part or in whole, on a belief in the importance of one or more of these three factors for student achievement, and for student failures, too.

This was a sad development—for American law as for American education—because, in fact, none of these three factors bears any clear or consistent positive relationship to academic achievement. To understand why this is so and how we know, it is necessary to look more closely at the theories and the evidence for each factor.

The Three-Factor Theory

The Resource Factor. Theories about the relationship between educational achievement and school resources are a good starting place. The notion that a shiny new school with a big library provides more educational opportunity than a creaky old building with a small library is intuitively plausible, to judges as to other people. It was to educational experts, too. In the 1950s and 1960s, they were sure that school "outputs" like achievement were related to school "inputs"—money and the sorts of resources money can buy. Sure, too, that predominantly black schools had lesser resources than predominantly white ones, certainly in the South and probably in the North as well, and that these differences were causally related to differences in achievement between black and white students in both regions.

A sociologist named James Coleman was sure too. The Civil Rights Act of 1964 required the U.S. commissioner of education to report to the President and the Congress within two years "concerning the lack of availability of equal educational opportunities for individuals by reason of race, color, religion, or national origin in public educational institutions . . . in the United States." Coleman headed the team of researchers who gathered the empirical data for that report, and they were very impressive data because they were derived from one of the largest representative samples of American schoolchildren ever assembled.[5] Coleman and his co-workers tested 570,000 students and 60,000 of their teachers. They also collected detailed data on resources in some 4,000 schools.

Interviewed in 1965, before this massive collection of data was analyzed, Coleman made his expectations clear: "the study will show the differences in the quality of schools that the average Negro child and the average white child are exposed to. You know yourself that the difference is really going to be striking. And even though everybody knows there is a lot of difference between suburban and inner-city schools, once the statistics are there in black and white, they will have a lot more impact."[6]

They did, too, but not the sort of impact that Coleman or anyone else expected. They showed that by the mid-sixties the resources available to students in predominantly black schools were as adequate as those available to students in predominantly white schools, in the South as in the North. Worse, they showed that there was no relationship between school resource levels and student achievement levels.

Of course, few people believed it, at first, and scores of highly trained researchers—many with passionate stakes in disproving the Coleman findings—pored over his data, rechecking and reanalyzing them in minute detail, making it the most intensely scrutinized study in the history of education.[7] Coleman's conclusion here withstood the scrutiny. And it was independently confirmed in many smaller but cumulatively impressive studies—130, at last count.[8] So far, there seems to be only one reasonably clear exception: class size, with smaller being better. Class size is fairly deemed a resource variable because it is determined by the number of teachers a system has funds to hire. That does seem to have a small but reasonably consistent positive relationship to achievement, at least when examined under the microscope of a new statistical technique known as meta-analysis. All other obvious and not-so-obvious resource variables—libraries, laboratories, gyms, bands, and what have you—have thus far proved to be unrelated. High levels of achievement seem to appear or fail to appear quite independently of anything money can buy, except teachers.

The Self-Esteem Factor. The belief in the importance of self-esteem for achievement was, if anything, even more fervent than the belief in the efficacy of resources. Experts in the 1950s and 1960s were convinced that low self-esteem was a major cause of low achievement. They were sure, too, that black self-esteem was lower than white self-esteem as a result of racial isolation and discrimination and that this—along with inadequate resources—caused the achievement gap between black and white schoolchildren. From this, it followed that in order to raise black achievement, it was necessary to raise black self-esteem. The experts were confident that integration would do both.

Doubters, in the 1940s, had argued that little children were not really aware of racial discrimination and could not, therefore, be adversely affected by it. By 1950, the work of two psychologists named Clark had laid those arguments to rest. Kenneth Clark and his wife, Mamie, had designed a disarmingly simple-seeming technique for getting at the feeling of very young children about race.[9] The great strength of their method, for that purpose, was that it was not dependent on a child's capacity to verbalize his feelings. All he, or she, had to do was to pick a doll in response to each of the Clarks' questions. For each, the Clarks gave the children a choice of two dolls, identical in every respect save one—color. They asked questions like these: "Which doll is nice?" "Which doll is pretty?" "Which doll would you like to play with?" "Which doll looks like you?" The Clarks asked these questions of black children in the North and in the South, in integrated and in segregated nursery schools, kindergartens, and primary schools.

They found that black children picked the white dolls more often than the black in response to every question except the last one, and even there a pro-white bias was often manifest, especially among the younger children. There was no confusion about which doll was black and which white, though. The Clarks asked those questions, too, and got consistently accurate responses from children as young as three.

The Clarks' data showed that little children were aware of racial stereotypes. They seemed to show that they were affected by them, too, in an obvious, adverse way. It is a classic illustration of the pitfalls of research interpretation. The first conclusion is there in the data. The second is not. To reach it, you must make an assumption. You must assume that a child's feelings about his own worth are the same as—or at least similar to—his feelings about the worth of his race or group. It is such a small, plausible assumption that it is easy to make. I made it myself, as did every other social scientist I knew in the 1950s. Nonetheless, it turned out to be mistaken. Children can and do evaluate themselves very differently from the way they evaluate others.

We learned that from thirty years of post-*Brown* research, and we learned a number of other unexpected, often theoretically unwelcome things about self-esteem and achievement and race. The first surprise was that the self-esteem of children everywhere was unexpectedly high, and buoyantly so. So, too, were their expectations; they generally bobbed along well ahead of actual skills and abilities. The second surprise was that, in study after study, the self-esteem of black children turned out to be just as high as that of white children. More often than not, it was higher, especially in predominantly black schools, and that was true for expectations, too.

Alas, high self-esteem and high expectations are not reliably associated with high achievement. Like impressive resources, they can and do coexist with quite low levels of achievement, among children of all races. That is what happened in American schools in the 1960s and 1970s. Self-esteem was high and rising; school resources increased substantially; achievement did not. Instead, it declined. The decline began in the mid-1960s and accelerated in the 1970s. The result was that, by 1980, millions of American high school graduates were looking for work without having achieved even minimal literacy and numeracy; millions more were entering college with verbal and mathematical reasoning skills that were half a standard deviation lower than those of their counterparts in the 1950s and the early 1960s.[10] They were lower than those of most of their contemporaries in the developed world, too, sometimes by as much as a whole standard deviation.[11] And the black-white achievement gap had not closed. At the start of the most intensive effort to achieve equality of educational opportunity in our history, it was approximately one standard deviation wide; a quarter of a century later, it still was.

The Freedom Factor. Resource and self-esteem levels may not have much positive impact on achievement—salaries for teachers aside—but they do not seem to have any negative impact either. The accumulated research evidence indicates that increases in these factors are irrelevant to achievement but not detrimental to it. This is true for integration, too. It is not true for factor three—student freedom from adult constraints, demands, and limits. Here, "more" is not just not better. It can be much worse. Converging evidence from three separate lines of research indicates that it was worse and that the great increases in student freedom in the 1960s and 1970s were a major cause of the great achievement declines of those decades.

The almost unlimited freedom of American students to do as they pleased in American schools in the 1960s and 1970s was largely a product of a kind of Deweyite revival among educational experts. This revival coincided in time with an upsurge of utopian activism in academic circles, and with a growing tendency to politicize all issues.[12] Poor John Dewey, dead and defenseless, was first reinterpreted and then embraced by a motley collection of improbable new adherents, alike only in their common insistence on the harmfulness of all academic demands, limits, and constraints. They included neo-Marxists, who saw children as an oppressed class and themselves as liberators; Summerhill Freudians, modern recruits to the cause of the noble savage; and sleek Carnegie Endowment types who reintroduced midwestern progressivism to us as a British import called the open schools movement.

The educational practices that these experts agreed were harmful included formal, structured classes with fixed time schedules and regular homework assignments. These were seen as constraints that prevented children from following their own interests and learning in an active, self-directed way. Required courses and sequences of courses were rejected for the same reason. So, too, was rote memorization, and boring work generally. Fixed standards—with objective tests to determine whether students had met them and with the withholding of passing grades when they had not—were also rejected. They were seen as oppressive and harmful. So, too, were disciplinary sanctions and suspensions. Failure was out. Sanctions were out. Social promotion and social diplomas were in.

Teachers who resisted these newly fashionable notions and continued to use the old methods were not excused as simply misguided. They were stigmatized as authoritarian bullies and, when they were white and the children they taught were black, as racists. There was no real

research evidence to support these beliefs—only theory, liberation rhetoric, and occasional anecdotes.

Evidence that at least some of these beliefs were mistaken came, initially, from studies undertaken to confirm them by demonstrating the
superiority of open classrooms to traditional ones. Researchers predicted that students in open classrooms would learn more than students
in traditional ones and that they would be more comfortable and more
creative, too. In study after disconcerting study, the results contradicted
these expectations. Student achievement was generally lower in open
classrooms; anxiety levels tended to be higher; and there were no discernible differences in creativity. Ideology did not seem to matter. Time
spent on schoolwork did, and it was consistently higher in traditional
classrooms. Left free to choose, most students chose to spend less time
on their schoolwork, in class and out.

Additional evidence that appropriate demands, limits, and sanctions
might be helpful rather than harmful emerged from the work of Ronald
Edmonds on effective schools [13] and from a new study by James Coleman comparing the performance of students in public and parochial
schools. [14] Edmonds undertook his work in hopes of disproving the conclusions that Christopher Jencks and a number of other researchers [15]
had drawn from Coleman's 1966 study—that schools don't matter.
Coleman's work had shown that resources and racial integration were
not related to achievement but that family background was. Jencks interpreted this to mean that the hope that schools could do an effective job
of educating the children of the poor was doomed to disappointment.
He called for a redistribution of wealth instead.

Edmonds's approach was to focus on public schools that bucked the
trend by getting impoverished minority group youngsters to perform at
or above national norms. He identified a small number of such schools
and studied them intensively, looking for common factors. He found
that all of the effective schools had principals and teachers who made
strong demands on students, setting out clear achievement goals, insisting that all students attain at least a minimum mastery of those goals,
and using objective, standardized tests to determine whether they had.
He also found that all of his effective schools had what he described as
"an orderly, safe climate conducive to teaching and learning," and he
concluded that this, too, made a positive difference.

Coleman's new study provided powerful independent confirmation
for Edmonds's conclusions, particularly the last one. He found that discipline was stricter in Catholic schools than it was in public ones and
that, as a result, the climate of order and safety that existed in Edmonds's exceptional public schools was the norm in parochial ones. He

also found that student achievement was generally higher in Catholic schools than in public ones and that this was especially true for impoverished minority group students.

Evidence in the Courtroom

A summary of research evidence like that presented in the preceding section is one thing; expert testimony in the trial courts is another. Its impact is dizzying, its accessibility is minimal, and no summary I have seen captures its flavor. My own first literal look at it—in education cases—was provided by Judge Bailey Brown of the Sixth Circuit Court of Appeals in Memphis, Tennessee. In his opinion in *Oliver* v. *Kalamazoo Board of Education* [16] in 1980, Judge Brown rendered friends of American law and education a service by doing something that is rarely done: reprinting substantial verbatim excerpts from the evidence plaintiffs' experts had presented in the trial court. I found it shocking at the time. I have since learned that it was quite typical. Accordingly, in offering the following verbatim excerpts from the *Debra P.* case, I have deleted the real name of the plaintiffs' expert referred to below as "Dr. Typical." His testimony, and my response to it and to similar testimony, came up repeatedly during my cross-examination.

Q.—Well, the phenomenon—you are familiar with Dr. Typical's testimony at trial here?

A.—I did read a transcript of his testimony.

Q.—You are familiar with his concerns about white teacher perceptions of black students coming into the system?

A.—Yes, I do recall reading his expressions of opinion on that.

Q.—In fact, you have read a great deal of opinions, I believe you say, from social science experts—or so-called social science experts who maintain that those kinds of problems, white teacher expectations of black students, have plagued the public school system since desegregation, is that right?

A.—Yes, indeed.

Q.—And you take very strong issue with that band of social science experts, is that right?

A.—I looked for any evidence that that is true, and I have searched as hard as I know how to for something other than subjective opinion and anecdotes. I emphasize the word, because I was somewhat concerned in the deposition transcripts that I read that the word—I must not have pronounced it clearly enough, but it keeps appearing as antidotes. The word I am using is anecdotes.

Q.—All right.

A.—And opinions.

Q.—And is it not your view of that body of knowledge which has been presented to the courts that it is largely anecdotal and unsupported by hard data?

A.—Yes. I recall Dr. Typical saying in response to a question, which I believe is on page 1075 of the transcript I saw, that the opinions he had been expressing in court that day were, I believe I am quoting accurately, purely subjective opinions.

Q.—All right.

A.—And I looked carefully at his testimony, and it seemed to me indeed that there was no research support that he cited. And so I would agree that they were indeed his purely subjective opinions, yes.

Q.—So that if you were to hear Dr. Typical testify that as late as 1979 there were in broad instances white teachers who simply didn't want to have black students there, you would take very serious issue with that in that it is simply not supported by the available data?

A.—Well, I would want to see the evidence he based that on. I would be glad to consider any evidence he had which suggested that that was true. But unless I did see such evidence, I could not reach that conclusion, no.

Q.—And you haven't seen any such evidence to date?

A.—No, sir, I have not.

Q.—Okay. And you have a great concern, do you not, that social scientists over the course of the last 10 or 15 years have, in your words, misled the courts with those anecdotal statements, opinions, is that right?

A.—Yes, sir, I do.

Q.—And led the courts into error?

A.—I believe that there has been a great—there have been many instances in which social scientists testified giving purely subjective opinions and presenting isolated anecdotes, which seem to me an inadequate basis for conclusions. And I am particularly concerned about those instances when social scientists do that when there is actual hard empirical data and when their opinions run contrary to solid scientific evidence.

I think in areas where we have no data, the best that honest social scientists can do is to use subjective professional judgment in attempting to answer questions. I am particularly concerned about instances when social scientists present subjective personal opinions that are contrary to widely available solid evidence.

And I think—yes, Your Honor, I do believe that it ill serves the court to present one's own opinion when it is contrary to the evidence, without also calling the court's attention to the evidence so that the court may judge for itself whether the empirical evidence or the personal subjective opinions—which constitutes the better evidence.

I think a minimal obligation would be to point out—point the court to the sources and to the data, so that the court can check for itself. It certainly is acceptable for an expert to have—to hold any opinion he cares to hold, but I do think the courts are ill served by experts who present their opinions and fail to present widely known massive data to the contrary.

There are—it is always possible—research is now terribly voluminous. None of us can keep up. Even those of us who specialize in one narrow area have a difficult time keeping up with all of the research. So, I am not criticizing people, because it is always possible to find a study that an expert hasn't read, and say, "Aha, did you mention this one?" I am not talking about that kind of thing.

I mean in areas like the effects of integration per se, racial integration on achievement, where you have hundreds of studies and where the literature is well-known, to point to none of those, it seems to me, yes, sir, a disservice to the courts and a serious one.

Areas like the relationship between school resources and achievement, again, where you have hundreds of studies and where these are not studies that were just done yesterday, but where you have these studies over a long period of time and where they are well and widely known, and when experts appear and testify and offer opinions contrary to that evidence, yes, sir, I do believe that they have an obligation to also advise the court that there is research literature to the contrary.

And I have very strong feelings on that. I think that social scientists disserve the court. And I think they disserve social science when they do that. And I am very distressed that there have been instances, a number of instances, where I believe that has occurred. And I think it is harmful to the law and for social science and for the relationship between them. Yes, sir.

. . .

Q.—I believe you testified earlier that Dr. Typical's conclusions on the relationship between students, particularly black student performance, and the lack of black administrators was something that Dr. Typical said was based—was purely his subjective opinion, right?

A.—That was my understanding.

Q.—Okay. Let me see if I can refresh your recollection a little bit on that, and review Dr. Typical's testimony at page 974 of the transcript here in 1979. Dr. Typical was asked, beginning at line 3, what effects if any would the demotion or the dismissal of black administrators have on students' perception, ability to achieve and desire to achieve:

"If you are a black student, let's say in a public high school in the State of Florida, or a middle school or even an elementary school for the most part, and you believe that you are entitled to an equal education and are in fact supposed to be getting equal education, and your perceptions and experiences and the perceptions of your parents whom you communicate with, supposedly, all are that blacks do not have an equal status in the administration of that district or in significant positions in that district, then this I think affects very seriously your perception of equity in your educational adventure, and in fact has a tendency to indicate to you that there is something that is not quite worthy of you as a black student and there must be something wrong with you or there must be something wrong with black administrators that they do not have equal access to this sort of job."

Dr. Typical goes on on page 975, line 3, "And there is a good deal of research that has been fairly well documented in the literature which indicates that this has a very serious detrimental effect on your academic achievement and your feelings as a result as a person, your self worth, this sort of thing."

Would you take issue with Dr. Typical on that with respect to the research that has been done in the field on that issue?

A.—I recall that specific passage, and that was because he did mention the word research. And that was why I read and reread the testimony and had one of my associates recheck, in case I had missed it, looking for a single cite to a single research study, and I found none. That was why I remember the precise page where he said that his opinions were purely subjective sometime later, because I was indeed interested to see that research. I could not find it, and he didn't cite it.

. . .

Q.—And in point of fact, during this entire point of time since integration, the social science testimony in front of what you have described as activist judges, and eventually reviewed by the 5th Circuit and the United States Supreme Court, was in stark contrast with the reality that was going on in the public school system at that time, is that right?

A.—No, Mr. Hanlon. I don't want to characterize all social science testimony and all—if you give me a specific example, I will do my best to comment on it—

Q.—Well, are you aware of—

A.—Many social scientists, thousands by now, have commented in thousands of cases, and I think it would be terribly unfair to condemn them all or to criticize them. I would have to see specific instances.

And the generalization that I would be willing to stand by is the one I made before, that when you have a social scientist testifying and offering his opinion, when his opinion is contrary to a well-established, well-known body of empirical fact, and he does not point out to the court that that body of research evidence exists, I object strongly to that.

Rereading that generalization a year later, I still believe that the adoption of the standard it calls for would be helpful. I do not believe that federal judges ought to be deciding educational policy for the nation, but, since they are right now, it would bode better for the nation if they had better evidence on which to base those decisions. Negative research results, like adverse legal precedents, ought to be reported to the courts.

The Constitutional Question

The word *education* is nowhere to be found in Article III of the Constitution of the United States—the part that defines the role of the federal judiciary in our tripartite system of government. It does not appear anywhere else in the Constitution either, not explicitly or implicitly. It is just not there. How, then, did we get where we are today, into a situation in which educational policy questions are routinely treated as questions of constitutional law to be decided by federal judges?

We got there, in major part, through a series of Supreme Court decisions interpreting one part of the Constitution of the United States, the Fourteenth Amendment. That is what permits people who favor some educational policy choices (e.g., open classrooms, social promotion, black English) and oppose others (e.g., minimum competence requirements, achievement grouping, disciplinary suspension) to bring their arguments into the federal courts and get federal judges to decide which choices are the right ones. They sue state and local public school officials who have opted for the policy choices they oppose, claiming that those choices violate the rights of schoolchildren under the Fourteenth Amendment.

The Fourteenth Amendment does not mention schoolchildren. It was added to the Constitution in 1868, three years after the end of the Civil War. Debate about its meaning began in Congress, prior to its passage, and continues still. Here is the full text of the most hotly debated part, Section 1:

> All persons born or naturalized in the United States, and subject to the jurisdiction thereof, are citizens of the United States and of the State wherein they reside. No State shall make or enforce any law which shall abridge the privileges or immunities of citizens of the United States; nor shall any State deprive any person of life, liberty, or property, without due process of law; nor deny to any person within its jurisdiction the equal protection of the laws.

How do those spare, bitterly fought-for words get federal judges into the educational policy-making business? The answer, I think, is that they do not when the Supreme Court endorses what I am going to call the neutral-law interpretation of the Fourteenth Amendment; they do when the Court adopts what I will call the special-benefit interpretation.

The neutral-law interpretation has a long history. There is little doubt that at least some of the congressmen who proposed the Amendment and some of the state legislators who ratified it had that sort of interpretation in mind. The Supreme Court acknowledged their existence in the *Brown* case in 1954 and characterized their position quite accurately: "The most avid proponents of the post-War Amendments undoubtedly intended them to remove all legal distinctions among 'all persons born or naturalized in the United States.'"[17]

If that interpretation had prevailed in the Supreme Court, there would have been no de jure segregation, in schools or anywhere else in America, in the first half of this century, and no educational policy-making by federal judges in the second half. That is so because under the neutral-law interpretation, the answer to a simple question—Has a legal distinction between American citizens been created or not?—decides the constitutionality of state actions challenged as incompatible with the Fourteenth Amendment. State-imposed segregation, in schools or anywhere else, obviously creates such a distinction, and is just as obviously unconstitutional under the neutral-law interpretation of the Fourteenth Amendment. On the other hand, state and local educational policy choices that apply to all public school children regardless of race do not create such distinctions. They are, for that reason alone, constitutionally sound, and federal judges do not need to decide whether they are educationally sound.

The special-benefit interpretation is very different, as are its implications. Those who espouse it see the Fourteenth Amendment as intended to apply primrily to black citizens and to benefit them, rather than to remove all legal distinctions between citizens. When this interpretation is applied, a new question becomes decisive: Does the legal distinction created result in a benefit to black citizens, a harm to them, or neither? That question is a much more complex one. The answers to it are never as clear, and, as a necessary consequence, judges who must answer it must also be given a high degree of discretion. Discretionary power, in legal terms, is power without any fixed limit on it. It is policy-making power, and judges bound by the special-benefit interpretation of the Fourteenth Amendment are not only permitted to exercise it, they are required to do so. In education cases, this means that federal judges must decide whether the policy choices of state and local school officials are educationally beneficial or educationally harmful to black students. Federal judges cannot do that without making educational policy choices for the nation.

Some federal judges believe that the neutral-law interpretation is the correct one; others prefer the special-benefit interpretation, but they are not free to choose, once the Supreme Court has spoken. They are obliged to follow its lead, as best they understand it. From the beginning, that usually meant deciding for the special-benefit interpretation. The *Slaughter-House* cases [18] were the beginning. They were the first Supreme Court cases interpreting the Amendment, and they were decided just five years after its passage.

The *Brown* Court tells us that the *Slaughter-House* Court "interpreted it [the Amendment] as proscribing all state-imposed discrimination against the Negro race." [19] An unwary reader might think that those cases were victories for black plaintiffs. They were not. There were no black plaintiffs in the *Slaughter-House* cases. The plaintiffs were white men who thought that the Fourteenth Amendment protected them, too, because they believed it was intended to remove all legal distinctions among "all persons born or naturalized in the United States," a category into which they thought they, too, fit. The *Slaughter-House* Court disagreed, five to four. It said that despite its clearly inclusive language, the Amendment was exclusive in its coverage, intended to apply primarily to black Americans and to benefit them, rather than to remove all legal distinctions between the races.

The next big loss for the neutral-law side came in 1896, in *Plessy* v. *Ferguson*.[20] This time, the plaintiff in the case was a black man, a Mr. Plessy, who refused to give up his seat on a train in Louisiana. Louisiana had a law providing "that all railway companies carrying passengers in their coaches in this state shall provide equal but separate accommodations for the white and colored races, by providing two or more passenger coaches for each passenger train, or by dividing the passenger coaches by a partition so as to secure separate accommodations. . . ." It was a criminal law, and Mr. Plessy was arrested for violating it.

He challenged his arrest, arguing that Louisiana's law was unconstitutional because it was clearly contrary to the Fourteenth Amendment. Under the neutral-law interpretation, it was. Mr. Plessy had been born in the United States, and Louisiana's law created a clear legal distinction between him and other American citizens, a distinction based on race. Alas, that argument had no force in the *Plessy* case because the *Plessy* Court, too, adopted the special-benefit interpretation of the Fourteenth Amendment. According to that interpretation, it was not enough for Mr. Plessy to show that a legal distinction between American citizens had been created. To win, under these circumstances, he also had to prove that the distinction had a specially harmful effect on black citizens. Obviously, equal physical accommodations, in and of themselves, could not have such an effect, so Mr. Plessy had to rely on psychological arguments to make his case. He did, and the Court also did, in rejecting them. Then as now, psychological arguments in court were long on theory, short on evidence. Here is the Court's argument:

> We consider the underlying fallacy of the plaintiff's argument to consist in the assumption that the enforced separation of the two races stamps the colored race with a badge of inferiority. If this be so, it is not by reason of anything found in the act, but solely because the colored race chooses to put that construction upon it.[21]

On this basis, the Supreme Court upheld the constitutionality of Louisiana's law. This decision was the green light for gathering post-Reconstruction forces. Twentieth-century misperceptions notwithstanding, segregation was not widespread in the United States or even in the American South in the nineteenth century.[22] The Louisiana law that Mr. Plessy challenged was not a centuries-old provision. It was a new law, passed in 1890, one of a scattered handful of similar new laws springing up in the aftermath of Reconstruction, straws in the wind, testing the limits imposed by the Fourteenth Amendment, two decades after its passage. Fine words, no doubt, but what, exactly, did they mean? What did they require? What did they prohibit? What limits did they actually impose on state action?

Plessy's case was the first case testing the constitutionality of these new laws to reach the Supreme Court. He was not fighting for a new right; he was fighting to retain one he already had. Under the special-benefit theory, he lost it, on the basis of a psychological argument, and a host of new laws sprang up in the wake of his defeat, making segregation a dominant pattern in large parts of the land, from the early decades of the twentieth century until 1954, when the Supreme Court finally agreed to reconsider its views, in the *Brown* case.

Plessy had won something, though. He won the most eloquent and precise statement of the neutral-law position ever made. Mr. Justice Harlan, the elder, made it, dissenting, alone, in the *Plessy* case. Unlike his brethren, Mr. Justice Harlan thought Louisiana's new law would have harmful effects on black citizens, but he was emphatic about the fact that he would have struck it down as unconstitutional in either event on the basis of his understanding of the impact of the Fourteenth Amendment on the larger document of which it is a part. He put it this way: "However apparent the injustice of such legislation may be, we have only to consider whether it is consistent with the Constitution of the United States. . . ."[23] He found that it was not, because: "Our Constitution is color-blind, and neither knows nor tolerates classes among its citizens."[24]

Did the Supreme Court in *Brown* vindicate John Harlan's vision of neutral law, making our Constitution color-blind at last? Or did it, once again, reaffirm the special-benefit theory, rejecting only the psychological argument adopted by the *Plessy* Court on the basis of evidence like the Clark study described earlier in this essay? Is school segregation unconstitutional because it hurts the self-esteem of black children, or is it unconstitutional irrespective of any or all presumed effects on their psyches or anyone else's?

The answer, alas, is yes, no, and maybe. There is language in the Supreme Court's opinion in *Brown* to support either conclusion. There is language in subsequent Supreme Court opinions and decisions to support either. Many federal judges are not clear. It is time for the Supreme Court to speak again, clearly.

PART EIGHT

Access and Academic Standards

10

Underprepared Students and Public Research Universities

MARTIN TROW

"The underprepared student" is a problem for systems of higher education that place strong emphasis on ease of access *and* also try to maintain certain academic standards. It is not a problem, say, in British universities, whose students enter only after passing at least two advanced-level examinations in their subjects of specialization; such students are, by definition, "prepared" for university level work. On the other hand, we do not hear much about underprepared students in most community colleges, which are designed to be open-door institutions and pride themselves on teaching their students at whatever the student's level of preparation may be. Students in community colleges may be underprepared for their academic courses, but not for the community college itself.

The stress created by a commitment both to broad access and to academic standards is a peculiarly American problem, and among American institutions it is especially acute in colleges and universities that by tradition and necessity have been relatively open to high school graduates, but whose research-oriented faculties and graduate schools create and maintain standards for academic achievement that are often at odds with their relaxed standards for admission. While the problem of the underprepared student is most widespread in the United States, it appears in other countries where comparable conditions exist or have been created. For example, the U-68 reforms of Swedish higher education were aimed at broadening access, in part to adults, workers, and housewives, who had not gained the necessary qualifications for entry to university from secondary school and who through the law have been granted special access as adults. That law has created a problem of the "underprepared student" (though on a very small scale) similar to that which faces American universities.

Where universities rest on a firm foundation of elite and rigorous academic high schools like the gymnasiums, lycées, the British grammar schools and direct grant schools as they were, and the sixth forms as they are—schools taught by university graduates for university entrants—or where institutions can be highly selective, such as the leading private colleges and universities in the United States today, the adequacy of preparation of their students does not arise as a serious issue. But that has not been true for most American colleges and universities for most of our history. Much of American higher education was established before a system of public high schools was created. Indeed, it was not until after the Civil War that there were many public high schools outside the big cities of the Northeast. Thirty years after that war ended, in 1895, only two out of five students admitted to American colleges and universities were drawn from public high schools. In that year only one in five came from the private preparatory schools, which were an outgrowth of the old academy and were also concentrated on the eastern seaboard. But the hundreds of modest state and denominational colleges that sprang up between the Revolution and the Civil War had to find some other way besides academies and high schools to bridge the gap between the primary schools and their own advanced classes. What many did was to create preparatory departments—a year or more, during which time the young, often very young, entering student was actually in residence but not enrolled in the college proper or doing work for the college's degree. These preparatory departments were "a bridge between the free public elementary school and the public university."[1] The absence of a national system of high schools, and the uncontrolled creation of public and private colleges and universities, created the need for what we now call "remedial education," in the form of a preparatory department in almost every college in the country.

"Insisting upon erecting colleges that neither need nor intelligence justified, college governing boards [before the Civil War] often had the choice of giving up or of taking any student who came along and starting him at whatever point his ignorance required. The result was that a college might not get around to graduating a class until it had been in operation for as long as eight years; in the meantime it had become the classical academy as well as college for the district that it served."[2] The practice of establishing preparatory departments, observes Frederick Rudolph, "has been something of a secret from history, but the colleges and universities knew what they were doing. They were laying their hands on every young man and woman they possibly could before their competitors did."[3] So remedial education, then as now, was linked to the market for students, as well as to academic standards. In 1870 only twenty-six colleges in the country, twenty-three of them in the Northeast, were not operating preparatory departments. As late as 1895, 40 percent of all the students admitted to the colleges and uiversities in the country were being admitted from the college preparatory departments of the colleges and universities themselves.[4] Once students of different ages and origins were entering college with very diverse backgrounds, preparations, and expectations, it became difficult to set any common standard for entry. As a result, in most public universities the real standards have been for the degree rather than for entry. In this century, after the public high school had replaced college preparatory departments, in universities that by law or custom have been required to accept all high school graduates, the freshmen year has been viewed in two ways. It has been a year for screening out those who are simply not able to do college level work—the notorious "slaughter of the innocents." For the rest, it has been a year for remedying the academic deficiencies they bring with them from high school.

American colleges and universities are no strangers to underprepared students or remedial instruction. Our problems, and indeed many of our responses, are today remarkably similar to those of the nineteenth-century college. We share with our academic forebears a powerful democratic ethos, weak secondary education, the pressure of the market felt through enrollment-driven budgets, and the absence of any central agency for setting or enforcing high school curricula or standards for college or university entry. Today, as in the past, all of these and other forces are bringing to our public colleges and universities many students who are not on entry prepared to do work at a standard that those institutions define as college level.

If the problem of the underprepared student is a perennial one for American higher education, as I have suggested, why is it that we seem to be especially concerned about the issue just now? The answer lies both in a set of realities and in a cluster of apprehensions. The realities we know. There is, first, the well-documented decline in basic skills across the country as measured by the College Board PSAT, SAT, and achievement tests, the American College Testing Program's tests, and the National Assessment of Educational Progress, among others.[5] To put the decline in another perspective, "In 1968, not one campus [of the University of California] had as many as half of its entering students scoring below 550 on the SAT-verbal; in 1979 more than half of the entering students scored below 550 [on the SAT verbal] on all eight UC general campuses, and on five of our campuses . . . at least *two-thirds* . . . scored below 550."[6]

In support of the evidence of the tests, there is the fact that larger numbers of entering freshmen on all UC campuses now need help with writing skills than five years ago, "and there is some evidence to indicate that the criteria for selecting students for [the remedial courses] may have changed over the years, which means that these numbers may be a conservative estimate of need."[7]

The faculty who teach freshmen at the University of California agree almost unanimously that students are on the whole less well prepared for college work than they were a decade ago, even when they have taken the college preparatory courses. For example, UC faculty in math and in English composition agreed that students have more trouble than they used to have "thinking abstractly and are not able to transfer their skills from one purpose to another, across disciplines."[8]

But the present concern among college and university faculty and administrators about the preparation for college work among undergraduate students arises as much out of apprehensions regarding the future as out of the experience of the present and immediate past. And these apprehensions are linked to notions about the causes of the underpreparation of students and to the sense that these forces are not, for the most part, responsive to actions by colleges or universities. Among the perceived causes of the inadequacy of preparation of students for college work are some that are linked to characteristics of the students and some that arise out of characteristics of the schools.

The gravest apprehension among academics is about the character and future of the public high school. The problem has many dimensions, but perhaps the most critical is the quality and morale of the teaching profession itself. From 1972 to 1980, SAT verbal scores for college-bound high school seniors planning to major in education dropped from 418 to 339, a loss of 79 points, while the SAT math scores in that population dropped 31 points, from 449 to 418. This is a much steeper decline than the national average for the SAT over the same time period, which dropped 21 points on the verbal and 15 on the math tests.[9]

Averages of 339 on the SAT verbal and 418 in math are figures to cause anxiety and indeed despair in anyone who reflects on them and on their implications for the primary and secondary schools. The negative selection to teaching that these figures indicate is, sad to say, a long-standing phenomenon in this country.[10]

Reflecting on the evidence available in the mid–1960s, I concluded then rather pessimistically that no matter how teacher education and secondary school curricula are reformed to strengthen the college preparatory function of the high schools, a substantial part of the actual teaching itself will be carried on by relatively poorly paid, low status, and academically less able people. This may not have mattered so much when secondary education was largely terminal—at least it can be argued that qualities other than academic ability, for example, a deep interest in young people and skills in working with them, are more important for teachers of students whose interests are not academic or intellectual. But this claim can hardly be made for teachers of college-bound youngsters whose success in college will rest heavily on the knowledge and intellectual habits they acquire in secondary school.[11]

That was written at a time when salaries for teachers and per capita expenditures for education were rising, when LBJ's Great Society and his War on Poverty were injecting substantial amounts of federal funds into the schools for the first time, and when the schools were accepting increasingly heavy responsibilities for combatting the effects of racial discrimination, class inequalities, family instability, the use of drugs, delinquent subcultures, and the tyranny of television. The schools still carry those burdens in a time of declining resources, worse (and more dangerous) conditions in the schools, and a large gap between the salaries of teachers and of other comparably educated professionals. The decline in the quality of our teaching profession overall cannot be reversed by pointing to its grave consequences. We have been doing that for a while without apparent results. And in our search for remedies, it may be the beginning of wisdom to accept that our teachers are, on average, *as* they are, and are likely to be as they are for as far ahead as we can see.

All other matters and troubles in the schools are secondary to the qualities and morale of the teaching staff. When we in colleges and universities look at the schools, we see with a mixture of anxiety and compassion a group of aging men and women (the average age of teachers in San Francisco high schools is fifty-five), ill paid and unrespected, the burden of whose work, physical and emotional, is of an order quite different from that of the daily experience of the university teacher, with his four to eight hours of classroom instruction, his department meetings and faculty senates. A moving document written by a Boston women teachers group [12] speaks again, as so many observers and participants have, to the loneliness, the helplessness, the rage and frustration, felt by teachers:

Even when their work has created a major program their contribution appears publicly as negligible and secondary. Their isolation from each other and the need to funnel any request and information up through the levels of the hierarchy and back down again, rather than directly to each other, has not allowed them to use their unique knowledge of classroom life, which they alone possess, as a basis for determining system-wide, or even school-wide policies.[13]

And this beleaguered work force, treated as employees rather than as professionals, and increasingly (especially its younger members) without security in their jobs or careers, clings to a union structure that further constricts opportunities for creative institutional responses; its contracts, for example, prohibit extracurricular activities like evening meetings with parents that creative principals see as crucial in involving parents in the education of their children.

Ironically, all the remedies that we propose for the schools seem only to generate more problems. In states that have introduced competency tests for graduation, it has been observed that the school curriculum and its resources increasingly focus on the numbers and proportion of students who can pass those tests and thus earn their diplomas, at the expense of more demanding academic and college preparatory courses. There has been in many places a steady shift of resources away from the gifted students and their college preparatory tracks, and even away from the average toward the slower and weaker students. Reports such as that of the National Assessment of Educational Programs in 1977, documenting that nearly half of the seventeen-year-olds tested could not read college freshman level materials or solve basic mathematical problems and that less than a third could write a unified and focused essay, understandably generate pressures from parents and school boards for more attention to the plight of the educationally disadvantaged and for a concentration in the high school on the most basic of basic skills. The result is what might be called the cult of remediation—a continued spiraling backward over the syllabus for the benefit of the slowest third of the class, while gifted and average students seek distraction elsewhere and anywhere outside the school to stave off the boredom of the classroom and curriculum. As a University of Wisconsin task force on basic skills put it, dryly:

> For whatever combination of societal reasons, the attitudes of many high school students have also shifted perceptibly, with apathy and disengagement from education prevalent. There has been a decline in student willingness to invest substantial work and effort in the learning process. Some academically talented students elect the less challenging paths and options created to serve the needs of those with other goals. Work-release programs and programs of reduced credits have encouraged the concept of education as a part-time phenomenon. Many teachers and students report a sense of postponement in secondary schools rather than a sense of serious responsibility for preparation.[14]

There is another source of worry among academics, which centers more on the behavior of our colleges and universities than on the schools and teachers. This is the concern that under the pressure of declining age cohorts and tight budgets, our enrollment-driven colleges and universities will subordinate everything, including academic standards, to the need to keep entering classes up to budgeted levels. And that, too, is an old American tradition.

In the face of all this, what can we do? By "we" I do not mean "we the people" acting through our political institutions to shape law and regulation and public expenditure as these might bear on the secondary school. Nor do I mean we the parents, or we the members of national organizations, or we the teachers and researchers in higher education. I mean we the faculty members and administrators of those public research universities (and that is most of them) which can neither screen out all underprepared students through selective admissions processes nor admit all high school graduates, however ill prepared, as a substantial part of our mission. The question I raise is not only what we can do for underprepared students and for secondary education but also whether we should do it. And how much of it, and what are its costs to our colleges and universities, to their resources of money, time, and energy, and to their capacity to teach and do research at high and demanding levels?

Many things are being done, and much of what we should be doing we are already doing. Perhaps the broadest consensus in the university on this issue is that we should make known more widely and effectively to school people, to parents, and to high school students just what the university expects of students when they enter. The task here is to define operationally what constitutes an "adequate" preparation for college and then to tell it to all the people—including principals, teachers, counselors, parents—who shape the decisions that students make and the courses that they take, decisions and courses that in turn affect what they know when they come to college.

An example of this kind of effort is the report of an advisory commission to the Ohio Board of Regents and the State Board of Education that was charged with "the task of developing a college preparatory curriculum that would clearly reflect collegiate expectations for entering students and, when followed, would reduce the need for remedial coursework at the collegiate level."[15] The report did that, not just by discussing in general terms the number of courses or years of English and mathematics that college-bound students should be taking, but also by specifying the skills and topics they should have mastered in their high school courses. The report develops a kind of normative syllabus for the high schools in algebra, geometry, trigonometry, and analytical geometry, and alongside that a statement, again quite specific, although rather differently couched, regarding the skills in English that are expected of students entering college. The report also includes a section on teacher training and in-service education, as well as one on communication to the educational community, students, and their parents. It is now widely recognized that a statement of academic expectations is no better than its dissemination.

A similar document was prepared in California by a committee composed of the representives of the academic senates of the California Community Colleges, the California State University and Colleges, and the University of California, and was adopted by all three segments.[16]

A statement of expectations can take the form of exhortations and warnings about the difficulties that students will experience on entering the university if they do not take certain courses and acquire certain skills in high school. Or it can take the form of tougher requirements for admission, as it has in California. In both cases the development of these statements, and the stress on their dissemination to the schools and the students, presupposes that there is an institution out there—the secondary school system—full of people who can prepare students appropriately if only they know what is expected. The schools surely have some potential for strengthening their college preparatory work. But it is not altogether clear what that further capacity of the schools, as they are currently staffed and organized, may be. The statement-of-expectations approach assumes that schools can adjust their curricula and courses if they are better informed about what the colleges think best for college-bound students, and that students and parents will also make better decisions as they come to know more about what colleges want. The motivation and desire of all parties to strengthen the college preparatory component of secondary education is assumed, as is the capacity of the schools to carry out those intentions. Most will warmly concur with the spirit of those sentiments. But we are wise if we recognize the limits of their efficacy. Not all teachers or principals want to strengthen their college preparatory work, and many may not be able to do it even if they want to. It is sobering to reflect that in the moderately selective University of California almost all entrants already meet the new and more stringent entry requirements of three years of high school math and that, nevertheless, large and increasing numbers of entering freshmen on examination show the need for remedial math work in the university. Just taking a course in high school does not ensure that the students learn the material or retain it until they enter college.

Alongside the clarification of expectations and their communication to students, parents, and schools, there are two other broad strategies colleges and universities can and to some degree do employ in response to this problem of the underprepared entering freshmen. One is familiar: the offering of remedial work in the colleges and universities themselves, programs and courses that try to remedy in college academic deficiencies accumulated in the primary and secondary years. The other is to develop services and programs for schoolteachers, for students, and for schools and school systems that aim at improving the quality of preparatory work in the schools.

In 1980–81, without any central direction or coordination, the number of remedial courses taught in colleges and universities across the country rose by 22 percent, 25 percent in private institutions and 19 percent in public. "Even the more selective private liberal arts colleges . . . offered twice as many remedial courses in the fall of 1980 as in the fall of 1979." [17]

Everyone is in favor of providing remedial work in college—at least until we begin to assess the costs. The decline in the ability and preparation of our entering students poses painful dilemmas for the faculty. A University of California report puts the issue very clearly:

> The effects of underpreparation are felt not only by students, but also by faculty. Those we interviewed told us, unequivocally, that teaching has gotten harder, that a professor can no longer assume a common level of knowledge or skill in a class because preparation is so varied, but more importantly, that faculty are now being asked to handle problems, especially in writing, that they were never trained to handle.
>
> The faculty we talked to who were affected most by composition problems seem to see two choices. They can either spend a great deal of time on an individual basis helping students and reconsidering their own teaching methods, or they can ignore it, keep going as they are, leave the problems to learning specialists trained to handle them and invest their time elsewhere where they feel more comfortable and productive. One English professor said, "I have a choice in my Shakespeare class; fake it and teach the course anyway, giving the students C's and B's or adjourn Shakespeare and teach writing."
>
> On top of this frustration, many faculty are also worried about class standards. If faculty members choose to spend their time working with students on writing, they have to assign less reading because students have a finite amount of time to spend on any course. If, on the other hand, the faculty chooses to ignore the problem, there is a fear they may assign easier reading, require less writing, and give more multiple choice exams, in order not to face problems in composition. And not assigning writing means less practice for students who need more, exacerbating the problem.
>
> . . . As one professor put it, "Everyone agrees that we should help

students who need it, but what concerns us is that there are *so many* students who need it. Offering precalculus classes has decreased the availability of the upper division courses that should be taught by anything calling itself a University math department. There is now a little resentment about what the increase in service courses is doing to our department, and alarm about what will happen if it gets worse."[18]

Looked at from a comparative perspective, American colleges and universities almost from their beginning have been oriented to markets in a way that Europeans can scarcely imagine.[19] Most European countries, at least in the modern era, have created systems of universities and colleges marked by a commitment to high and fairly uniform academic standards, in their requirements both for entry and for gaining a certificate or degree. (There are exceptions: for example, the Open University in England is less stringent than other British universities in its requirements for entry, though equally stringent in its requirements for the degree. Attrition rates are high; as for the rest, they just have to pass the examinations, if and when they can.) Throughout Europe, efforts to greatly expand access to higher education or to make it more equitable have been constrained by those academic standards.[20] The United States, by contrast, and almost uniquely in the world, has from its beginning taken ease and breadth of access to some kind of higher education as desirable, and its colleges and universities have, for the most part, struggled to achieve as high a standard of student performance as possible, given the ease of access. As the demand for higher education has grown, the society has not let standards of achievement, either at entry or for the earned degree, stand in the way of enrollment growth, although there is a relatively small number of highly selective institutions to which this does not apply. Whereas European universities have been noted for high standards and constrained access, our system is characterized by ease of access and variable standards.

The comparatively high attrition rate in American universities (as compared with European universities), especially in the less selective public universities, is one consequence of the tension between ease of access and the maintenance of standards. And the growth of remedial work in colleges currently is another response to this same tension. A report of the University of Wisconsin's task force on basic skills, while urging the "clarification of expectations" about college work, and a greater emphasis on compensatory or remedial courses in the university, specifically recommends that the university *not* raise entry standards, for fear of reducing intake. But the difficult question then arises of whether to give credit for these compensatory courses and basic skills. Some universities have come down on one side of that question, some on the other, while a few, like Wisconsin's task force, recommend giving elective credit for compensatory courses but within defined limits. The fact that there are differences on this matter, both of views and of practice, is the best evidence for how soft the concept of academic standards in higher education is, and consequently for how vulnerable those standards are to market pressures, especially the pressure to maintain enrollment at all costs.

There are good arguments on both sides of the credit issue. The obvious objection to offering credit for remedial work in college is that this reduces the amount of "college level" "nonremedial" work a student will need for a degree. In a system that awards undergraduate degrees on the accumulation of credits rather than, as in Europe and in most graduate work in this country, on the demonstration of competence in an examination or essay, a lowering of the level of some of the credits will arguably reduce the level or quality of the work that the degree reflects.

The trouble is that what first degrees represent in knowledge and skill varies so much between different institutions, and between different departments and disciplines within the same institution, that a certain dilution for a subset of students in the level of the work they take is probably not discernible after four years of college anyway. Moreover, the assumption on which our credit system is based is that students learn only what they are taught in credit-carrying courses. And we know that that is not true. On the other hand, the firmness (or rigidity) of some university faculties in resisting the awarding of credit for remedial work arises directly out of their sense of the vulnerability of the standards for college level work, standards already weakened by diversity, competition, a shocking grade inflation since the mid-1960s, the powerful pressure of the market for enrollments, and the call for "relevance." If we grant credit for any remedial work, many faculty members ask, where will it stop? And we have before us the cautionary lessons of the secondary curriculum, and its debasement under slightly different pressures, almost undefended by any conception of what constitutes standards for secondary school work or a high school diploma.

The academic arguments for credit are hard to disengage from the financial and political pressures behind them. If you do not grant credit for remedial work, who will teach the courses and who will pay for them? Can you legitimately charge students for courses for which they do not earn credit? And if not from students, where will the money come from, if state governments object, as some do, to paying twice for skills and knowledge that should have been gained in the high schools?

Moreover, it is argued, these remedial courses lay a foundation for the rest of college work; colleges teach these basic courses differently than the high schools do; and they are no easier, and rather more important, than many other things taught in college. And if one institution does not give credit for this work and delays the student's progress toward the degree, other institutions *will* give them credit and thus gain an advantage in recruiting students. This latter argument will become sharper and more persuasive over the next ten or fifteen years, as age cohorts decline and the numbers needing remedial work increase.

But quite apart from the issue of credit, there are a host of problems for colleges in their remedial work. As these precollege level courses grow in number, who should teach them? Is this a responsibility of the regular faculty, recruited for the most part for their scholarship and research skills, and not on the whole enthusiastic or even particularly gifted as teachers of the regular college level introductory courses? Or should it be some volunteer subset of the faculty? If the latter, what of the effect of those decisions on their careers, and of that on the numbers volunteering? Or should it be a special group of teachers hired for remedial courses outside the ordinary appointment procedures of the university and without regular departmental affiliation or tenure? What, then, of the dangers of a body of second-class citizens within the university, doing a crucial job for it but inevitably enjoying less compensation and status and feeling more resentment? To what extent can the remedial work be shifted where possible to neighboring community colleges, whose faculty members presumably have more experience and interest in students without strong academic preparation? Moreover, community colleges can often get state compensation for remedial courses when the university cannot. In my own university, though, there is strong resistance on the part of at least some experienced faculty to subcontracting to the community colleges what they see as an absolutely vital part of the introduction to the work of the undergraduate curriculum.

Whether in a community college or university, students can learn intermediate algebra in 30 hours of class time, whereas it may take 200 hours in high school—and even then may never really "take." What does that tell us about the effects of different expectations, or motivations, of schools and colleges as learning environments, or the quality of teaching, or the braking effect of the bottom third in school? We do not yet understand adequately why a college (almost any college) is so much more effective than high school in teaching the basic academic skills. Whatever the reasons, colleges are so much more effective (and cost-effective) in preparing their own students for their own programs that they will surely continue to offer remedial work and to expand those offerings until they are constrained by the demands of their own advanced work. Where that line is drawn will differ from institution to institution, and is already a source of controversy in some.

Colleges and universities have a variety of ways of responding to the problems of poorly prepared high school graduates:

- They can spell out more clearly what level and quality of high school work is necessary for success in college, and urge schools and students to meet those expectations.

- They can exclude poorly prepared students by raising their admissions requirements.

- Where they cannot or may not exclude poorly qualified students, they can admit them and dismiss on academic grounds those unable to meet their standards during or after the first year.

- Groups of university-based scholars and scientists can prepare better materials in their own fields for adoption and use by the schools, as groups of mathematicians, physicists, chemists, biologists, and teachers of English did during the reform movement following Sputnik.

- Or they can try to develop new and stronger links with the secondary schools (or parts of them). This means working directly with high school students, their teachers, and the schools themselves in an effort to strengthen the academic preparation of students before they enter college. These "outreach programs" can be designed to serve selected students, teachers, or, more rarely, whole schools and school districts.

Services by universities to schoolteachers are familiar to all: many schools of education have programs of in-service training, and the summer institutes in science and mathematics supported by the National Science Foundation in past years are well known. Many such programs, large and small, spring up to put into effect some new form of relationship between university and school people or to improve the quality of teaching in the schools through new skills or perspectives that have been developed in the university. The Bay Area Writing Project, with its origins at Berkeley, but now spreading all over the United States, is a good example of this kind of program targeted directly at teachers.

Some programs are aimed primarily at students in high schools, and only secondarily at their teachers. Many of these are part of affirmative efforts to increase the numbers of minority students entering college or university. An example is the well-known MESA program (Mathematics, Engineering, and Science Achievement), which originated in the Berkeley School of Engineering but now is located in sixteen MESA centers throughout the state of California. This program, "designed to increase the number of underrepresented minorities in professions related to mathematics, engineering, the physical sciences, economics and business administration," targets talented minority high school students and provides additional tutoring and other services to those students and to their teachers. The MESA program is typically focused on a teacher in a participating school who has a special relationship with a small number of mathematically talented and motivated minority students, the teachers and students together creating a kind of cocoon in which these students' talents and motivations are nurtured, looking toward their entry into college and a math-based career. Another and similar program, the Professional Development Program at Berkeley, also seeks out minority students with high academic potential and draws them into a range of activities—summer workshops, Saturday classes, tutorial work, and the like, outside the school—designed to introduce them to the climate and expectations of the university.

These programs, which focus on high school students and teachers, are often seen as, and often in fact are to some degree, "change agents" in the life of the student. On the whole, those programs take the school, its structure, and its mode of operation as given; they either try to enrich the chosen students' education, taking them out of the school into the university and its labs and museums, or they create within the school a special protected and enriched environment for a small number of specially talented students.

But there is a third "outreach" model, less common as yet, in which the university takes as its target not so much the student or the teacher as a whole school or a group of schools or a school district; it aims to strengthen the academic preparation of students by strengthening the schools in which that education is provided. If successful, the college or university can after a period of years withdraw its support and resources and hand over to the now strengthened schools the continued management of what is intended to be a permanently strengthened educational program. This is a different model from the university lab school or preparatory department of the past; the relationship with the schools is a cooperative one, it is partial rather than total, and it is temporary. I want to describe one such program, located at Berkeley, and then to identify four problems, or at least potential problems, that arise in this area of university-school relationships.

The Cooperative College Preparatory Program (CCPP), based in

Berkeley's Lawrence Hall of Science, was founded in 1980, like many other outreach programs, "to address the continuing underrepresentation of minorities at the University and, in particular, an accelerating decline in numbers of Bay Area minority students sufficiently prepared to enter college and study math-based fields."[21] In 1983–84 the program had a staff of about fourteen and a budget of roughly $375,000.

Although the program is directed primarily toward two predominantly black high schools, eight of their feeder junior high schools, and six feeder elementary schools in Oakland, there is in principle no reason that such programs could not link universities with high schools of any racial or ethnic mix. And a great many schools and colleges in this country need help, especially with their math programs. At the beginning of the 1980s, only a third of all American high schools required more than one year of math for graduation. Less than a third even taught calculus. In that same year only one-third of all high school students had completed three years of math. And students in the general and vocational tracks (who make up 60 percent of all high school students) were worse off: only one in five of those students had graduated with three years of math. Half of all high school graduates in the United States took no math or science beyond the tenth grade.

As for the teachers of math, in the decade 1972–82 the number of secondary level math teachers being prepared in teacher education programs declined by 75 percent. Almost five times more science and math teachers left teaching in 1982 for employment in nonteaching jobs than left because of retirement. Nationwide, almost a quarter of the teaching posts in math were unfilled. And in 1981 half the teachers newly employed to teach secondary science and mathematics were not fully qualified to teach their subjects.[22]

But the need for special assistance to predominantly black central-city schools all over the country is clear. For example, at the start of the program in Oakland in 1980–81, of the 1,304 ninth-graders in the first six junior high schools served by the CCPP, only 114 (less than 9 percent) took algebra. At the two high schools fed by these junior high schools, only 36 of 1,308 (2.8 percent) tenth-graders took geometry; 21 out of 1,095 (2 percent) in the eleventh grade took advanced algebra/trigonometry; and only 3 out of 819 twelfth-graders in the two high schools (0.4 percent) took precalculus. At one of the high schools, only 3 out of 680 tenth-graders were prepared to take geometry. "At the two high schools, there were virtually no students progressing toward being prepared to take calculus during their first year of college." Indeed, only 21 students at both schools combined were in a position to complete advanced algebra/trigonometry by the twelfth grade and thus to take precalculus in their freshman year in college.[23]

These figures, which could be matched in many inner-city high schools, reflect the near absence of a college preparatory program in mathematics. Virtually all the graduates of these schools who go on to higher education will need remedial math work in college. Why should this be so?

University people who are currently grappling with these problems report that inner-city schools (always allowing for exceptions) are characterized by a set of conditions and events that constitute a kind of "vicious system," which defeats the best efforts of individual teachers and students. They describe some of the elements of that vicious system as follows.[24]

First, teachers in those schools who teach the early courses in the college preparatory math sequence confront students whose abilities and motivations differ widely. In the process of addressing the various deficiencies of their students, and especially of the slower ones, teachers tend to fall behind and rarely cover all the required material in a course. "As a result, students who are prepared to take a course on one level move on to the next level with gaps in their backgrounds, building up an increasing deficit year by year. Eventually, course titles misrepresent what is being taught and grades become difficult to interpret because it is not really known what they are measuring. At this point we say, 'standards have dropped.'"

A number of other conditions contribute to the erosion of the mathematics curriculum in these schools:

· They lack an efficient way of identifying talented students.

· They do not have good ways of grouping students by mathematical ability.

· They are handicapped by policies requiring a minimum class size, so that to make up the required number in the college preparatory math courses, unqualified students are enrolled in them, which further complicates the existing problems of identifying, counseling, and grouping the abler students.

· There is a severe shortage of trained mathematics teachers in these inner-city schools, as elsewhere in American secondary education. This results in the assignment of inadequately trained teachers to the college preparatory math courses. Those teachers tend to avoid teaching material that they themselves are not sure of. Moreover, some of them transmit their own negative attitudes toward math to the students and encourage the students to avoid more difficult math.

· Finally, open enrollment policies in school districts accelerate the decline of academically weak schools. As such a school develops a poor reputation for its college preparatory program, it tends to lose its most capable students to other schools in the district, and its capacity to develop a strong program and attract good students is further diminished.

Add to all this a generally unfavorable climate of learning and often poorly trained and insecure administrators, and it is not difficult to see why so few students from these schools are adequately prepared for college level work on graduation.

The academic climate and performance of school administrators, along with the school curriculum and teaching staff, are increasingly of concern to universities. For example, Berkeley's College Cooperative Preparatory Program (CCPP) was created to be "a means whereby the university could assist the schools to initiate and follow through a complex and long-range process of change involved in developing their autonomous capacity to maintain a high level of operation."[25] And that "high level of operation" is defined operationally: it is not just to create a basic college preparatory math program in grades seven through twelve, but specifically to increase the number of students moving through these programs on track—that is, taking college preparatory courses in math in the seventh and eighth grades, algebra in the ninth grade, and so on, to precalculus in the twelfth grade.[26]

The CCPP model in operation is based on two central elements: project coordinators, instructors, and mentors in the schools, and the School-University Institute. The coordinator for each school is an experienced professional math educator employed by the university, who works half-time every day at a school site, offering advice and assistance to students, faculty, staff, and administrators. Coordinators work directly with students, both individually and in small groups in the classrooms, before and after school and during lunch hours; they team teach with members of the school's math department; they train, students to be peer teachers; they coordinate the work of counseling teachers; and they assist school administrators with general management administrative problems. They are also a key link between the school and the Institute.

CCPP instructors are young college graduates, working full-time on the project and assigned roughly half-time to a given school, where they work primarily in the classrooms with the local teachers, tutoring individual students, and teaching small groups. They also train peer teachers. Project mentors are part-time staff, usually graduate or undergraduate students at the university in math, engineering, or science departments, whose work resembles that of staff instructors but who are more likely to confine their work to the classrooms and to the direct instruction of students individually and in small groups. On the average, any given school will have a half-time coordinator and a half-time instructor or mentor in the school each day.

The other major component of the program, the School-University Institute, holds monthly meetings during the school year and a two-week workshop at the Lawrence Hall of Science during the summer. The Institute "brings together faculty, staff, and parents across schools, district staff, CCPP staff and University faculty" to talk about secondary education, their schools, the problems in their schools and solutions to them. The coordinators at the school sites provide the detailed follow-up work required for the effective implementation of any plans developed at the meetings of the Institute.

So far, the program seems to be successful by its own criteria. In the first two and a half years of its operation, the number of seventh-grade students in the first six junior high schools that it serves increased from 165 to 246; of eighth-graders taking college preparatory math, from 178 to 331; and of ninth-graders taking algebra, from 114 to 280. At the two high schools served by the program over the period, the number of tenth-grade students taking geometry rose from 36 to 83; of eleventh-graders taking advanced algebra/trigonometry, from 21 to 70; and of twelfth-graders taking precalculus, from 3 to 28. The numbers and proportions are still small: the increase in the students taking precalculus in the two twelfth grades represented a growth from 0.4 percent to 3.3 percent of those classes. But a beginning has been made; moreover, it has already become necessary for this university-based program to move down into the elementary schools in order to prepare larger proportions of students to enter the base of an expanding pyramid of on-track enrollments in mathematics in junior high and high school. It is only in that way, by starting in elementary school, that more students can be prepared to enter colleges and universities with an adequate background to begin college level mathematics.[27]

The CCPP is designed to strengthen the schools and the school district, to give them the ability to raise the quality and level of their own teaching of mathematics, and to sustain the level of work in that district after the university connection has been withdrawn. Many other programs are aimed at enriching the work of the school, at bringing students out of the school into other teaching environments, essentially bypassing the school and its limitations, or at creating cocoons, special protected environments in which a few selected students and teachers work with university staff members, insulated from the broader environment of the school. The CCPP has taken on the much bolder and more ambitious task of trying to make a substantial and permanent gain in the capacity of these schools and their district to solve their own problems. Many of those problems are not directly math related. But the program director and his staff have had to address those problems; they could hardly deal with the mathematics problems if they had not been prepared to do so. And high among those tasks is helping the school principals and vice-principals strengthen their leadership and management skills—for example, by helping them plan so that things work well on the very first day of school in the fall. If a school does not get off to a good start, if classes are not well organized and grouped, and if programs are not articulated, these management failures then take a very great toll in faculty morale and in the general school climate. The program assists school management in identifying academically talented students and developing appropriate course work for them; it helps to articulate the work of the junior high schools with the high schools, and of each course with the next. It creates conditions in which school people learn to talk to one another, and develops lines of communication between teachers and counselors, links that in many of these schools are inadequate. It also pays continued attention to the infrastructure of school management and administration. At the same time, the director of the program, through his work with the district superintendent and his staff, has gained a credibility and an authority that enable him to make suggestions about staffing, programmatic change, and the like—suggestions that are beginning to have effects throughout the district.

The role of parents in the program is interesting. Two from each participatory school are members of the Institute. As might be expected, they have become strong supporters of the program. And collectively, parents have political clout in the superintendent's office. The parents' representatives are crucial allies of the program; when one of the participating schools refused to send teachers or administrators to the Institute, the parents from that school who did go to meetings of the Institute complained loudly, and school officials changed their minds.

The success of this program, if it is achieved, will be the result not only of its goals and change agents—the CCPP staff, the coordinators, instructors, and mentors working in the schools and district office, the University-School Institute for planning and coordination, and so on. Behind these elements of the program, indeed of any successful program of this kind, is a dense mesh of relationships, developing and changing over time, between the program staff and the people in the schools and district office that the program is serving. The staff is not just giving advice and helping in the classrooms. It is also intervening at crucial points to call meetings, to initiate the discussion of problems leading to decisions, and then to help create the organizational machinery and arrangements that will ensure that something will actually happen to implement those decisions. That takes knowledge, skill, and time; substantial effects are not achieved through a few workshops. There is no quick fix for our schools.

But there are major problems in these outreach programs that bring university people into close and continuing relationships with school people. One problem lies in the difficulties of writing about these programs so that other university and school people around the country who have interests in developing similar projects can learn from the experience of those already in the field. It is not particularly difficult to describe the aims of such programs and their special treatment models or strategies. Nor is it difficult to report their record of achievement over time, whether it is measured by the growth of enrollments in on-track courses, the performance on achievement tests, or the number of students entering colleges or universities. The difficulty is in describing how the treatment models have whatever effect they do have. In addition to the ordinary problems of understanding complex social situations in the process of change, one here faces that of writing about the events and processes with truth and candor in ways that do not injure the people in the schools or deeply offend them. These outreach programs are likely to encounter school situations that are less than satisfactory, and teachers and administrators whose performance is less than adequate. The success of these programs is closely related to their ability to raise the quality of performance of some of these actors, to find ways of removing others, and to develop structures that bypass still others. The development of relationships of trust between the project staff and the people who make real decisions in the schools is a crucial part of the story. Paradoxically, though, to describe all this in detail and with candor is to threaten the very activities and relationships on which the whole enterprise is based.

I see no easy solution to this problem; indeed, only Americans believe that every problem has a solution. But if we are to learn more about how colleges and universities can serve to strengthen and not merely to enrich the schools, we will have to find ways of describing and analyzing those projects and programs that are in the field, and to do so with enough courage to report their failures and errors along with their successes.

The second problem such programs face arises out of the sharp differences that exist between universities and secondary schools, both as organizations and as cultural systems. The program that I have been sketching could not have achieved even its preliminary success if its director had not had ten years of experience in the school district that the program is serving, and as much knowledge of the culture of those schools as of the culture of the university that employs him. Barbara Nelson has described some of the differences in attitudes and values between MIT professors and the staff and teachers of a public high school in Boston with which it was linked.[28] The differences between big public universities and central-city high schools may be equally great. It is crucial that the university people engaged in these "outreach" programs know the culture of the schools, and not assume that the schools can and will adapt to the very different styles of life and work, conceptions of the nature of knowledge, and attitudes toward authority and rank, toward time, toward the use of scientific equipment, that characterize universities and university people.

Third, the broad-spectrum programs aimed at strengthening schools and school systems exist in the university alongside a very large number of other kinds of outreach programs, aimed at students and teachers in the schools, though in different ways. Many of these serve specific groups—physically handicapped students, recent immigrants from Asia, young musicians, and so on. But the tendency of programs to proliferate and overlap calls for some measure of central coordination within the university, so that outreach programs do not compete for the same clientele and resources. Even when an outside observer can see that different university-based programs are not competitive but potentially complementary and mutually supportive, the staffs of those programs often see their neighbors as threats to their own missions and budgets. Turf defense is a classic and perennial problem in large organizations, especially in an era of contracting resources. We have within the university what might be called the political problems of programmatic diversity.

Again, there is no general "solution" to the problem of coordinating many programs, each of which is (or fears it is) more or less temporary and in competition with similar programs for scarce resources. Senior administrators who oversee such programs have to find ways to encourage and reward cooperation between them, and that may require that the several project leaders and their staff members feel, and indeed be, relatively secure in their own areas of activity. Fear and anxiety encourage the defense of turf rather than the pursuit of programmatic goals. The bold and creative university programs that they and the secondary schools need also require rewards and encouragement from top university leadership, which people in the schools so rarely get from their own top leadership. If higher education aims to strengthen the capacities and leadership skills of the secondary schools, it must look first to its own.

Fourth, there is the question of how to staff these programs. Very commonly, remedial and outreach programs in universities use not regular "tenure-track" faculty but staff members who are not regular members of academic departments and do not belong to the academic senate or hold tenure. As these programs grow, there is danger of the emergence of a "subterranean university," cut off from the academic community, though providing vital academic services, and staffed by second-class citizens who over time come to resent the attitudes and privileges of the regular "tenure-track" faculty. These ancillary staff members may be recruited from and remain attached to the counterculture, and bring from it a hostility toward the very institutions for which they are presumably preparing undergraduate students. If the staff members of these remedial and outreach programs are not to be latent enemies of the institutions that employ them, they must have appropriate status and recognition, a measure of job security, and frequent interaction with regular faculty members. Even then, the uncertain funding of these programs, and the reluctance of many regular faculty members to become involved in them, almost ensures a measure of insulation of the programs and isolation of their staff members from the university as a whole.

What the nature of the relationships between higher education and secondary schools should be is a difficult and sensitive matter. In a relationship that has not, on the whole, been notably successful in the recent past, the clear need is to create a variety of connections and learn which are more and which are less successful.[29] Indeed, many different kinds of such ties already exist throughout the country. Some universities may enter into a very close association with one or more nearby high schools, accepting primary responsibility for their support and management, operating them as extended versions of the preparatory departments that were so common in the nineteenth century. Or a college or university may take on the guidance and supervision of the junior and senior years of a number of feeder high schools, perhaps those with special concern for college preparation. Alternatively, a university may want to develop links with high schools along disciplinary lines, developing ties between, say, its own math department and a number of high school math departments and, in those departments, with the math teachers who have the strongest professional interest in college preparatory work. Berkeley's various outreach programs offer a wide range of consultative services to the schools, all the way from assistance in strengthening the curriculum to sharing classroom instruction and advanced study groups before and after school and providing planning and management support for school administrators. We know that many high school teachers want more professional and collegial support, intellectual stimulation, and some relief from their heavy teaching loads within the confines of their own classrooms. The active interest of university faculty might be the catalyst that can create such professional communities in the high schools for the teachers of English or math or science whose interests run more toward college preparatory programs than toward remediation or vocational training.

The difficulties and pitfalls in any such relationships that cut across segmental lines are real. Nothing could be more destructive than an approach by academics as Lady Bountifuls bringing welfare baskets to their benighted brethren in the schools. Even when spared such insulting condescension, high school teachers may well respond to initiatives from the universities with the reply "Please don't help us just now; we haven't quite recovered from the last time." The well-intended interventions of experts of all kinds in recent decades have not on the whole made the life of ordinary high school teachers much easier or happier. Moreover, as I have noted, colleges and high schools are profoundly different kinds of institutions, governed by different norms and attitudes, marked by different institutional cultures. The differences in, for example, their attitudes toward time, rank, and knowledge all create unanticipated difficulties in the relations between academics and school people.

Despite all the problems and difficulties, though, both sides can gain much if the historic dividing lines between school and college are blurred and breached *selectively*, if those schools and school people who share concerns about academic work are brought more closely into touch with academics who have a genuine interest in the preparation of students in secondary schools. Establishing those links may begin to restore some of the rewards and status to secondary school teaching that it has lost, and may even help to retain in the schools those teachers with academic interests and talents who currently leave faster than they can be replaced.

But those links, in whatever form, should not be made solely or primarily through our schools of education. The problem of the underprepared student is a problem for a college or university as a whole. A school of education may have a natural interest in the sources of the difficulties of teaching and learning in the schools, and in remedies for them. And such a school may play a useful role in helping, through its research, illuminate the problems of the schools for an academic audience. But in the perennial tension between access and achievement, the schools of education on the whole have been a democratizing force, concerned more with the expansion of educational opportunity than with academic values. The actual institutional links between school and college must be with the university as a whole and with those academics and departments (including education) that have a special interest in the problems of articulation between high school and college.

In the United States, the close ties between upper secondary education and the colleges and universities were weakened by the growth of mass terminal secondary education between 1890 and 1940. During that half-century much of the authority exercised by the academic community over the schools, their curriculum, and their teachers was surrendered to professional educators, often the products of the schools and departments of education that had sprung up in public as well as private universities after the Civil War.[30] By contrast, in most European countries those ties were never wholly severed; the lycée, the gymnasium, and the British sixth form are still the institutional forms that the university takes in secondary education. These schools are in one way or another selective, not least for motivation; they are intensive and demanding both in the level of effort they require and in the content of their academic work, which is oriented toward an examination—the *Abitur*, the *baccalauréat*, the A-level exams—which is the universities' screening mechanism for entry into the university. Most important, their teachers are essentially academics, trained in the universities for which they prepare their students.

We in the United States are not likely to create a system of selective public secondary schools (though we should cherish the ones that have survived), and we have our own traditions of articulation between school and college stemming from the old academies, the preparatory departments of the colleges, and the college preparatory tracks of public high schools. If we can reestablish such links and create new ones, we may contribute materially to the college preparatory work of the high schools. We still need our statements of expectation, clearly articulated and widely communicated to schools and students and parents, as well as the costly and difficult remedial work in the universities and colleges. Universities have little influence on the level of funding of education, which so greatly affects the recruitment of teachers. But universities may be able to help the schools themselves—their organization, curriculum, and staff. If we can improve those aspects of secondary education, we might actually see the effects on our entering freshmen.

We should not underestimate the costs and difficulties of such an effort, not least of determining who in the university will actually reach out and establish the links with the high schools and their staffs. But these links are being forged now; we need to learn more about what is happening and how these efforts can be improved and extended. That may be the greatest service we can perform for the secondary schools, for their college-bound students, and ultimately for ourselves in the colleges and universities.

The continuing crisis of secondary education will require public colleges and universities to play a larger role in the preparation of students for college level work. But apart from clarifying and disseminating our expectations for college entrance, the other functions that we can serve are in varying degrees expensive, and each has its costs and dangers to our central mission of advanced teaching and research. We have no choice but to do more to raise the level of preparation of our entering students. But we must keep in mind what it is they are being prepared for. If we do not find and keep the right balance, if we allow our remedial roles and services to grow without constraint, then we may find our colleges and universities surrendering the very qualities that have enabled them to respond quickly and effectively to the crisis of American secondary education. Our enormously successful system of mass higher education has been both a cause of and a compensation for the weakness of the college preparatory role of our junior and senior high schools. It would indeed be a tragic irony if our colleges and universities went the way of the high schools in the course of trying to remedy their deficiencies.

11

The Problem with Competence

NATHAN GLAZER

A modest aim, increasing the average level of competence in educational tasks of America's youth, runs up against a peculiarly difficult, indeed intractable, problem. This is not to suggest that nothing can be done—in the conclusion I will suggest what, in view of the intractabilities I will outline—but it is to suggest that the enormous recent outpouring of reports, and the massive amount of work being done by state educational boards and commissions, will result in much less than we expect. Many reasons will be given by various analysts on the basis of their own special insights. But one overwhelming reason appears to me decisive, and that is the substantial differences in levels of educational achievement by race and ethnic group that now exist in the United States and that can be expected to exist for some time. The demand for competence meets as a first barrier the fact that different percentages of key ethnic and racial groups achieve different levels of competency. In a society reaching for equality, despite the recent shift in our concerns about quality, this is a difficult problem indeed.

I do not use as our objective "excellence." This is a peculiar term for an objective in education, or in any other social policy affecting a large and varied population. It was the National Commission on Excellence in Education that issued the most publicized and important of the reports urging a modest increase in competence.[1] Another of the recent education reports also uses the term. I hope it will be replaced by the more modest term, and objective, of competence. To speak of "excellence" in education is to speak, necessarily and unless we insist on distorting language, of peaks of achievement: Nobel Prize winners. The best school.

The best secondary school. The best college. Inevitably excellence implies distinction, the greatest distinction. But the greatest distinction cannot be uniform among a large population, unless one blinds oneself to the differences within it. When a substantial crowd is given the degree summa cum laude at a college, one knows that yet another and higher distinction is necessary in order to communicate what must be a differential range of achievement. One hundred people do not reach a summit. If they do, a higher summit whose scaling represents a higher achievement will be set. The history of the use of the term *excellence* would make an interesting essay. Its entry into this discussion can be dated from John Gardner's 1961 book *Excellence*.[2] But Gardner's aim was not really excellence: it was raising the level of achievement of a large number of students, particularly black and other minorities, who were achieving poorly. The aim was, in my view, not excellence but competence, a decent objective and yet one that we seem to have enough difficulty in reaching.

The use of *excellence* had the effect, even if not the intention, of eliciting exaggerated praise for modest achievements. The praiser understands, one likes to think, that the praised really has not done all that much, but hopes that his enthusiastic approval will spur the praised on to greater efforts. The praised, however, may misunderstand the praise as indicating really superior achievement—"excellent!"—but if young and in a continuous process of education will soon understand where he or she stands in relation to others. The danger is that in a situation in which almost everyone is engaged in giving praise, the student will never understand that even mere competence, let alone excellence, is a difficult achievement requiring substantial work.*

So, then, *competence:* the ability to read and write with some accuracy and celerity; the ability to fill out an employment questionnaire; the ability to read a newspaper, and the political news in it; the ability to calculate moderately accurately, to add, subtract, divide, and multiply, to take a percentage, to understand a fraction and the relation between a percentage and a fraction. One hesitates to propose that we include in competence algebra and geometry, even though every state in the union demands education to the age of sixteen, or some two years of high school, during which, traditionally, these elements of mathematics were

---

* I cannot forbear mentioning another case of the depreciation of language: the use of the term *genius* for those who win MacArthur awards. In the first set of awards, one could set aside one's doubts about one or another grantee: perhaps the mysterious process of selection and choice had discerned talents one was not aware of. By the time the fifth distribution rolled around, one could no longer do this, and even the newpapers were putting *genius* in quotation marks.

taught. The ability to read a graph, directions. Some modest knowledge of the formal aspects of government, of the key events in American and world history. Some knowledge of elementary science (once again, scarcely physics or chemistry). I have a very modest definition of competence. It consists of the skills that permit one to be a delivery boy, a mailman, a clerk, and the female equivalents. It turns out that many American youths, despite ten years of compulsory education, do not achieve these modest levels of competence.

The reports that came out in such profusion during 1983 did not consider the college or university level. Conceivably there are many failures there, as well. Too many Americans study business, too few engineering and the hard sciences, but one can, it seems, count on the signals of the market to some extent to make adjustments.[3]

The issues that concerned the commissions and the reports were further down the line: at the level of the elementary school and the high school, and quite properly. If the great education fright of 1957 was that the Russians were doing better at putting objects into space—and that called for attention to science and mathematics at higher levels, support of advanced college and graduate studens who had already achieved a high level of competence, and more—the great education fright of 1983 focused on Japan. Japan produces very few Nobel Prize winners in science as yet, but it is awesomely efficient at producing very good automobiles, television sets, computers, cameras, and a variety of other kinds of sophisticated hardware that require very competent workers. Our concern in 1983 was not that American military technology would not remain the best in the world—it probably would—but that American soldiers would not be competent enough to know how to use and repair the equipment. It was that American workers did not seem able to turn out a bus that did not fall apart, a subway car that did not malfunction, automobiles that could compete with those from Japan and Germany. It was embarrassing that the United States had to go to Japan and Canada and France and Hungary for its mass transportation equipment and had to control the number of Japanese automobiles Americans wished to buy.

The explanations for American failure in international competition were legion, and perhaps education had little to do with it. Perhaps the arcane analyses of rates of saving and investment, as affected by levels and types of taxes, or the equally arcane proposals of how to get good management, explained a great deal of what was going wrong with the American capacity to compete. But a large number of people thought it had something to do with American education. Indeed, it is revealing that the movement to raise levels of competence by testing teachers, by requiring exit examinations from high school, by raising requirements for college—and all through 1983 and the first months of 1984 one saw story after story from state after state on what we might call the competency movement—was inspired not by the search for "excellence" but by the fear of declining levels of competence.[4]

The movement for competency exams, exit tests, and teacher testing was not, obviously, a movement led by teachers; nor was it a movement led by educators and theorists of education. They desperately sought to stem a popular demand for competency, insisting that the tests were being misused, or that emphasizing tests would distort teaching, or that education meant more than cognitive competence, and that all these other elements were being ignored in the mad rush in the states to raise the level of literacy and numeracy. The experts were ignored, though they did slow and affect the movement somewhat. This was a movement of the ordinary nonexperts. Whatever the more sophisticated explanations, they knew that too many youngsters coming out of high school as graduates or dropouts did not have the competence necessary for ordinary tasks: and they ignored totally the education establishment in designing what measures they thought might redress the situation.

The contrast with 1957 could not be more striking. Then attention was directed at the highest reaches of education and of achievement. In 1983 it was directed at the lowest. In between these two drives for greater competence, there was another education furor: we seem to have almost forgotten it, yet the issue to which it was addressed is the stumbling block that will lay this new drive for competence in ruins unless we can find ways to address it. It is the issue of the educational deficit of blacks and some other minority groups, but in particular blacks.

I concentrate in this article on the impact that competence tests will have on blacks. That is where the main problem of low scores is found. One cannot speak of a *general* minority problem in achieving minimum competence. The educational debate often lumps blacks with Hispanics, but the term *Hispanics* covers a multitude of ethnic groups, and there is no reason to expect any special problem in educational achievement for some of them, such as Cubans, descendants of immigrants from Spain, immigrants from some Latin American countries south of Mexico. The two large groups of Hispanics with special educational problems are Mexican Americans and Puerto Ricans. These problems seem in part to be related to language and to the rate at which students acquire competence in English. Undoubtedly the special problems of many Mexican Americans and Puerto Ricans in education are serious and should be addressed. But there is no such thing as a general minority problem in education. As is well known, some minorities (e.g., immigrants from

Asia) do not have problems in getting high scores on tests, particularly tests of competence in mathematics and science. Indeed, the success of these groups raises sharply the question of why they do so much better not only than long-settled American minorities but also than the majority of American whites. The minority problem in education is overwhelmingly, though by no means exclusively, a problem of blacks. It is also blacks who, because of slavery and the legal enforcement of minority status for a century after slavery, quite properly make the most powerful claim on American conscience and pose most strongly to policymakers the need—for political, historical, and moral reasons—to raise levels of educational achievement.

The great educational drive of the mid-1960s and early 1970s was addressed in the largest sense to the gap in educational achievement between blacks and whites. And in the largest sense it was a failure. The Civil Rights Act of 1964 banned segregation in school systems receiving federal assistance—modest at the time. The Elementary and Secondary Education Act increased greatly the flow of federal funds to public school systems and became the club whereby segregation was overcome in the southern states. Federal aid to local school districts, the fulfillment of a movement that had been checked for many years by the refusal of congress to support segregated school systems, became aid for poor children when it emerged as enacted legislation—and poor children were going to be in large measure black and minority children. This is not the place to analyze the failure of these programs to make much headway in overcoming the huge differences in educational achievement between blacks and whites. These differences were documented by an enormous report, *Equality of Educational Opportunity,* in 1966.[5] The report showed how serious the problem of overcoming these gaps would be. It demonstrated that black students did worse than minority students with language handicaps. It demonstrated that the differences in achievement increased with years of education. It demonstrated that no simple relation between sums spent on education and achievement could explain the differences and that therefore no substantial increase in expenditure, or at least any increase within the realm of political possibility, would do much to overcome it. Even though enormous changes did take place in reducing the difference in the years of education received by blacks and whites in the later 1960s and 1970s, the differences in achievement persisted. By the early 1980s blacks were receiving almost as much education as whites, attending institutions of higher and post-secondary education in numbers not far short of those for whites. Yet this gap closing was deceptive, if one considered the content of education received and real achievement. Blacks entered the less demanding institutions (such as community colleges) disproportionately, and the less demanding fields of specialization, such as education and social science. In highly selective institutions, the numbers of blacks were kept up through special recruiting efforts, programs to provide tutoring or summer instruction, or the acceptance of blacks whose grades and scores would not normally have gained them admission.

The federal commitment to desegregation established in 1964 with the Civil Rights Act has, with all its ups and downs, continued. There is no longer today any publicly imposed segregation. There is a heritage of historically black and white institutions of higher education in the South, and a problem of high concentrations of students by race caused by residential concentrations in the central cities, which is not segregation in the sense of 1954, or 1964, at all.

The flow of federal funds to improve the education of poor children began in 1965 and reached a substantial volume in the 1970s. By 1974, no less than $363 of Title I ESEA funds was available for each eligible pupil; by 1978 , $421. This was a considerable federal effort, when compared with the average spent at the time for each pupil in U.S. public schools, which was $2,000. Other programs (education for the handicapped, Emergency School Aid Assistance, vocational education, bilingual education) added other funds that were directed in large measure to poor children.[6]

In the early 1980s, there was considerable discouragement over the effects of this fifteen-year effort in closing the gap between black and white achievement. A modest ray of hope was signaled only in 1982.[7] But because of this continuing gap any effort to apply a standard of competency across the board means that more blacks must fail. Whether we apply that standard to competency tests for high school diplomas, or exit examinations from high school, or math and science requirements for entry into college, or requirements for higher SAT scores for entry into college, or law school or medical school admission tests, or requirements for entry into graduate programs of any kind, or minimal qualifications for teachers, or qualifications such as the Ph.D. for college teachers—wherever we try to apply a standard we can be sure, with the present distribution of testable capacities, that more, considerably more, blacks than whites will fail. The implications of such a certain outcome have not been sufficiently considered.

This reality affects every effort to raise achievement, even one so modest as the attempt to impose minimal academic qualifications for college athletes. The minimal standards proposed to permit athletes to play were very low indeed. The problem was that a disproportionate number of black athletes, particularly in black colleges, would have become ineligible.

Consider one effort to raise the quality of teachers, in Georgia: "A newly released five-year summary of Georgia's teaching-testing program reveals . . . only 34 per cent of black students passed it on the first try, compared with 87 per cent of white students. . . . State officials said that great care was taken, when the test was developed, to avoid racial bias. . . . Other states with teacher testing programs have had similar experiences with disproportionately low numbers of minority candidates passing the examinations. In Florida, results form a similar certification test, released early this year, showed that 35 per cent of the black candidates passed on the first try, compared with 90 percent of the white candidates. . . ."[8]

The issue exists not only in the South. The gaps may be somewhat less in the North, but New York and Illinois will, we can be sure, show the same problem as Georgia and Florida. With the same inevitable results: there will be suits to put aside the tests as discriminatory, and, in the present state of the law, we have good grounds for believing they will be so put aside.[9]

The barriers to using minimum competency tests for teachers come not only from the courts. The Educational Testing Service itself resists the use of its National Teacher Examination to evaluate teachers already employed. It asserts that this would be a misuse of a test. Why a test designed for entering teachers would be misused if used for teachers already in service is not immediately clear. The president of the ETS, Gergory Anrig, said that "classroom supervision and other evaluation techniques" were available to "assess those essential qualities of teaching competence, in addition to academic knowledge, that cannot be measured effectively by any paper-and-pencil examination—qualities such as dedication, sensitivity, perseverance, caring."[10]

The explanation does not really hold water. It is true there are many important teacher qualities that cannot be measured by a pen-and-pencil test. But the concern of parents and businessmen is that students are being taught by teachers who cannot spell properly or do not write grammatically, or do not know simple arithmetic and grade-school mathematics, and these concerns can indeed be addressed by paper-and-pencil tests. The issue raised by the ETS action is a larger one that the explanation does not reach: we see a general refusal to face the size of the problem because of the fear that facing it will occasion the charge of racism. It seems safer to refuse to find out the size of the gap between black and white.

Teacher competency is properly seen as a key point of leverage for establishing competency among students. Tests are not the only way to promote teacher competency. One may make great play with tests, regardless of which side of the dispute one is on. Those who oppose them can point out ambiguities in the answers considered correct. Those who support them can point out how simple they are. It is very difficult politically for teachers to argue that tests are unfair to them: parents want to be assured that teachers at least know what is right, even before knowing the degrees of their sensitivity, understanding, empathy, caring qualities, or other valued psychological traits. Tests are certainly one way of excluding the truly incompetent. Nevertheless, the fact that radically different proportions of white and black will achieve whatever passing grade is set will raise grave barriers to their use.

One of the points made in considering the crisis caused by high black teacher failure rates in tests for teachers is that they have attended inadequate colleges, which have not taught them properly.[11] Why not, then, try to raise the standards for college education? There is no strong demand that colleges test graduates for competency. But colleges are increasingly requiring a more solid high school education for entering students. That, too, comes up against the reality that black and Hispanic students characteristically avoid the courses in mathematics and sciences that are now being required by state boards of high school students for admission to college. Commission members who are fifty or sixty years old remember when standard requirements for college admissions included two and a half years of mathematics, two of science, four of English, two of history, three years of one foreign language, two years of another. This was long before driver training and marriage and family living were credit courses in high school taken by large numbers. It therefore seems reasonable to them to reestablish this level of academic work for college admission. Once again, the problem is, as in teacher competency tests, differential impact by race.

Thus, the New York State Board of Regents, the most powerful state education board in the country, went further than most. It proposed two years of mathematics, two of science, four of social studies, and proficiency in a foreign language by the end of grade nine. For the Regents diploma, a more prestigious one and the one that was characteristically taken by students aiming for college in the days before open admission, it added an additional year of math or science and three years of a foreign language. Such requirements would make hash of the City University of New York's Open Admission program, already substantially modified by economic crisis. They would exclude students with vocational, arts, and music specializations. But they would also exclude large numbers of black and Puerto Rican students. The Board of Regents had clearly overreached itself in trying to reestablish the requirements of a few decades before.[12] Issues of competency apart, the mere requirement to *take* two years of mathematics or science would disproportionately exclude black students from the benefits of diploma or college admission, if such were the requirements.

Consider: the National Assessment of Educational Progress reports that 37 percent of all black students took only one math course, compared with 24 percent of all white students; that only 13 percent took three math courses, compared with 32 percent of whites. Math requirements for diploma or college admission mean that fewer blacks can qualify.[13]

Lucy W. Sells has given perhaps the most impressive demonstration of the seriousness of the problem. Her major interest is in the under-enrollment of women in math and science and the impact this has upon their job opportunities, but her studies also deal with minorities. A study in a Northern California high school in a district "with a long commitment to equal opportunity" shows the familiar pattern. In this school, there are three types of mathematics courses, which in effect serve as tracks. One is for those who need remedial courses, which she labels the "Off the College Track." None of the courses taken in this track (remedial math, applied math, consumer math) serve for admission to the University of California system. A second, which she labels the "Terminal Track," provides the minimal math required for admission to the University of California. It precludes access to freshman calculus. The third, the "Calculus Track," enables students to enter college mathematics.

The figures are as follows:

Race	Off the college track	Terminal track	Calculus track	Total	Number
Asian	4%	17%	79%	100%	218
White	5%	23	72	100%	1,239
Hispanic	31%	44	25	100%	59
Black	34%	47	20	100%	1,016
All students	17%	32%	51%	100%	2,532

These findings are worth pondering because in this district we find perhaps the greatest level of commitment to, and the greatest achievement of, minority students in California, in a state in which, proportionately, as Sells demonstrates, many more students go on to advanced mathematics than even in a progressive southern state like North Carolina.[14]

The critics of the rising tide of new high school requirements as a prerequisite for graduation and entry to college have a point, though it is not the point they emphasize. In their frequent attempts to prevent these new requirements from coming into effect through litigation, their major resort must be to the claim of discrimination: black students are being unfairly treated, either because the tests are racially biased or because the black students who are taking them attended segregated schools. The first claim is generally nonsense: tests of numeracy can scarcely be racially biased. Tests of reading comprehension and spelling are often attacked for bias, but the claims are exaggerated and far-fetched, and even so these tests are under continuous revision to remove possible bias. The claim that black students received an inferior education because they attended segregated schools—or for some other reason—is better founded. This was the basis for the extended *Debra P. v. Turlington* litigation in Florida, against Florida's high school exit exam, and for some time a federal judge suspended its operation on this basis. The most recent decision in the case, however, perhaps influenced by the rising wave of competency requirements, accepts the Florida test on the ground that students who must take it have now received all their education in integrated schools.

All emphasis in the competency movement is now being placed at the high school graduation level—exit tests from high school, minimal high school course requirements for college entry. But the problem begins long before high school. The gap in achievement begins at the beginning of school experience, and widens thereafter, though there has been some lessening of the gap in recent years. This is not to say that high school remediation cannot overcome it, but presumably the more effective place to reach the deficiency is in elementary school, which has escaped much recent reform vigor, largely because we do not have such radical evidence of inadequacy as that demonstrated by the decline in SAT scores and the experience of employers of high school graduates and dropouts. Nevertheless it would be a mistake to emphasize high school alone as the stretch of education in which such deficiencies can be overcome. They rest on a base of weakness in literacy and numeracy that it is the proper function of the elementary school to cure.

We have pointed to problems in teacher testing in high school requirements, exit testing, and increased college requirements. At the far end of the educational chain, the gap shows up in its most striking form. Neglected in much of the discussion that ranged around the landmark *Bakke* decision was a sobering table in Justice Powell's majority opinion that described graphically the problem that a medical school like that of the University of California at Davis faced in recruiting a substantial number of non-Asian minority students.

"The following table," Justice Powell wrote, "compares Bakke's . . . MCAT scores with the average scores of regular admittees and of special admittees in both 1973 and 1974." [15]

	Class entering in 1973			
	MCAT (percentiles)			
	Verbal	Quantitative	Science	General Information
Bakke	96	94	97	72
Average of regular admittees	81	76	83	69
Average of special admittees	46	24	35	33
	Class entering in 1974			
Bakke	96	94	97	72
Average of regular admittees	69	67	82	72
Average of special admittees	34	30	37	18

The gap is truly startling. Whatever the deficiencies of these tests, they must in some way relate to knowledge of science and quantitative skills, which are not very difficult to test and which all agree are important for the student physician. Doctors may manage with fewer verbal skills, but even these are important for explaining symptoms and reporting or understanding findings. The family doctor in particular must choose words carefully and subtly. Whatever one may say—and one may say a great deal—for using a more relaxed standard in order to recruit a larger number of black and minority candidates into medical schools, this degree of relaxation seems excessive. Had the differences in percentile scores been of the order of 10 or 20 rather than 35 or more, it is possible there would not have been a *Bakke* case. The fact that the admissions committee had to reach so far down into the pool of potential medical students indicates how radical the deficiencies in academic skills of aspiring black and non-Asian minority students are.

One could tell a similar story for law school admissions tests. Once again, the tests can be attacked. It is easier to criticize law school than medical school tests, for there is little disagreement over the need for medical students to have a base of scientific knowledge. A very extended attack on the LSAT has been launched by the National Conference of Black Lawyers, and its analysis does score some points against the test makers. Test makers are often prissy in insisting that one answer and one alone is correct.[16] Yet there is no reason to believe that changes in how tests are constructed and scored would help blacks. And even if one were to succeed in removing the burden of the LSAT, one would have to face the subsequent burden of the state tests for admission to the bar, in which blacks do poorly and which are also under legal attack.

It is easy to attack tests: the question is whether there is an alternative. Tests correlate roughly with some kind of ability. Even if it is not the ability to be a concerned family doctor, or to be an effective trial lawyer, the qualities tested for are reasonably important for the professions in question, and are in any case the only qualities that can be tested. To attempt to introduce other qualities means to depend on the uncertain outcomes of interviews and other kinds of qualitative assessment. At one time these were considered biased against blacks and other minorities—which is one reason why tests became so important. It is possible now that interviewers and assessors, understanding the crucial political and social importance of larger numbrs of blacks in key positions, would favor blacks. Critics of tests sometimes talk as if they have greater trust in sympathetic judgments by whites of black capacities than in objective measures.

There is much to be said for placing less emphasis on tests in schools, more emphasis on observation and on samples of work. Whether blacks would do better with such approaches to selection is indeed a good question. If they would, we should count this as one advantage to moving to other bases of selection. It is true that tests offer the benefit of greater objectivity, and lesser cost, but these should not stand in the way of methods of selection that seem generally as useful and have the further benefit of not penalizing blacks and non-Asian minorities.

But it is questionable whether such forms of selection are available. They are easier to institute for the selection of jobs than for further academic work. Academic work does depend on academic skills, and objective tests are rather better measures of these than observation is. It is true that if one is selecting for professional education for fields in which science and writing ability are not as important as they are in medicine and law, it should be possible to reduce reliance on tests. The school superintendent, the social worker, the business executive, needs a variety of skills, and may manage well with lesser competence in the kind of abilities that SATs, MCATs, and LSATs test. Indeed, it is my impression that, in the selection for admission to such programs, tests do count for less, and skills and recommendations—which penalize blacks less—do count for more. But even in professional training for professions that do not require strong quantitative and writing skills, the academic work itself is inevitably . . . academic. For example, one may see candidates for an administrative program in education who might do quite well in the posts such a program leads to, but the academic skills are so low that one may have serious doubts whether the candidate can get through the program.

There is some, but not much, opportunity to increase black representation in professions that are now heavily based on strong academic skills by a shift from testing. In any case, such an approach would work only for some professional programs. When it comes to exit exams from high school, admission exams for college, or college requirements that insist on math and science courses, there is no alternative to improving academic skills.

The attack on testing seeks an alternative to testing. There is no clear alternative for the high school exit and college entrance level. Despite this, the attack proceeds. There is a certain amount of hypocrisy in this attack. The critics of testing do not say directly that they think the qualities being tested are unimportant: rather, they attack the tests as discriminatory because more blacks fail them. But there are no alternatives in the form of *tests* that can be used to replace present tests. We have seen in certain cases (for example, tests for police officer or fireperson) tests ruled out by courts again and again as discriminatory, and their replacements also ruled out as discriminatory, until no test is considered suitable, and direct employment by racial quota is instituted.

This seems the unstated but clear objective of the attack on testing. If no alternative test is satisfactory—and no one can guarantee that a meaningful test can be devised that will select the same proportions of whites, blacks, Hispanics, Mexican Americans, Chinese Americans, Japanese Americans, Indian Americans, and so on—tests are subject to legal attack as discriminatory. This may or may not lead to the test's being set aside, or to a lower passing score's being set for blacks; it depends on the judge and the case, and the Supreme Court refuses to give clear guidance. But despite doubts as to what the law is, one thing is clear: if the replacement of tests by quotas becomes general, if this is to be sought as the solution to the problem of black underachievement, it will create—in a measure it has created—a two-class system in education in which it is taken for granted that blacks lack the ability to succeed in fair competition.

One can envisage such an approach becoming general: passing and admission scores' being set lower for blacks than for whites (and raising the unwelcome question of what to do about groups, such as Asian, that characteristically get more than their "proper" share). We have been debating this problem under the general rubric of "affirmative" action for fifteen years or more, and we have still not reached a general solution. Other countries have gone that route—India in an effort to increase the numbers of scheduled castes and tribes in higher education, Malaysia in an effort to increase the number of Malays in higher education. The general result is extensive doubt as to the quality of the group aided in this manner. This approach does not reduce faith in tests (which is generally higher in other countries than in the United States). Rather, it reduces faith in those who enter selective institutions of higher education and competitive occupations from the aided group. This is not what blacks want, and such a general solution to the problem of black underachievement might be as severe a disaster for good race relations as the continuance of the present low proportions of blacks in selective institutions and competitive occupations.[17]

The one alternative that could achieve general acceptance is an honest effort to raise black achievement, in the belief that this is possible. It is an effort that must begin at the beginning. It must make use of all the varied experiments we have tried in the last twenty years. A few of them have had some success. It requires undoubtedly greater financial resources for the education of blacks. This need not be invidious: greater resources for the education of central-city poor children today generally means greater resources for the education of black and Hispanic children. How to spend these resources is not a simple matter: a mere across-the-board increase does not assure any improvement. One could raise teachers' salaries across the board with no change—at least not in any measurable time—in the achievement of black children. One can multiply the number of personnel in ineffective ways—more administrators, more specialists drawing up grant proposals, more accountants keeping track of different sources of money, more lawyers arguing over the legitimacy of expenditures, and so on. The way federal money has flowed to urban school districts has not been terribly efficient. There are many reasons for this: congressional insistence on special authorization, appropriations and regulations for scores or hundreds of programs to be kept distinct; conflicts between contradictory objectives (Keep all the children together so they can educate each other? Pull out the Title I recipients so it is unarguable that Title I aid is targeted on them alone?); political conflicts in local districts over the best way to spend money; ideologists in Washington insisting exclusively on one or another approach, as in the case of bilingual education. It would be hard now, on the basis of the evidence, to argue that the federal contribution has hurt poor children, somewhat easier to argue that it has been responsible for some marginal improvement. But the price has been excessive. It has been pointlessly expensive in administrative time and costs. Paul Peterson quotes research by J. Meyer to the effect that "each new dollar or federal funds creates nine times the increase in administrative personnel that each new dollar of local money creates." Peterson estimated that increased administrative costs to public schools from this source may have amounted to $500 million in 1977–78.[18]

I believe the greatest effort, the greatest investment, must be at the level of elementary education. By the time high school is reached, the foundations for further education have been set or not. The administrators and superintendents and principals and educationists now protesting in vain against the requirement that high school students must take two years of math, two of science, three of a foreign language, and the rest, are right, even if they have not yet given a forceful and persuasive explanation of their objections. They are right because they know it is out of the question for many of the students who enter their high schools conceivably to undertake studies for which they have no preparation, of which they have no understanding, for which they have no incentive.

This is not the place to propose a program for the elementary schools, and I am not capable of proposing one. The one thing that seems undeniable is that we do not have a formula to impose. Many things that have been tried in the past fifteen years show some promise. Many things we have done we know were foolish and, if anything, contributed to poorer education. In a situation where no formula exists, one must accept diversity: private schools, independent schools, community-run schools, principal authority, teacher authority, community involvement, all of which must inevitably mean diversity of approaches.

The tests can be used to inform how the different approaches are working. But if they are to serve this function the unremitting attack on testing and its legitimacy—an attack in which not all black parents, I believe, join—must come to an end. One cannot know how one is doing if one refuses to accept any measure as legitimate. The educationists, in their fear that they will never be able to bring the black children up to snuff, insist that there are all those wonderful other things in education—sensitivity, caring—that they are doing, and on this ground they sometimes join in the attack on testing They should desist. First of all, it is doubtful they are any better at achieving the untestable objectives than the testable ones. Second, all these wonderful qualities will be to no effect if numeracy and literacy are not present.

Competency tests at this point designed for everyone are, alas, somewhat beside the point. To protect colleges and universities and to provide them with prepared students, it is reasonable to propose stronger requirements for college admission. But then we must be prepared to accept the fact that we will see a reduction in the number of blacks and Hispanics eligible for college entry. We can hope that this reduction occurs only for a while. If it is unaccompanied by substantial measures that truly educate larger numbers of minorities, these new requirements will simply not survive. No court will allow them; no politically prescient elected official could defend them; American society generally would not be willing to accept the consequences of such requirements now. And quite properly. We can raise the required levels of competency only if we simultaneously attack, on a scale and with an effectiveness we have not yet been able to muster, the educational problems of blacks.

Notes

1. Four Surprises, or Why the Schools May Not Improve Much

1. National Commission on Excellence in Education, *A Nation at Risk: The Imperative for Educational Reform* (Washington, D.C.: Government Printing Office, 1983).
2. James S. Coleman, Thomas Hoffer, and Sally Kilgore, *High School Achievement: Public, Catholic, and Private Schools Compared* (New York: Basic Books, 1982).
3. Harold Stevenson, "The Educational Achievement of American, Japanese and Taiwanese Elementary School Students," mimeographed (Univ. of Michigan, 1984).
4. Stanford Univ. News Service, Aug. 17, 1983.
5. An upbeat but far more evenhanded view of the schools can be found in the *Time* cover story of Oct. 10, 1983.
6. Anne Remley, "The Push for Rigor," Ann Arbor *Observer*, Sept. 1983.
7. Walter Goodman, "Some Intellectuals See Conservatism as Ominous," New York *Times*, Feb. 1, 1984. Howe is reported to have said, "The very word 'excellence' ought to make us cringe a little, so thoroughly has it been assimilated to the prose styles of commission reports, letters of recommendation and hair spray commercials." He also said that *excellence* was a code word for "educational Reaganism." Phyllis Franklin, a functionary of the Modern Language Association, said that the commission reports, in the words of the story, "treated the humanities in images drawn from the marketplace and the military," a truly astonishing assertion.
8. Herbert J. Walberg, "We Can Raise Standards," *Educational Leadership*, Oct. 1983, pp. 4–6.
9. Herbert J. Walberg, "Synthesis of Research on Teaching," in *Handbook of*

233

Research on Teaching, ed. M. C. Wittrock (Washington, D.C.: American Educational Research Association, 1983).

2. A Strategy for Revitalizing Public Education

1. Denis P. Doyle, *Debating National Education Policy: The Question of Standards* (Washigton, D.C.: American Enterprise Institute, 1981), 7.
2. Paraphrased from Vincent Ostrom, *The Intellectual Crisis in American Public Administration* (Tuscaloosa: Univ. of Alabama Press, 1973), 28–29.
3. David B. Tyack, *The One Best System* (Cambridge, Mass.: Harvard Univ. Press, 1974), 14.
4. Jonathan P. Sher, ed., *Education in Rural America: A Reassessment of Conventional Wisdom* (Boulder, Colo.: Westview Press, 1977), 24.
5. Ibid.
6. Ibid.
7. James B. Conant, *The American High School* (New York: McGraw-Hill), 1959.
8. Edgar L. Morphet, Roe L. Johns, and Theodore L. Reller, *Educational Administration: Concepts, Practices, and Issues* (Englewood Cliffs, N.J.: Prentice-Hall, 1959), 226.
9. See ibid., see chap. 10, for a good outline of this approach to school district politics and administration.
10. National Center for Education Statistics, *Digest of Education Statistics, 1981,* comp. W. Vance Grant and Leo J. Eiden (Washington, D.C.: Government Printing Office, 1981), 65.
11. Ibid., 64.
12. Werner Hirsch, "Determinants of Public Education Expenditures," *National Tax Journal,* 13 (March 1960), 39.
13. William Niskanen and Mickey Levy, "Choosing the Structure of Local Governments" (Unpublished MS).
14. Roger G. Barker and Paul V. Gump, *Big School, Small School* (Stanford: Stanford Univ. Press, 1964).
15. Sher, *Education in Rural America,* 64.
16. Niskanen and Levy, "Choosing the Structure."
17. NCES, *Digest of Education Statistics, 1981,* 75.
18. Marsha Levine and Denis P. Doyle, "Private Meets Public: An Examination of Contemporary Education," in *Meeting Human Needs: Toward a New Public Philosophy,* Jack A. Meyer ed. (Washington, D.C.: American Enterprise Institute, 1982), 286.
19. American Enterprise Institute, "Are Public Schools Making the Grade?" *Public Opinion,* 4, no. 5 (Oct.–Nov. 1981), 21–26.
20. Robert Nozick, *Anarchy, State, and Utopia* (New York: Basic Books, 1974), xi.
21. Alexander Hamilton, "Federalist One," *The Federalist Papers,* ed. Jacoby E. Cooke (Middletown, Conn.: Wesleyan Univ. Press, 1961), 3.
22. James S. Coleman, Thomas Hoffer, and Sally Kilgore, *High School Achievement: Public, Catholic, and Private Schools Compared* (New York: Basic Books, 1982).
23. John I. Goodlad, *A Place Called School: Prospects for the Future* (New York: McGraw-Hill, 1983), 310.
24. Ibid., 309.

25. Amitai Etzioni, "The Role of Self Discipline," *Phi Delta Kappan*, 64 (Nov. 1982), 185.

26. Goodlad, *A Place Called School*, 275.

27. Prepared testimony of Sen. Leroy Greene, California State Senate, Sacramento.

28. Diane Ravitch, "On Thinking about the Future," *Phi Delta Kappan*, 64 (Jan. 1983), 319.

29. Goodlad, *A Place Called School*, 274.

30. Jessica Shaten and Ted Kolderie, *Contracting with Teacher Partnerships* (Sacramento: Sequoia Institute, 1984).

31. Goodlad, *A Place Called School*, 189–90.

32. Ibid., 276.

3. Changing Our Thinking about Educational Change

1. National Commission on Excellence in Education, *A Nation at Risk: The Imperative for Educational Reform* (Washington, D.C.: Government Printing Office, 1983).

2. Ernest L. Boyer, *High School: A Report on Secondary Education in America* (New York: Harper & Row, 1983).

3. John I. Goodlad, *A Place Called School: Prospects for the Future* (New York: McGraw-Hill, 1983).

4. Mortimer Jerome Adler, *The Paideia Proposal* (New York: Macmillan, 1982).

5. College Entrance Examination Board, *Academic Preparation for College: What Students Need to Know and Be Able to Do* (New York: College Board, 1983).

6. *Report of the Twentieth Century Fund Task Force on Federal Elementary and Secondary Education Policy* (New York: Twentieth Century Fund, 1983).

7. National Science Board Commission on Precollege Education in Mathematics, Science and Technology. *Educating Americans for the 21st Century* (Washington, D.C.: Govrnment Printing Office, 1983).

8. Education Commission of the States, *A Summary of Major Reports on Education* (Denver, 1983).

9. Conrad Carlberg and Kenneth Kavale, "The Efficacy of Special versus Regular Class Placement for Exceptional Children: A Metaanalysis," *Journal of Special Education*, 14 (Fall 1980), 295–309.

10. National Center for Education Statistics, *The Condition of Education* (Washington, D.C., Government Printing Office, 1982).

4. Curriculum in Crisis:
Connections between Past and Present

1. College Board, *On Further Examination: Report of the Advisory Panel on the Scholastic Aptitude Test Score Decline*, (New York: College Board, 1977), 31.

2. Annegret Harnischfeger and David E. Wiley, *Achievement Test Score Decline: Do We Need to Worry?* (St. Louis: CEMREL, 1976), 91, 107.

3. President's Commission on Foreign Languages and International Studies, *Strength through Wisdom: A Critique of U.S. Capability* (Washington, D.C.: Government Printing Office, 1979), 6; National Science Foundation and the

Department of Education, *Science and Engineering Education for the 1980s and Beyond* (Washington, D.C.: Government Printing Office, 1980), chap. 5.

4. Berman, Weiler Associates, "Improving Student Performance in California: Recommendations for the California Roundtable" (Berkeley, Calif., Nov. 1982).

5. National Commission on Excellence in Education, *A Nation at Risk: The Imperative for Educational Reform* (Washington, D.C.: Government Printing Office, 1983), 5; Ernest L. Boyer, *High School: A Report on Secondary Education in America* (New York: Harper & Row, 1983).

6. National Commission on Excellence, *Nation at Risk*, 18–19; Boyer, *High School*, 71–77.

7. National Center for Education Statistics, "How Well Do High School Graduates of Today Meet the Curriculum Standards of the National Commission on Excellence?" (Sept. 1983).

8. National Science Board Commission on Precollege Education in Mathematics, Science and Technology, *Educating Americans for the 21st Century* (Washington, D.C.: Government Printing Office, 1983), 1, 40.

9. *Education Week*, Dec. 7, 1983, pp. 6–17.

10. I. L. Kandel, *History of Secondary Education* (Boston: Houghton Mifflin, 1930), 394–422.

11. Edward A. Krug, *The Shaping of the American High School, 1880–1920* (New York: Harper & Row, 1964), 34.

12. Ibid., 48–49; William Humm and Robert L. Buser, "High School Curriculum in Illinois," *Educational Leadership*, 37 (May 1980), 670–72.

13. U.S. Bureau of Education, *Report of the Committee on Secondary School Studies* (Washington, D.C.: Government Printing Office, 1893), 17, 51, 173–74.

14. Krug, *Shaping of the American High School*, 68, 84–85.

15. Ibid., 84.

16. National Education Association, *Report of the Committee on College-Entrance Requirements* (Washington, D.C.: NEA, 1899).

17. Krug, *Shaping of the American High School*, 145, 192.

18. Ibid., 225.

19. Ibid., 240.

20. Ibid., 251, 276.

21. Ibid., 282.

22. Ibid., 354.

23. U.S. Office of Education, *Cardinal Principles of Secondary Education* (Washington, D.C.: Government Printing Office, 1918), 22.

24. Krug, *Shaping of the American High School*, 398–99.

25. Daniel Tanner and Laurel N. Tanner, *Curriculum Development: Theory into Practice*, 2d ed. (New York: Macmillan, 1980), 103–14.

26. Krug, *Shaping of the American High School*, 287, 341–42.

27. Diane Ravitch, *The Great School Wars: New York City, 1805–1973* (New York: Basic Books, 1974), 224–25.

5. The Fourth R: The Repatriation of the School

1. See, e.g., the work of Peter Laslett, Anthony Wrigley, Alan Macfarlane, and Ferdinand Mount in England; Philippe Ariès, Jean-Louis Flandrin, and Em-

manuel Le Roy Ladurie in France; Lutz Berkner, Hans Meidick, Peter Liette, and Jürgen Schlumbohm in Germany; and Michael Mitterauer in Austria.

2. This process has been brilliantly described by Philippe Ariès, *Centuries of Childhood: A Social History of Family Life* (New York: Knopf, 1962), and Peter Laslett, *The World We Have Lost* (New York: Scribner, 1965).

3. Brigitte Berger and Peter Berger, *The War over the Family* (Garden City, N.Y.: Doubleday, 1983).

4. Richard Coleman and Lee Rainwater, *Social Standing in America: New Dimensions of Class* (New York: Basic Books, 1978).

5. See Diane Ravitch, *The Troubled Crusade: American Education, 1945–1980* (New York: Basic Books, 1983).

6. James S. Coleman, *The Adolescent Society: The Social Life of the Teenager and Its Impact on Education* (Glencoe, Ill.: Free Press, 1961); Urie Bronfenbrenner, *Two Worlds of Childhood: U.S. and U.S.S.R.* (New York: Russell Sage, 1970).

7. A good summary of the ambiguity of research can be found in Hope Jensen Leichter, ed., *The Family as Educator* (New York: Teachers College Press, 1974).

8. See in particular John Seeley et al., *Crestwood Heights: A Study of the Culture of Suburban Life* (New York: Basic Books, 1956), which clearly demonstrates the middle-class family's relation to the schools.

9. Examples of this type of attempt can be found in Christopher Jencks, *Inequality: A Reassessment of the Effects of Family and Schooling in America* (New York: Basic Books, 1972); Christopher Jencks et al., *Who Gets Ahead? The Determinants of Economic Success in America* (New York: Basic Books, 1979); Kenneth Keniston et al., *All Our Children: The American Family under Pressure* (New York: Harcourt Brace Jovanovich, 1977); Richard De Lone, *Small Futures: Children, Inequality, and the Limits of Liberal Reform* (New York: Harcourt Brace Jovanovich, 1979).

10. The agreement on this point is wide among practitioners of child and youth care. Such divergent analysts as Ernest Boyer, Neil Postman, Robert Levine, Robert Hill, Andrew Billingsley, and Robert Coles have recently confirmed this premise.

11. Robert Woodson of the National Center of Neighborhood Enterprise, Washington, D.C., has frequently brought together during the past few years inner-city women who are heads of household. The tapes and summaries of interviews are illuminating indeed. The materials that Robert Hill of the Bureau of Social Science Research, Washington, D.C., is currently collecting strongly support this claim as well.

12. The school board meetings of the towns of Brookline, Newton, and Wellesley, Massachusetts, may serve as a typical reference here.

13. J. S. Fuerst, "Report Card: Chicago's All-Black Schools," *Public Interest*, no. 64 (Summer 1981), 79–91; Martin Kilson, "Black Social Classes and Intergenerational Poverty," ibid., 58–78. See also the reports on George Washington Preparatory High School, in the Watts section of Los Angeles, as reported by Alfred S. Regnery at the Jan. 25, 1984, hearing of the Senate Committee on the Judiciary, Subcommittee on Juvenile Justice.

14. In addition to the sources cited in note 13, see David L. Kirp, *Just Schools: The Idea of Racial Equality in American Education* (Berkeley: Univ. of California Press, 1982).

15. James S. Coleman et al., *Public and Private Schools* (Washington, D.C.: NCES, 1981).

16. See the various publications and research reports of Andrew Greeley for the National Opinion Research Center at the University of Chicago.

17. Peter Skerry, "Christian Schools versus the I.R.S.," *Public Interest*, no. 61 (Fall 1980), 18–41.

18. National Center for Neighborhood Enterprise, Washington, D.C., Conference Report prepared by Joan Rafferty for the National Conference on Grass Roots Schools, 1983.

19. Michael Rutter et al., *Fifteen Thousand Hours: Secondary Schools and Their Effects on Children* (Cambridge, Mass.: Harvard Univ. Press, 1979).

20. Ibid., 168.

21. See, e.g., reports on Peter L. Benson's (Search Institute, Minneapolis) research with 8,165 adolescents and 10,467 parents in 950 places, published by many daily papers around the country in Feb. 1984.

6. Teacher Unions and School Quality: Potential Allies or Inevitable Foes?

1. Accurate, unduplicated membership tallies are elusive. Each of the major unions has—and counts—members who are not schoolteachers, including college professors, teacher aides, school bus drivers, and even nurses. Some teachers belong to more than one organization. Some union locals are affiliated with more than one national; the major California teachers' union, for example, is affiliated with both NEA and AFT. Membership figures change frequently, as one union ousts the other in a representational battle in one city, only to be upset in a similar contest in the next state. No aggregate data at all exist for the independent unions. The NEA claims a total membership of about 1.6 million, the AFT nearly 600,000, but probably not more than 85 percent of these are classroom teachers.

2. Indeed, it is more likely that unionism will spread among the nation's 280,000 private school teachers, relatively few of whom currently belong to unions or bargain collectively.

3. Such "recognition," in turn, entails both winning an election among workers, conducted in accordance with the applicable state law, and then successfully negotiating a contract with the employer—typically the local school board.

4. As the NEA evolved into a full-fledged union in the 1960s and 1970s, it became increasingly awkward for "management" to belong to the same association. Accordingly, the various supervisory and administrative groups split off and formed separate organizations of their own.

5. See, inter alia, Marshall O. Donley, Jr., *Power to the Teacher* (Bloomington: Indiana Univ. Press, 1976); Wayne J. Urban, *Why Teachers Organized* (Detroit: Wayne State Univ. Press, 1982).

6. These and related matters are discussed at greater length in my article "Teacher Politics," *Commentary*, Feb. 1983, 29–41. See also Gilbert T. Sewall, "The National Education Association," *Journal of the Institute for Socioeconomic Studies*, 8 (Spring 1983), 36–45; Robert W. Kagan, "A Relic of the New Age: The National Education Association," *American Spectator*, Feb.

1982, pp. 14–18; Eugene H. Methvin, "The NEA: A Washington Lobby Run Rampant," *Reader's Digest*, Nov. 1978; Phil Keisling, "The Class War We Can't Afford to Lose," *Washington Monthly*, June 1982; Stephen Chapman, "The Teachers' Coup," *New Republic*, Oct. 11, 1980, pp. 9–11.

7. Susan Moore Johnson, "Teacher Unions in Schools: Authority and Accommodation," *Harvard Educational Review*, 53 (Aug. 1983), 309–26; idem, *Teacher Unions in Schools* (Philadelphia: Temple Univ. Press, 1984); Douglas E. Mitchell and Charles T. Kerchner, *The Dynamics of Public School Collective Bargaining and Its Impacts on Governance, Administration and Teaching*, multilith (U.S. Department of Education, National Institute of Education, Dec. 1981); Lorraine McDonnell and Anthony Pascal, *Organized Teachers in American Schools*, multilith (Rand Corporation, Feb. 1979); William L. Boyd, "The Public, the Professionals, and Educational Policy Making: Who Governs?" *Teachers College Record*, 77 (May 1975), 539–77; Ida Klaus, "The Evolution of a Collective Bargaining Relationship in Public Education: New York City's Changing Seven-Year History," *Michigan Law Review*, 67 (March 1969), 1033–66.

8. The preamble to the Tennessee "professional negotiations" act, for example, speaks of "establishing, maintaining, protecting and improving educational standards," but in the operative passages concerning "scope of negotiations" only eight specified "conditions of employment" are mandated. Although "other terms and conditions" may be negotiated, the law is clear that "it shall not be bad faith" for either side to refuse to do so.

9. This is quite an intricate program, one that also includes union participation—via the "review panel"—in the supervision and evaluation of new "intern" teachers, and it remains to be seen what will happen if an incorrigibly "incompetent" veteran teacher, marked for dismissal by the school system, appeals to the union to represent his interests. Under judicial interpretations of the Taft-Hartley Act, unions have a duty to provide "fair representation" for their members. See "Teacher Excellence: Teachers Take Charge," *American Educator*, 8, no. 1 (Spring 1984), 22–29.

It should also be understood that, regardless of what the AFT national leadership may say, few of the union's state and local affiliates are yet facing up to the "incompetence" problem in ways the public would applaud. One continues to hear many anecdotes, told by frustrated principals and angry parents, of individual teachers with grave classroom deficiencies who remain in the schools because of union-won constraints on efforts to do anything about them.

10. That the Tennessee plan dealt with these concerns was not altogether coincidental. I helped devise it—and benefited hugely in the process from the intense discussion of teacher career ladders that took place under Ernest Boyer's leadership during the period when I and many others were assisting him and the Carnegie Foundation for the Advancement of Teaching with the study that eventually yielded his fine book *High School* (New York: Harper & Row, 1983). The reader will discover therein a somewhat bobtailed version of the teacher career ladder concept.

11. Evidence is contained in the results of a poll conducted by the National School Boards Associaton in May 1983. Asked whether "teachers who are more effective in the classroom should receive larger salary increases than

teachers who are less effective," 61.5 percent of all NEA members and 62.1 percent of all AFT members said yes—as did 76.4 percent of the handful of teachers who belong to neither union. Marilee C. Rist, "Our Nationwide Poll: Most Teachers Endorse the Merit Pay Concept," *American School Board Journal*, Sept. 1983, pp. 23–27.

12. The problem the AFT faces is that Shanker towers above his own ranks. If he were to be hit by a truck—or made ambassador to Poland—tomorrow, the union would experience an acute leadership vacuum.

13. At least one prominent longtime advocate and analyst of collective bargaining by teachers and other public employees, Myron Lieberman, disagrees. He believes that public employee bargaining is, on the whole, pernicious and will diminish in scope and significance as the public comes to reject it. See Myron Lieberman, *Public-Sector Bargaining: A Policy Reappraisal* (Lexington, Mass.: D. C. Heath, Lexington Books, 1980); idem, "Teacher Bargaining: An Autopsy," *Phi Delta Kappan*, 63 (Dec. 1981), 231–34.

14. See, inter alia, Victor S. Vance and Phillip C. Schlechty, "The Distribution of Academic Ability in the Teaching Force: Policy Implications," *Phi Delta Kappan*, 64 (Sept. 1982), 22–27, and a number of the essays in Lee S. Shulman and Gary Sykes, eds., *Handbook of Teaching and Policy* (New York: Longman, 1983), including Sykes's superb essay, "Public Policy and the Problem of Teacher Quality: The Need for Screens and Magnets." For the most recent survey of teacher attitudes toward education and toward policy changes, see *The Metropolitan Life Survey of the American Teacher*, conducted by Louis Harris and Associates (New York: Metropolitan Life Insurance Co., June 1984).

15. Among the best recent summaries of this research is the "research brief" *Effective Schools: A Summary of Research* (Arlington, Va.: Educational Research Service, 1983).

16. Thomas J. Peters and Robert H. Waterman, Jr., *In Search of Excellence* (New York: Warner Books, 1984). See also, inter alia, Frank M. Gryna, Jr., *Quality Circles: A Team Approach to Problem Solving* (New York: American Management Association, 1981); *Japanese Quality Control Circles* (Tokyo: Asian Productivity Organization, 1972); Robert E. Cole, *Work, Mobility and Participation* (Berkeley: Univ. of California Press, 1979). For some of the educational implications of quality circles, see Larry Chase, "Quality Circles in Education", *Educational Leadership*, Feb. 1983, pp. 18–26, which includes a sizable bibliography.

17. Clinton S. Golden and Harold J. Ruttenberg, *The Dynamics of Industrial Democracy* (New York: Harper, 1942), xxvi.

18. Kerchner and Mitchell, *Dynamics of Public School Collective Bargaining*, esp. chaps. 3, 6, and 7.

19. Ibid., pp. 7–4 and 7–5.

20. Kerchner and Mitchell are inclined to see the intrusion of "policy" issues into the bargaining process as generally a means by which management seeks to increase its control over teachers. My own impression is that the union is equally apt to be "the aggressor" in these matters. The more important point, however, is that the image of "aggression" contradicts the spirit of mutuality, participation, and shared decision making that is an essential

feature of modern organization theory as I understand it, and of such techniques as quality circles.

21. A number of NEA school systems continue to function in a traditional "professional" mode, which, at least with respect to education policy issues, may resemble the Third Generation of labor-management relations but is, I think, more properly viewed as a stage antecedent to the First Generation, in which collective action by teachers is prompted by collective discontent.

22. See, e.g., Bob Kuttner, "Can Labor Lead?" *New Republic*, March 12, 1984, pp. 19–25.

23. Obviously, the NEA is not part of "organized labor" in the usual sense, but it can scarcely fail to be affected by developments a couple of blocks south on Sixteenth Street, N.W.

24. As a matter of philosophical preference and political taste, I much prefer the analysis—albeit far gloomier in its contemporary implications—of the problem of public service in a "liberal" society set forth by Harvey C. Mansfield, Jr., in his superb essay "The Prestige of Public Employment," in *Public Employee Unions: A Study of the Crisis in Public Sector Labor Relations*, ed. A. Lawrence Chickering (San Francisco: Institute for Contemporary Studies, 1976), 35–49. Mansfield contends, "The real question is whether we can solve the problem of public employee unions without a concept of public spirit. And that problem leads in turn to the question whether public spirit can be resurrected in a large society like America, based on liberal principles. . . . In particular, it is time to recognize that liberal principles, in deriving the public good from private interests, may have taken for granted a public spirit in ambitious men and an uncalculating affection in the citizens at large which cannot be derived from self-interest. We may have been living off the moral capital—meaning the public spirit—of pre-liberal times, so that we now face a crisis from the exhaustion of this human resource."

7. Schools That Make an Imprint: Creating a Strong Positive Ethos

I would like to thank the Ford Foundation and the National Institute of Education for their support of the research on which this article is partly based. Portions of this essay are adapted from two articles of mine published in *Daedalus* and the *Bulletin of the National Association of Secondary School Principals*.

1. Frances Taliaferro, "Blackboard Art," *Harper's*, Oct. 1981, pp. 89–92.
2. Thomas Hughes, *Tom Brown's School Days* (London: J. M. Dent, 1957), 65.
3. Evelyn Waugh, *Decline and Fall* (Boston: Little, Brown, 1977), 8.
4. David Tyack and Elisabeth Hansot, *Managers of Virtue: Public School Leadership in America, 1820–1980* (New York: Basic Books, 1982), 23.
5. Robert S. Lynd and Helen Merrell Lynd, *Middletown: A Study in Contemporary American Culture* (New York: Harcourt, Brace, 1929), 203.
6. Lester F. Ward, *Dynamic Sociology* (1883), excerpted in *Children and Youth in America: A Documentary History*, ed. Robert H. Bremner (Cambridge, Mass.: Harvard Univ. Press, 1971), II, 1104.
7. E. Digby Baltzell, *Philadelphia Gentlemen: The Making of a National Upper Class* (Glencoe, Ill.: Free Press, 1958), 10.

8. Survey by the National Catholic Education Association, reported in *Education Week*, May 9, 1984.

9. James Coleman, Thomas Hoffer, and Sally Kilgore, *Public and Private Schools* (Washington, D.C.: National Center for Education Statistics, 1981).

10. See the symposium on Coleman's report by Richard J. Murnane et al. in *Harvard Educational Review*, 51 (Nov. 1981), 483–564, and Karl L. Alexander, "How Schools Differ: A Review of the Evidence Comparing Public and Private School Effectiveness" (Report to the National Institute of Education, Feb. 1984).

11. My colleagues—Urmila Acharya, Sharon Franz, Richard Hawkins, Wendy Kohli, and Madhu Prakash—and I visited thirty-three public and private schools in the northeastern United States. In the second year of study, we chose five schools to study more intensively, spending one day a week in each throughout the school year. Three of these were public schools, one was Catholic, and the other was a non-Catholic private school. For an overview of the themes of our work, see Gerald Grant, "The Character of Education and the Education of Character," *Daedalus*, Summer 1981, pp. 135–49.

12. "On Generativity and Identity: From a Conversation with Erik and Joan Erikson," *Harvard Educational Review*, 51 (May 1981), 268.

13. Burton Clark, *The Distinctive College: Antioch, Reed and Swarthmore* (Chicago: Aldine, 1970).

14. Judith Smilg Kleinfeld, *Eskimo School on the Andreafsky: A Study of Effective Bicultural Education* (New York: Praeger, 1979), esp. chap. 4.

15. Phillips Academy, Andover, *Catalog*, 1979–80, p. 12.

16. David R. Satterthwaite, "Thanks for the Memories, Palmer," *Georgian*, 55, no. 2 (April 1984), 1.

17. Thomas F. Green, "The Formation of Conscience: Moral Education in an Age of Technology," (Syracuse Univ., 1984).

18. Tyack and Hansot, *Managers of Virtue*, 239–40.

19. Janet Ward Schofield and Andrew Sagar, "The Social Context of Learning in an Interracial School," in *Desegregated Schools: Appraisals of an American Experiment*, ed. Ray C. Rist (New York: Academic Press, 1979), 155–99.

20. Richard S. Peters, *Authority, Responsibility and Education* (London: Allen and Unwin, 1973), 140–56.

8. The Storm before the Lull:
The Future of Private Schooling in America

1. Denis P. Doyle, "A Din of Inequity? Private Schools Reconsidered," *Teachers College Record*, 82 (Summer 1981), 661–73.

2. See Susan Abramowitz and Stuart Rosenfeld, eds., *Declining Enrollment: The Challenge of the Coming Decade* (Washington, D.C.: National Institute of Education, 1978).

3. Virgil Blum, *Inner City Private Education: A Study* (Milwaukee: Catholic League for the Religious, 1982); James S. Coleman, Thomas Hoffer, and Sally Kilgore, *High School Achievement: Public, Catholic, and Private Schools Compared* (New York: Basic Books, 1982); Andrew Greeley, *Catholic High Schools and Minority Students* (New Brunswick: Transaction Books, 1982).

4. Michael Rutter et al., *Fifteen Thousand Hours: Secondary Schools and Their Effects on Children* (Cambridge, Mass.: Harvard Univ. Press, 1979).

5. See Chester E. Finn, "Trashing the Coleman Report," *Education Week*, Sept. 7, 1981.

6. Some of the continuing limitations in federal data collection are discussed in a recent op-ed piece in the Washington *Post*. See Denis P. Doyle and Terry W. Hartle, "Where Invidious Comparisons Work," Washington *Post*, Feb. 19, 1984.

7. Daniel Patrick Moynihan, "Government and the Ruin of Private Education," *Harper's*, April 1978, pp. 28–38.

8. For a more complete description, see Denis P. Doyle, *Family Choice in Education: The Case of Denmark, Holland, and Australia* (Washington, D.C.: American Enterprise Institute, forthcoming).

9. Constitution of the State of California, Article 9, Section B.

10. The data are from statistics compiled by the Catholic Schools Office of the Archdiocese of Washington, D.C.

11. See Abramowitz and Rosenfeld, *Declining Enrollments*, 81–127.

12. See note 3.

13. Bruce S. Cooper, Donald H. McLaughlin, and Bruno V. Manno, "The Latest Word on Private-School Growth," *Teachers College Record*, 85 (Fall 1983), 88–99.

14. Ibid., 93–94.

15. Ibid., 94.

16. Ibid., 97.

17. Blum, *Inner City Private Education.*

18. Ibid., 61.

19. For an in-depth analysis of Coleman's findings, see Denis P. Doyle's review of *High School Achievement* in *Teaching Political Science*, 10, (Summer 1983), 201–2.

20. The Gallup poll asked Americans, "Would you like to see [a voucher system] adopted in this country?" Some 51 percent replied yes. George H. Gallup, "The 15th Annual Gallup Poll of the Public's Attitudes toward the Public Schools," *Phi Delta Kapan*, 65 (Set. 1983), 38.

21. Quoted in Stephen Arons, *Compelling Belief: The Culture of American Schooling* (New York: McGraw-Hill, 1983), 195.

22. Albert O. Hirschman, *Exit, Voice, and Loyalty: Responses to Decline in Firms, Organizations, and States* (Cambridge, Mass.: Harvard Univ. Press, 1970); Charles L. Schultze, *The Public Use of Private Interest* (Washington, D.C.: Brookings Institution, 1977); and John Coons and Stephen Sugarman, *Family Choice in Education* (Berkeley: Univ. of California Press, 1982).

23. For an elaboration of this idea, see Denis P. Doyle and Chester E. Finn, *Educational Quality and Family Choice: Toward a Statewide Public School Voucher Plan* (Washington, D.C.: American Enterprise Institute, forthcoming).

24. For an analysis and description of these reports through Aug. 1983, see Marsha Levine, "School Reform: A Role for the American Business Community," unpublished paper (New York: Committee for Economic Development, 1983).

25. The results appear each year in the Sept. issue of *Phi Delta Kappan*.

26. Gallup, "15th Annual Gallup Poll," 39.

27. See James Reichley, *Church and State in Modern American Democracy* (Washington, D.C.: Brookings Institution, forthcoming); Doyle, *Family Choice in Education*.
28. For a more complete discussion of the separation of church and state, see John W. Baker, Thomas Sieger Derr, and A. E. Dick Howard, *Church, State, and Politics: Chief Justice Earl Warren Conference on Advocacy*, ed. Jaye B. Hensel (Washington, D.C.: Roscoe Pound–American Trial Lawyers Foundation, 1981).
29. See *Danish Education* (Copenhagen: Danish Ministry of Education, 1980).
30. Simon Bolivar, from his address to the Congress of Angostura, Feb. 15, 1819.
31. Coleman now has at his disposal new data sets, which will permit him to extend his original analysis and address his original conclusions with greater authority.
32. Glen Macnow, "Twice as Likely to Send Kids Elsewhere: Teachers Shun Own Schools," *Detroit Free Press*, Sept. 1983, p. 6A.
33. Mueller vs. Allen, 463 U.S. (1983).

9. Our Black-Robed School Board: A Report Card

1. 474 F. Supp. 244 (M.D. Fla. 1979).
2. 564 F. Supp. 177 (M.D. Fla. 1983).
3. *Public Interest*, no. 60 (Summer 1980); 119–47.
4. Barbara Lerner, *Minimum Competence, Maximum Choice: Second Chance Legislation* (New York: Irvington, 1980). See also idem, "The Minimum Competence Testing Movement: Social, Scientific, and Legal Implications," *American Psychologist*, 36 (Oct. 1981), 1057–66.
5. James S. Coleman et al., *Equality of Educational Opportunity* (Washington, D.C.: Govenment Printing Office, 1966).
6. See interview with James Coleman in *Southern Education Report*, 1 no. 3 (Nov.–Dec. 1965), 2–7.
7. See, e.g., Daniel P. Moynihan and Frederick Mosteller, eds., *On Equality of Educational Opportunity* (New York: Random House, 1972).
8. Eric A. Hanushek, "Throwing Money at Schools," *Journal of Policy Analysis and Management*, 1 (Fall 1981), 19–41.
9. "Racial Identification and Preference in Negro Children," in *Readings in Social Psychology*, ed. Theodore M. Newcomb and Eugene L. Hartley (New York: Holt, 1947), 169–78.
10. Barbara Lerner, "American Education: How Are We Doing?" *Public Interest*, no. 69 (Fall 1982); 59–82.
11. Ibid.
12. See esp. Joseph Adelson, "How the Schools Were Ruined," *Commentary*, July 1983, pp. 45–54, and Chester E. Finn, Jr., "Teacher Politics," ibid., Feb. 1983, pp. 29–41.
13. "Programs of School Improvement: An Overview" (Paper delivered at the National Institute of Education Conference on the Implications of Research for Practice, Airlie House, Va., Feb. 1982).
14. James S. Coleman, Thomas Hoffer, and Sally Kilgore, *High School Achieve-*

ment: *Public, Catholic, and Private Schools Compared* (New York: Basic Books, 1982).

15. Christopher Jencks et al., *Inequality: A Reassessment of the Effects of Family and Schooling in America* (New York: Basic Books, 1972).

16. 640 F. 2d 782.

17. 347 U.S. 483 at 489.

18. 16 Wall 36 (1873).

19. 347 U.S. at 490.

20. 163 U.S. 537 (1896).

21. Ibid. at 551.

22. C. Vann Woodward, *The Strange Career of Jim Crow* (New York: Oxford Univ. Press, 1957).

23. 163 U.S. at 553.

24. Ibid. at 559.

10. Underprepared Students and Public Research Universities

1. Frederick Rudolph, *The American College and University* (New York: Knopf, 1962), 281.

2. Ibid., 282.

3. Frederick Rudolph, *Curriculum* (San Francisco: Jossey-Bass, 1977), 160.

4. Ibid., 158.

5. *Report to the Policy Committee on the University of California's Activities to Assist Underprepared Students* (Univ. of California, March 1981), pt.1, p.7.n.1.

6. Ibid., p. 14.

7. Ibid., p. 17 and table D-14.

8. Ibid., p. 18.

9. See Gary Sykes, "Teacher Preparation and the Teacher Workforce: Problems and Prospects for the Eighties," mimeographed (National Institute of Education, Sept. 1981), 1; idem. "Contradictions, Ironies, and Promises Unfulfilled: A Contemporary Account of the Status of Teaching," *Phi Delta Kappan*, 65 (Oct. 1983), 87–93; J. Myron Atkin, "Who Will Teach High School?" *Daedalus*, Summer 1981, p. 91.

10. See Henry Chauncey, "The Use of the Selective Service College Qualification Test on the Deferment of College Students," *Science*, July 4, 1952, p. 75; Robert North, "The Teacher Education Student: How Does He Compare Academically with Other College Students?" in *The Education of Teachers: New Perspectives* (Washington, D.C.: NEA National Commission on Teacher Education and Professional Standards, 1958); R. L. Thorndike and Elisabeth Hagen, "Men Teachers and Ex-Teachers: Some Attitudes and Traits," *Teachers College Record*, 62 (Jan. 1961), 311.

11. Martin Trow, "Two Problems in American Public Education," in *H. Social Problems*, ed H. Becker (New York: Wiley, 1966), 105. Ironically, the growth of mass education, and the increased opportunities for women and minority members over the past two decades, has further weakened the teaching profession by draining off able people from groups that formerly saw in teaching one of the few easily accessible professions.

12. Sara Freedman et al., "Teaching as an Imperilled Profession," mimeographed (Boston Women's Teachers' Group, Jan. 1981).

13. Ibid., 15. See also Rose Scherini, *High Schools Today: Overview and Implications for the University of California, Berkeley* (Berkeley: Office of Student Research, May 1981).

14. University of Wisconsin System Basic Skills Task Force, *Final Report* (Madison: Univ. of Wisconsin, May 1979), 4.

15. Advisory Commission on Articulation between Secondary Education and Ohio Colleges, *Report* (Ohio Board of Regents and States Board of Education, April 1981), 1.

16. "Competencies Expected of Entering Freshmen" (Notice of Meeting, Univ. of California Academic Senate, Dec. 2, 1981), 51–76. See also *Preparation for College in the 1980s* (New York: College Board, 1981).

17. *Chronicle of Higher Education*, June 1, 1981, p. 8.

18. *Report to the Policy Committee*, 24.

19. See Martin Trow, "Comparative Perspectives on Access," in *Access to Higher Education*, ed. Oliver Fulton (Guildford, Eng.: Society for Research into Higher Education, 1981),89–121.

20. Ibid., 95–104.

21. Louis Schell, "The Cooperative College Preparatory Program: A Comprehensive Model for School Change," mimeographed (Berkeley: Univ. of California, Lawrence Hall of Science, Oct. 1982); idem, "The Cooperative College Preparatory Program: A Collaborative School-University Program to Increase School Effectiveness and Minority Enrollment at the University," mimeographed (Berkeley: Univ. of California, Lawrence Hall of Science, Jan. 1984).

22. *Higher Education and National Affairs*, Oct. 1, 1982.

23. Schell, "CCPP: Comprehensive Model," 1.

24. This section draws on and quotes ibid., 23–24.

25. Ibid., 5.

26. Ibid., 6.

27. Schell, "CCPP: Collaborative Program."

28. See Barbara Nelson, "Making Problems: The Social Construction of Problems by Members of School and University in the Joint Planning of a School," Center for Studies in Higher Education, Occasional Paper no. 13, mimeographed (Berkeley: Univ. of California, March 1980).

29. See Clifford Adelman, *Starting with Students: Notable Programs, Promising Approaches, and Other Improvement Efforts in American Postsecondary Education*, vol. 1 (Washington, D.C., National Institute of Education, Dec. 1983). This document describes over a hundred programs, most of which link specific colleges and universities to nearby secondary schools in some supportive way.

30. See Martin Trow, "The Second Transformation of American Secondary Education," *International Journal of Comparative Sociology*, 11 (Sept. 1961), 144–66; Richard Hofstadter, *Anti-Intellectualism in American Life* (New York: Knopf, 1963), 323–58.

11. The Problem with Competence

1. Task Force on Education for Economic Growth, Education Commission of the States, *Action for Excellence: A Comprehensive Plan to Improve Our Schools*, (Denver, 1983).

2. John W. Gardner, *Excellence: Can We Be Equal and Excellent Too?* (New York: Harper & Row, 1961).

3. "Top Students Move to Science Studies, Leave Humanities," *Chronicle of Higher Education,* Feb. 22, 1984, p. 1. "The officials said employment prospects—or lack of them—were responsible for the changes in student interest."

4. See the section entitled "Aiming for Excellence," in *Education Week,* Dec. 7, 1983, pp. 5–17, for a summary of action in the fifty states.

"In the last 11 months, 54 state-level commissions have been formed to study various aspects of education improvement; many have been formed since the April report of 'A Nation at Risk,' the report of the National Commission on Excellence in Education. . . .

"[S]ince 1981, . . . [m]ore demanding requirements for high school graduation have been established in 26 states. . . . Twenty-four states are considering recommendations to increase graduation requirements.

"Seven states have enacted or are considering a requirement that students take an 'exit test' before receiving a diploma. They join 19 states that had enacted such measures earlier. . . .

"Fifteen states report they have taken new teacher-evaluation requirements and eight are considering doing so . . . seven have enacted competency requirements for certification."

5. James S. Coleman et al., *Equality of Educational Opportunity* (Washington, D.C.: Government Printing Office, 1966).

6. See Paul E. Peterson, "Background Paper," in *Making the Grade: Report of the Twentieth Century Fund Task Force on Federal Elementary and Secondary Education* (New York: Twentieth Century Fund, 1983), tables on pp. 95, 46, 65.

7. See Nancy W. Burton and Lyle V. Jones, "Recent Trends in Achievement Levels of Black and White Youth," *Educational Researcher,* April 1982, pp. 11–14; and for further research by Lyle Jones along the same line, "Achievement Gap between Blacks, Whites Continues to Narrow," *Education Week,* Sept. 7, 1983.

8. "Few Blacks Passing Ga. Teacher Test, Study Finds," *Education Week,* Nov. 6, 1983.

9. See "U.S. Judge Halts Use of N.T.E. in Mobile County," *Education Week,* Sept. 7, 1983: ". . . a federal appellate court refused to temporarily overturn a district court's decision to stop the Mobile County (Ala.) School System from requiring teachers to pass part of the National Teacher Examinations before they can be employed or receive tenure. . . . Judge Myron Thompson of the U.S. District Court . . . issued a preliminary injunction barring the 66,000-student school system from further use of the test on the grounds that its current use of the test apparently violates Title VII of the Civil Rights Act of 1964, which prohibits racial discrimination in employment. In his opinion, the judge wrote: 'In view of the fact that the Mobile County School system is 26 per cent to 39 per cent black, but 66 per cent to 67 per cent of those denied re-employment because of the test requirement were black, the conclusion is inescapable that when all the evidence is in, adverse racial impact will probably be found in the Mobile County School system.'" A judge ruled similarly a few weeks later in Marion County, South Carolina.

See "U.S. Judge Rejects Use of Examination to Fire Teachers," *Education Week*, Oct. 12, 1983.

10. "ETS to Withhold Teacher Tests to Bar Misuse," *Education Week*, Nov. 30, 1983.

11. See, e.g., arguments in Dorothey Gilliam's column "Teacher Test," *Washington Post*, Nov. 14, 1983.

12. "Alvarado Says Regents' Plan Deprives the Poor and Gifted," New York *Times*, Nov. 18, 1983; "New York Regents Climb Down from Their Ivory Tower," ibid., Nov. 20, 1983.

13. "Achievement Gap between Blacks, Whites Continues to Narrow."

14. Lucy W. Sells, "Leverage for Equal Opportunity through Mastery of Mathematics," in *Women and Minorities in Science: Strategies for Increasing Participation*, ed. Sheila M. Humphreys (Boulder, Colo.: Westview Press, 1982), 7–26. The table is taken from p. 12.

15. 94 *Supreme Court Reporter* 2742.

16. David M. White, ed., *Towards A Diversified Legal Profession: An Inquiry into the Law School Admission Test, Grade Inflation, and Current Admissions Policies* (National Conference of Black Lawyers) (San Francisco: Julia Richardson Associates, 1981).

17. I have discussed these issues at length, more often in the context of selection for jobs than in that of selection for education, but there is much in common in the two realms. See *Affirmative Discrimination: Ethnic Inequality and Public Policy* (New York: Basic Books, 1975, 1978), and *Ethnic Dilemmas, 1964–1982* (Cambridge, Mass.: Harvard Univ. Press, 1983).

18. Peterson, "Background Paper," 101.